7th edition

P9-ELO-415

Nolo's Simple Will Book

By Attorney Denis Clifford

NOLO

SEVENTH EDITION	NOVEMBER 2007
Editor	BETSY SIMMONS
Cover Design	SUSAN PUTNEY
Production	MARGARET LIVINGSTON
Proofreader	PAUL TYLER
CD-ROM Preparation	ELLEN BITTER
Index	THÉRÈSE SHERE
Printing	DELTA PRINTING SOLUTIONS, INC.

Clifford, Denis.
    Nolo's simple will book / by Denis Clifford. -- 7th ed.
        p. cm.
    ISBN-13: 978-1-4133-0713-9 (pbk.)
    ISBN-10: 1-4133-0713-2 (pbk.)
    1. Wills--United States--Popular works. 2. Wills--United States--Forms. I. Title:.
II. Title: Simple will book.
    KF755.Z9C54 2006
    346.7305'4--dc22

                              2007018038

Quantity sales: For information on bulk purchases or corporate premium sales, please contact the Special Sales
Department. For academic sales or textbook adoptions, ask for Academic Sales. Call 800-955-4775 or write to
Nolo, 950 Parker Street, Berkeley, CA 94710.

Acknowledgments

Thanks to all those friends who helped me put together the 7th edition of *Nolo's Simple Will Book*, and who've helped over the years:

First, my Nolo colleagues who worked with me so productively, patiently, cheerfully: My current editor Betsy Simmons, a superb editor and a pleasure to work with; Shae Irving, Mary Randolph and Steve Elias, great editors; Terri Hearsh and Stephanie Harolde, production (and also great editors); and Ely Newman and André Zivkovich, my computer gurus.

Next, to all my fellow Noloids, who make this such a special—indeed, unique— place to work.

Then, to Naomi Puro, Amy Pine, Carol Pladsen, Katherine and Paul Clifford and Marilyn Putnam.

About the Author

Denis Clifford practices law in Berkeley, California, specializing in estate planning. He is the author of several Nolo books, including *Plan Your Estate, Make Your Own Living Trust* and *Form a Partnership* with Ralph Warner. A graduate of Columbia Law School, where he was an editor of *The Law Review*, he has practiced law in various ways, and is convinced that people can do much of their own legal work.

Table of Contents

Glossary

Appendixes

Index

Your Will-Making Legal Companion

You're thinking about writing your will—good for you! Many of us know it's something we should do for our families, but just never get around to it. After all, we're all busy and have lots of chores just waiting to be tackled.

So why should making a will move to the top of your to-do list? Because estate planning, including preparing a will, is about keeping control over crucial parts of your family's life. You're the one who should decide what happens to your property and what would happen to your children if for some reason you couldn't raise them. But if you don't make these decisions, a judge could do it—without any idea of what you would have wanted.

When you make a will with this book, you'll be able to:

- Determine who gets your property when you die.
- Name personal guardians for your minor children.
- Name an adult to manage property you leave to your minor or young adult children.
- Name an executor.
- Forgive debts.
- Designate how to pay your final bills and taxes.

You'll also get an overview of estate planning, so you can figure out what other steps you might need to take. Other documents—for example, a health care directive and power of attorney—can be just as important to your family as a will. We'll explain why, and point you in the right direction if you want to prepare those documents yourself, too. And you may want to consider some additional estate planning tools, such as a living trust, that can make things simpler for your family later.

The wills in this book are legal in every state except Louisiana (which has its own set of estate planning laws that differs from all other states'). These wills are fine for most folks with a modest to moderate amount of property and typical assets. If you have a more complicated situation, or a large estate—say, more than $2 million—you will probably want some additional help from a lawyer or tax expert.

Making a will is a significant matter, worth serious thought. Happily, however, writing your will does not have to be difficult, and most people don't need a lawyer to do it. Nolo has been helping people make their own legally valid wills for more than 25 years, and *Nolo's Simple Will Book*, remains one of our most popular estate planning books—for good reason. It has clear, easy-to-understand instructions, and it explains when you might need a lawyer's help.

Your biggest challenge will probably be making some personal decisions—for example, deciding how to leave property, or who will care for your young children if you can't. However, the sooner you make these important decisions, the better. And when you're finished, peace of mind will reward your effort. You'll know you've taken an important step toward your family's security. Good luck! ●

Making Your Own Will

This book enables you to write your own will, valid in every state except Louisiana. If you're temporarily residing outside the United States for work, study, travel, or military service, you can also use *Nolo's Simple Will Book* to make a will that's valid for property you own in the U.S.

Living Overseas

You do not have to live in the U.S. to prepare a will that is valid in this country. To prepare a valid will if you live abroad, you must follow the formal will requirements presented in this book and maintain legal residence in a U.S. state. If you live overseas temporarily because you are in the armed services, your residence is the "Home of Record" you declared to military authorities.

If you live overseas for business, education—or just for the fun of it—you probably still have sufficient ties with a U.S. state to make it your legal home (called your "domicile" in legalese). For example, if you were born in New York, lived in New York, and are registered to vote there, then your residence is New York for will-making purposes.

> **CAUTION**
>
> **If your choice is not clear.** If you do not maintain continuous ties with a particular state, or if you have well-established homes both in the U.S. and in another country, consult a lawyer before preparing your will.

Using this book, most people can safely prepare a will without hiring a lawyer. In your will you can make legally binding provisions for who gets your property—real estate, heirlooms, and whatever else you own. You can also specify who will care for your minor children, if the need arises, and leave property for the benefit of your children. And by following the book's detailed instructions on signing and witnessing, you can be sure your will is legal.

What a Will Can Do for You

Most people know what a will does, at least in a general way—they understand that it's a document created to make binding provisions for who receives property after death.

Estate Planning Vocabulary

"Estate" is the legal term for all the property you own. You have an estate whether you're wealthy or impoverished, as long as you own something. "Estate planning" means arranging for the transfer of your property after your death. The phrase also includes related concerns, such as providing for minor children. The planning involved can be just making a will, or it can involve more complex matters, such as creating trusts to benefit a disabled child or reduce estate taxes.

A will is the simplest estate planning device, and the easiest to prepare. If you're like many people, a will is all the estate planning you need or want, at least for a long time. Most younger people (roughly, under age 50) want to be certain their desires regarding their property will be carried out if they die; they also know that, statistically, it's highly unlikely that they'll die for decades. So they decide to postpone the cost and hassles of more complex estate planning until their autumnal years. A will is all they need for now.

Similarly, the primary estate planning goal of many younger couples is to ensure to the best of their abilities that their minor children will be well cared for—and financially provided for—if both parents should die together. Of course, a single parent has the same concerns. A will enables a parent to handle these matters.

Finally, many people simply don't want the bother and cost of extensive estate planning, no matter what their age or health. Fortunately, preparing a will achieves their basic goal of distributing their property as they see fit, with as little hassle now as possible. If you don't need or want comprehensive estate planning, or have been postponing or procrastinating considering it, be sure you at least have a will.

> *The French philosopher Rabelais wrote a one-sentence will: "I have nothing, I owe a great deal, and the rest I leave to the poor."*

Vocabulary—Gifts

Throughout this book, except where otherwise indicated, the word "gift" means any property you leave by your will, whether left to individuals or institutions. Sometimes, lawyers distinguish between "devises" (gifts of real estate, also called real property) and "bequests" (gifts of personal property, meaning everything but real estate). This book uses "gift" to cover both types of property.

What Your Will Can Do

When you prepare a will using this book, you can accomplish all these goals:

- Leave your property, including your home, to those you choose—your spouse, partner, children (including minor children), grandchildren, other relatives, friends, organizations, or charities.

- Provide for an alternate person or organization to inherit something if the first person you pick to receive it fails to survive you.

- Appoint your executor—that is, the person who handles your property after you die and makes sure the terms of your will are carried out.

- Nominate a personal guardian to care for your child or children, should you die before they reach age 18 and the other parent is unable or unwilling to care for them.

- Choose someone to manage property you leave to a minor or young adult. You can select the management method you decide is best for your situation. Your choices are to set up an individual child's trust or a "family pot trust" (all property left to minor children is put in one pot), leave a gift using the Uniform Transfers to Minors Act, or leave the property directly to your minor children, to be supervised by the property guardian you name in your will.

- Revoke all previous wills.

- Forgive debts owed to you.

- Handle what happens to your property if you and your spouse die simultaneously.

- Disinherit anyone you want to, except where state law restricts your power to disinherit your spouse.

Using the "Right" Language

Many people worry that the gifts they want to leave in a will they prepare themselves may not turn out to be legally binding. This worry is expressed in many ways, such as:

"I'm concerned about legal requirements. How can I leave gifts so that I know my wishes will be followed? What's the right language to use to leave my property?"

"I want to leave many specific gifts to family and friends. I have pictures, mementos, heirlooms, and antiques. How can I ensure that the proper people get them, and that no one else can claim them?"

Using the will forms in this book, you can be sure that all gifts you make in your will are legally binding. To accomplish this, you need only write your intentions in plain English. No "legalese" is required. The will forms contain all the technical language required for a valid will.

When You May Want More Estate Planning

A will is an indispensable part of any estate plan, and it's all the estate planning many people do. Other people decide they need to do some additional planning.

Here are the most common estate planning issues that prompt people to go beyond making a will:

- reducing probate costs and delays (probate is the court process your will must usually go through after your death)
- reducing federal estate taxes, which may affect estates worth $2 million or more, depending on the year of death
- protecting your assets, as far as possible, from being depleted if you or your spouse suffers a catastrophic illness.

You may also want more than a will if you have a personal situation that requires specialized and sophisticated legal work. For example, if you have a child with a disability, you'll want to provide for that child while at the same time preserving his or her eligibility for government benefits. You can accomplish this through a special trust, which you can prepare yourself or have prepared by an expert. (See Chapter 14 for more on special needs trusts.)

Another situation in which you may need a trust is if you're married and have children from a prior marriage. However, some people in second or subsequent marriages need no more than a will. If you just want to divide your property, leaving some to your spouse and some outright to children from former marriages, a will from this book will work fine. For instance, a woman can safely use a will to leave her share of a co-owned house and an investment in a limited partnership to her husband, and leave other major items of her property, including jewelry and stocks, to her children from her first marriage.

If you want to leave property in a more complex manner, however, you'll need arrangements beyond what's possible with this book's will forms. For example, you may want to leave property for the use of your spouse during her or his life, with the property to go to your children after death of the spouse. Accomplishing this requires a trust, often called an "AB" trust. A property control trust must be drafted by a knowledgeable attorney; there are too many complexities and individual differences for a standardized, do-it-yourself form.

If you don't know now whether or not you want more than a basic will, relax. As you work through this book, you'll get a good idea of whether or not a will can satisfy all your estate planning concerns. Chapter 14 discusses estate planning issues in more detail.

RESOURCE

More information about estate planning. All these estate planning matters, and many others, are discussed in great depth in *Plan Your Estate*, by Denis Clifford (Nolo).

Protecting Assets: A Catastrophic Illness Clause

The will forms in this book do not contain what some people call a "catastrophic illness clause." This term is commonly used to mean a will clause that tries to preserve assets from being used for the costs of a major illness that strikes oneself or one's spouse. More particularly, many people want to preserve their eligibility for Medicaid or Medicare without having to use up all (or even any) of their assets. Married couples want to protect, at least, the assets owned by the healthier spouse.

A catastrophic illness clause certainly sounds like a good idea. But unfortunately, no simple will clause can protect your assets. Simply put, the law doesn't allow you to easily retain your assets and still be eligible for federal aid.

RESOURCE

Getting expert help. There are various ways of protecting some of your assets from huge medical bills: making gifts, paying children for services, and using certain complex types of trusts. These methods are discussed in *Long-Term Care: How to Plan & Pay For It*, by Joseph Matthews (Nolo). If you want to take such concrete actions, see a lawyer knowledgeable in this distinct legal area. To help you, a lawyer must be up to date on relevant federal and state statutes and regulations, which can change fast.

Property You Can't Leave by Will

A will usually doesn't affect certain kinds of property that you've legally bound yourself to transfer by other means, including:

- Property held in joint tenancy, which will automatically belong to the surviving joint tenants at your death. A will provision leaving joint tenancy property would have no effect unless all joint tenants died simultaneously.

- Property you've transferred to a living trust.

- Proceeds of a life insurance policy where you've already named a beneficiary for the policy.

- Money in a pension plan or in an individual retirement account such as an IRA, 401(k), or profit-sharing plan, or any other retirement plan for which you've named a beneficiary.

- Money in a pay-on-death bank account or stocks held in a transfer-on-death account, for which you have named a beneficiary to receive whatever is in the account when you die.

- Property specifically controlled by a contract. For example, if you are a partner in a small business, the partnership agreement (a contract) may limit your ability to dispose of your interest in the business by will. The surviving partners may have the right to buy a deceased partner's interest at a "fair market value." You can, of course, specify in your will who is to receive the money from this sale.

If you live in the state of Washington, however, there's an exception to this general rule: you are allowed to leave some of the property listed above by will.

For more general information on the kinds of property discussed above, see Chapter 14.

Illegal or Unenforceable Will Provisions

There are also a few legal limitations on what you can do in a will. You cannot:

- Encourage or attempt to restrain certain types of conduct of your beneficiaries. For example, you cannot leave a gift contingent on the marriage, divorce, or change of religion of a recipient. You can, however, make a gift contingent on other behavior—for example, "to John, if and when he goes to college." Why this distinction? Because courts say that "public policy" prohibits attempts to coerce fundamental rights like the choice of spouse or religion. But it's allowable to try to control lesser matters, like going to school. However, you cannot use this book to impose controls over your beneficiaries or property, except leaving property in a trust for children. Making contingent gifts almost always opens a can of worms—for instance, who will enforce the will's conditions, and for how long?

- Leave money for an illegal purpose, such as encouraging minors to smoke tobacco.

- Leave property to felons convicted of certain crimes. These rules vary from state to state.

Dying Without a Will

As one incentive to writing your will, let's pause for a moment and consider what happens if you die without one. If you don't make a will, or use some other valid method to transfer your property after you die, your property will be distributed to your spouse and children under the "intestate succession" laws of your state. If you have neither spouse nor children, your property will go to other close relatives according to law. If no relatives qualify under law to inherit your property, it will go to your state (this is called "escheating"—one of my favorite legal words). Similarly, in the absence of a will, a state court judge determines who will care for your children and their property, and also who supervises the distribution of all of your property.

Because you bought this book, I won't bother with sermons on how foolish it would be for you to die without a will. But obviously, the division of property according to state intestate succession laws is highly unlikely to coincide with your

---

Why Many People Don't Write Wills

Among the famous people who have died without a valid will are Presidents Abraham Lincoln, Andrew Johnson, and U.S. Grant, as well as Howard Hughes and Pablo Picasso.

Though most people are aware that they need a will, many Americans don't have one. (Over 40% of Americans over age 45 don't have a will according to an AARP study; younger people are even less likely to have one.) Why? No one knows for sure, but here are some likely reasons:

- The legal establishment has managed to mystify the process of writing a will. People fear that "making

it legal" is a terribly complicated task and are frightened of writing a will themselves for fear of making mistakes.

- People believe that if they go to a lawyer to have a will prepared, they'll be charged a substantial fee. There's considerable basis for this fear.

- Lurking beneath many people's failure to make a will is the superstitious fear that thinking about a will or preparing one may somehow hasten death. Though this fear is plainly irrational, it's surely caused some people to put off writing a will.

personal desires. If you want to distribute any of your property to friends or organizations, intestate succession laws won't do it. If you're living with a partner to whom you aren't married, that person usually can't receive any of your property if you die intestate, absent a contract. In states that offer registered domestic partnerships and civil unions, a surviving partner has intestate inheritance rights. (See "Same-Sex Couples" in Chapter 3.) And if you have minor children, you will have left the judge no written guide as to who you want to raise them—something no parent wants. In sum, dying intestate is as unwise as it is unnecessary.

The Human Element

In the face of the overwhelming emotional force and mystery of death, the act of making a will may seem minor indeed. The larger questions and meanings are appropriately left for philosophers, clergy, poets and, ultimately, to you. For many, death is a painful subject to think about, to talk about, and to plan for. The ancient Greeks believed the inevitability of death could best be faced by performing great deeds. Christian religions offer the promise of eternal life; preparing for death means preparing to "meet your maker." Other cultures prepare for death in a wide variety of ways.

However you choose to prepare spiritually for death, many practical matters must be dealt with. For example, your property will have to go to someone. It's no denigration of death, or life, for you to be concerned with the wisest, most desirable distribution of your property. Writing a will is an act of concern, or love, to ensure that the people (and organizations) you care for receive the property you want them to have.

Discussing your wishes with close family members, if you choose to do so, can be worthwhile. Most couples discuss their wills with each other. You may want to discuss your will with other people, particularly family members you

name as beneficiaries. Of course, you don't have to discuss the contents of your will with anyone. Even your executor needs to know only that you wrote a will and where it's located—not what's in it. Haven't we all seen some Hollywood potboiler where the will of the deceased is read to the shock or dismay of would-be inheritors and perhaps the executor as well?

I suggest that in real life it's often wise to go further. Before making final decisions about your will, candor is often sensible for several reasons, ranging from the pleasure of letting people know what they'll inherit to clearing up confusion to reducing tensions. Maybe you'll learn how much two children really love and want that heirloom artwork. Or perhaps you'll learn that nobody cares that much. Isn't it better to know the desires of your loved ones before you write your will, or at least let people know what you intend to do?

Most of this book is devoted to the mechanics of will preparation. But don't let the technical aspects of will making overshadow the personal ones—which, after all, are why you're writing a will.

How to Get the Most From This Book

You may be tempted, especially if you think your situation is uncomplicated, to skip most of this book and go straight to the fill-in-the-blank wills. After all, filling in those blanks doesn't look too hard, does it?

I urge you to you slow down and take advantage of the information in the book first. The book's chapters are designed to be read sequentially. They start with some important background material about wills and pertinent state property laws, and then cover inventorying your property. Then you'll be ready to move to the core of will writing: choosing your beneficiaries (your inheritors), choosing your executor (the person who carries out the will's terms), and providing for any minor children you have, including nominating someone to raise them in the event you and their other parent can't.

TIP

This is a workbook. Don't be afraid to mark up this book. Many readers find that it helps them to write down facts, make notes, and record decisions as they proceed through the book.

A number of worksheets are provided to aid you with this process. You may want to print them out with the CD-ROM at the back of the book, tear them out of Appendix B (they're perforated), or photocopy them and work on the copies. Of course, use of the worksheets isn't mandatory—this isn't school. It's up to you to decide how much you want to use them.

So take out a pencil, eraser, and some scratch paper, and get ready.

After you've read through the material that applies to your personal situation, proceed to the will forms. The book gives you two ways to prepare a will. You can:

- Choose a fill-in-the-blank form, if one fits your family situation, from Chapter 10; or

- Create a customized will clause by clause, choosing from an extensive variety of options presented in Chapter 11. Sometimes I also refer to this as an assemble-the-clauses will.

Both the fill-in-the-blank will forms and the create-your-own-will clauses are on the CD-ROM in the back of this book. In either case, you must use a computer or typewriter to prepare the final version of your will.

Next, pay close attention to the discussion of the rules that dictate what you must do to make your will valid under state law (signing and witnessing), and read the suggestions on what to do with your will after it's been finalized.

Finally, there's information on estate planning and using lawyers.

CAUTION

Don't wing it. If you jump right to the forms without knowing what you're doing, you're flying blind. For instance, take the issue of naming someone to receive a beneficiary's property if he or she predeceases you. This is called naming an alternate beneficiary. Do you want to bother with this? What do you risk if you don't? Can you name more than one alternate beneficiary for the same gift? Clearly, it's better to know what your choices are than to decide by hunch or guess.

It's really not very demanding to go through this book and grasp the information you need. So take an hour—or three—to do it. Sure, skim or skip materials that clearly don't apply to you, but remember, your purpose here is not speed, but effectiveness; you want a will that is both legally valid and achieves your personal desires. That will take a little time (probably less than you expect) but will be well worth it.

Will You Need a Lawyer?

Most people can draft their own will without any aid except this book. The will-making process does not inherently require a lawyer. After all, for most people, making a will involves absolutely no conflict with others—the most common reason for hiring an attorney. No state law requires that a will be prepared or approved by a lawyer. In reality, only occasionally does a will require the sort of complex legal maneuvering that can necessitate a lawyer's skills. This book alerts you when drafting your will may require a lawyer's assistance.

SEE AN EXPERT

Notice the briefcase. This is the symbol you'll see throughout this book when consulting a lawyer is suggested. Though you'll find quite a few of these symbols in the book, you'll probably not be affected by any of them. How to find and work with a lawyer is discussed in detail in Chapter 15.

Wills have been a part of Anglo-American law for hundreds of years, in more or less the same basic form. For centuries, self-help was the rule in this country and lawyer assistance the exception. Even as late as the Civil War, it was unusual for a person to hire a lawyer to write a will. However, in more recent times, the legal profession has frightened the public into thinking that lawyers must prepare wills. This is nonsense.

The heart of making a will is deciding who you want to leave your property to. No lawyer can determine that for you. Similarly, a lawyer is obviously not the best person to decide who should raise your children if you can't. While working these matters through may be difficult, you can probably state your decisions in a sentence or two. And the plain truth is that turning those sentences into a formal will is usually not very complicated.

In any case, a will drafted by a lawyer is probably not as custom-tailored as you might imagine. Lawyers generally prepare wills by adapting previous clients' wills. And those wills probably originated from a standard attorney's form book containing the same types of clauses you'll find in this book (except that we've removed considerable amounts of unnecessary legal-sounding verbiage). Very likely, the lawyer has created a standardized form on computer. All that's left to be done is to type in your name, the names of the people you want your property to go to, and other necessary information, and then to print out the document. There's nothing wrong with this approach—but you can do it yourself just as well, using the forms in this book, and much more cheaply.

Some members of the legal establishment have tried to frighten the public with horror stories of disasters that befell some benighted person with a self-drafted will. A renowned lawyer once remarked that anyone who can take out his own appendix can write his own will. This analogy is false. If you can decide on which over-the-counter remedy to buy for a cold, or complete

> ## When to See a Lawyer
>
> Here are common situations when the services of a lawyer are usually warranted:
>
> - Your estate will be worth $2 million or more and may be subject to federal estate tax unless you engage in tax planning.
> - You want to establish a trust other than a simple family pot trust or child's trust (which are discussed in Chapter 7).
> - You own a part of a small business and have questions as to the rights of surviving owners, your ownership share, or another business matter.
> - You must arrange for long-term care of a beneficiary—for example, a disadvantaged child.
> - You fear someone will contest your will.
> - You wish to disinherit, or substantially disinherit, your spouse.

simple tax forms, preparing your own will should present no problems, unless yours is an unusual situation. (As I've said, throughout the book I flag potentially complex situations where you might need the help of an expert.) Drafting a valid will takes intelligence and common sense, but doesn't normally require sophisticated legal skills.

If you do decide at some stage that you want a lawyer's assistance, educating yourself will still be beneficial. If you are fairly knowledgeable about wills, or, better yet, if you prepare a draft of what you want, you may substantially reduce the lawyer's fee. And you'll be better able to tell whether the lawyer is being straightforward or is trying to bamboozle you into an overly complicated and expensive approach.

One piece of advice: In a will, you're expressing your own intentions. No one else can know those intentions. Sometimes, when people think, or fear, that they need a lawyer, what they're really doing is longing for an authority figure (or believing one is required) to tell them what to do. By buying this book, you've demonstrated that you're not willing to turn such basic decisions as the distribution of your own property over to someone else. Good. Keep that firmly in mind when considering whether you actually need a lawyer's help.

A Look at a Basic Will

Seeing a will drafted from this book may take some of the mystery out of the document—and reassure you that you can safely write your own will. At this point, some phrases or terms may not be crystal clear to you, but rest assured that every one will be thoroughly explained before you actually begin drafting your will.

Let's take as our example Jane Martinez, a woman in her mid-30s. Jane is married to Michael Francois. They have no children. She has several good friends and a cherished older sister, Martha Dougherty.

Jane's major assets are the expensive tools and other business assets she uses in her solely owned woodworking company, her sports car, and $65,000 in savings. She also values her extensive library, several pieces of jewelry, and one Thomas Hart Benton etching she inherited from her aunt.

This sample will is complete except for the formula language defining the executor's powers, which is the same for all wills in this book and is omitted here to save space.

Will of Jane Martinez

I, Jane Martinez, a resident of Montclair, Essex County, New Jersey, declare that this is my will.

1. Revocation of Prior Wills. I revoke all wills and codicils that I have previously made.

2. Personal Information. I am married to Michael Francois, and all references in this will to my husband are to him.

3. Specific Gifts. I leave the following specific gifts:

I leave $5,000 to my good friend Amy Wolpren, or, if she does not survive me, to my sister Martha Dougherty.

I leave $5,000 to my good friend John McGuire, or, if he does not survive me, to my sister Martha Dougherty.

I leave all my woodworking tools and business interest in Martinez Fine Woodworking and my car to my husband, Michael Francois, or, if he does not survive me, to my sister Martha Dougherty.

I leave my Thomas Hart Benton etching to my sister Martha Dougherty, or, if she does not survive me, to her daughter, Anita Dougherty.

I leave my gold jewelry and my books to my good friend Jessica Roettingen, or, if she does not survive me, to my sister Martha Dougherty.

4. Residuary Estate. I leave my residuary estate, that is, the rest of my property not otherwise specifically and validly disposed of by this will or in any other manner, including lapsed or failed gifts, to my husband, or, if he does not survive me, to my sister Martha Dougherty.

5. Beneficiary Provisions. The following terms and conditions shall apply to the beneficiary clauses of this will.

A. 45-Day Survivorship Period. As used in this will, the phrase "survive me" means to be alive or in existence as an organization on the 45th day after my death. Any beneficiary, except any alternate residuary beneficiary, must survive me to inherit under this will. If there are no surviving beneficiaries for a specific gift, that gift shall become part of my residuary estate.

B. Shared Gifts. If I leave property to be shared by two or more beneficiaries, it shall be shared equally between them unless this will provides otherwise.

If any beneficiary of a shared specific gift left in a single paragraph of the Specific Gifts clause, above, does not survive me, that deceased beneficiary's portion of the gift shall be given to the surviving beneficiaries in equal shares.

If any residuary beneficiary of a shared residuary gift does not survive me, that deceased beneficiary's portion of the residue shall be given to the surviving residuary beneficiaries in equal shares, unless this will provides otherwise.

C. Encumbrances. All property that I leave by this will shall pass subject to any encumbrances or liens on the property.

6. **Executor.** The following terms and conditions shall apply to the executor of this will.

A. Nomination of Executor. I nominate my husband, Michael Francois, as executor of this will to serve without bond. If Michael Francois shall for any reason fail to qualify or cease to act as executor, I nominate Martha Dougherty as executor, also to serve without bond.

B. Executor's Powers. I direct that my executor take all actions legally permissible to have the probate of my estate done as simply as possible, including filing a petition in the appropriate court for the independent administration of my estate.

[This clause is completed by the executor's powers provisions contained in all wills in this book.]

Signature

I subscribe my name to this will the 23th day of May, 2008, at Montclair, Essex County, New Jersey, and do hereby declare that I sign and execute this instrument as my last will and that I sign it willingly, that I execute it as my free and voluntary act for the purposes therein expressed, and that I am of the age of majority or otherwise legally empowered to make a will, and under no constraint or undue influence.

Jane Martinez
_____

Witnesses

On this __23rd__ day of __May__, __2008__, __Jane Martinez__ declared to us, the undersigned, that this instrument was her will and requested us to act as witnesses to it. She thereupon signed this will in our presence, all of us being present at the same time. We now, at her request, in her presence and in the presence of each other, subscribe our names as witnesses and declare we understand this to be her will, and that to the best of our knowledge the testator is of the age of majority, or is otherwise legally empowered to make a will, and under no constraint or undue influence.

We declare under penalty of perjury that the foregoing is true and correct, this __23rd__
day of ___May___, __2008__, at _____Montclair, New Jersey_____.
    month   year   city and state

___*Tom Warton*___
  witness's signature

___Tom Warton___ residing at ___10 Marion Ave___,
  witness's typed name   address

___Montclair___, ___Essex___, ___New Jersey___
    city   county   state

Jim Riodan
_____
witness's signature

Jim Riodan   residing at   275 Lorraine St.   ,
witness's typed name   address

          Montclair   ,   Essex   ,   New Jersey
               city   county   state

Linda O'Shea
_____
witness's signature

Linda O'Shea   residing at   23 Croissy Lane   ,
witness's typed name   address

          Montclair   ,   Essex   ,   New Jersey
               city   county   state

An Overview of Wills

Most people find it helpful to have a general view of what will making involves before focusing on specific components of their own wills. This chapter looks at several major concerns, starting with the one people most worry about: What makes a will legal?

How to Make a Valid Will

The legal requirements for drafting a valid will aren't nearly as complicated as many people fear. Carefully read what follows and you'll be reassured.

Age Requirements

To make a will you must either be:

- 18 years of age or older, or
- living in one of the few states that permit younger people to make a will if they're married, in the military, or otherwise considered "emancipated."

SEE AN EXPERT

Getting help. If you're under 18, don't make a will unless you've checked with a lawyer.

Mental State

You must be of "sound mind" to make a valid will. The fact that you're reading and understanding this book is, as a practical matter, sufficient evidence that you meet this test. The legal definitions of "sound mind" are mostly elaborations of common sense. The standard interpretations require that you:

- know that you're making a will and what a will is
- understand the relationship between yourself and the people who would normally be provided for in the will, such as a spouse or children

- understand what you own, and
- be able to decide how to distribute your property.

In reality, a person must be pretty far gone before a court will rule that she lacked the capacity to make a valid will. For example, forgetfulness or even the inability to recognize friends doesn't, by itself, establish incapacity. Also, it's important to remember that in the vast majority of cases, there's no need to prove to a court that the will writer was competent. It's presumed that the will writer was of sound mind, unless someone challenges this and proves otherwise in a court proceeding—which very rarely happens.

A will can also be declared invalid if a court determines that it was procured by "fraud" or "undue influence." This usually involves some evildoer manipulating a person of unsound mind to leave all, or most, of his property to the manipulator. Will contests based on these grounds are also quite rare.

SEE AN EXPERT

If you suspect someone might challenge your will on the basis of your mental competence or fraud, be sure to see a lawyer. For example, if you plan to leave the bulk of your property to someone you know is disliked and mistrusted by some close family members, work with a lawyer to minimize the possibility of a lawsuit, and maximize the chances your wishes will prevail if there is one.

Legal Requirements

You won't be around to vouch for your will's validity when it takes effect. Because of this stark truth, every state has laws designed to make sure that nobody can pass off a phony document as your will after your death. Most states' rules (except Louisiana's) are very similar, and they are less onerous than many people imagine.

Contrary to what some people believe, there's no requirement that a will be notarized to be valid. Here are the rules:

- The will should be typewritten or computer-printed. ("Types of Wills," below, discusses oral and handwritten wills, which are valid in some states.)

- The document must expressly state that it's your will.

- The will must have at least one substantive provision. A clause that leaves some, or all, of your property to someone is the most common substantive provision. However, a will that only appoints a personal guardian for your minor children and doesn't dispose of any property is also valid.

- You must appoint an executor (called a "personal representative" in some states). This person is responsible for supervising the distribution of your property after your death and seeing that your debts and taxes are paid. Nevertheless, in most states, even if you fail to name an executor in an otherwise valid will, a court will appoint one and then enforce the will.

- You must date and sign the will in the presence of at least two witnesses. Your witnesses cannot be named to receive property in your will. The witnesses watch you sign your will, and then sign it themselves. Witness requirements are covered in detail in Chapter 12.

- Although there is no legal requirement that a will be notarized, in most states if you and your witnesses sign an affidavit (a sworn statement) before a notary public, you can help simplify the court (probate) procedures required for the will after you die. This use of the "self-proving" affidavit is covered in Chapter 12.

- A will doesn't need to be filed with any court or government agency.

Will-Writing Vocabulary

In these first two chapters, I've introduced a bit of the basic lingo lawyers and courts use when discussing wills. Learning this vocabulary and the concepts behind the words is a significant step towards gaining the self-reliance necessary to write your own will. It's easy to be intimidated and uncomfortable when we don't know what lawyers' talk means. This obfuscation can be consciously, even cynically, used to keep people dependent on lawyers, particularly with a subject like will drafting. People fear that will writing must inherently require a lawyer, because the lawyers' language pertaining to wills can seem so forbidding.

Don't let them scare you. Beyond being written in (I believe) clear English and explaining in the text the most important will-writing terms, this book contains a Glossary that defines all significant terms that might arise when you're preparing your will. If you're unsure of the meaning of any legal term used in the text, please turn to the Glossary to aid your understanding.

The State Law That Governs Your Will

Generally, a will is valid in any state in the U.S. if it was valid under the laws of the state (or country) where you were "domiciled" when the will was made. Your domicile is the state where you have your principal home—that is, the place where you spend most of your time, as opposed, say, to a summer home. You can have only one domicile. When preparing your will, follow the rules of the state of your domicile even if you work in another state.

SEE AN EXPERT

If you're not sure where you're domiciled. If there's any doubt in your mind about which state is your permanent home—for example, if you divide your time roughly equally between houses in two states—and how that might affect your will, check with an attorney.

What happens if you move to another state after signing your will? The short answer is that you should review your will in light of the new state's laws, especially property ownership laws. (See Chapter 13 for a discussion of what to look for.) Fortunately, you'll probably determine that your original will does not need to be changed.

Types of Wills

This book enables you to prepare a normal typewritten will. Other types of wills, none of which I recommend, are also discussed below.

Typewritten "Witnessed" Wills

This is the conventional will, the kind this book enables you to prepare. Once prepared, it must be properly signed and witnessed. This type of "formal" will is familiar to courts and is what most people mean when they speak of a will. (Specific requirements for your will are covered in Chapter 10.)

"Pour-Over" Wills

Many people have heard of this form of will, but aren't quite sure what it does, so I'd like to clear up any mystery about it here. A pour-over will is simply a conventional will that names another entity—usually a "living trust" that the will writer has established—to receive the property subject to the will.

Few readers of this book need concern themselves with a pour-over will, for the simple reason that they are not setting up a living trust. Even if you decide to set up a living trust, a pour-over will may not accomplish anything desirable, as I discuss in Chapter 14.

Statutory Wills

A statutory will is a printed, fill-in-the-blanks, check-the-boxes form. It is authorized by state law in six states: California, Maine, Massachusetts, Michigan, New Mexico, and Wisconsin. In theory, statutory wills are an excellent idea—inexpensive, easy to complete and thoroughly reliable. Unfortunately, in practice, statutory wills aren't useful for most people. The main reason is that the choices provided in the statutory forms as to how property can be left are quite limited. And because these statutory forms cannot legally be changed, you can't customize them to fit your situation. Any attempts to alter a statutory will risk negating the entire will.

As an example of a restriction in a statutory will, with the California version you cannot leave your automobile and household property, including jewelry, separately—it must go as one gift. There are also restrictions on leaving real estate other than your personal residence. (If you want to look at the will itself, see Section 6240 of the California Probate Code.) The California statutory will is primarily useful to people who are married and want to leave the bulk or all of their property to the other spouse. If you want to leave some of your property, beyond a few gifts, to relatives, friends or institutions, the statutory will doesn't do the job.

Because of its limitations, the movement to adopt statutory wills has slowed. Only two states have adopted a fill-in-the-blanks will form since the mid-1980s.

Stationery Store Wills

Many stationery stores or legal supply stores offer a one- or two-page printed will form, with blank spaces, sometimes quite large, for you to complete. In my opinion, these forms are far too oversimplified. They contain no instructions for filling them in and no information regarding a host of reasonable concerns you might want to know about, ranging from leaving shared gifts to witnessing requirements.

Handwritten Wills

In a minority of states, handwritten, unwitnessed wills, called "holographic" wills, are valid. This type of will must be written, dated, and signed entirely in the handwriting of the person making the will. It is definitely not recommended by, and is not covered in, this book. Probate courts traditionally are very strict when examining holographic wills after the death of the will writer.

Because holographic wills are not witnessed, they're often thought to be less reliable. Cross-outs may invalidate the entire will. Further, it may be difficult to prove to the court's satisfaction that the document is actually in the deceased person's handwriting, and was intended to serve as his will.

Video Wills

You cannot create a valid will with a video recording. To be valid, a will form must be authorized by state law, and no state has authorized videotaped wills. While it would be convenient to just speak and be filmed to make a will, it simply isn't allowed. That's not to say that you can't make a video for your loved ones expressing thoughts and feelings. (See "Explanatory Letters," below.) But that video won't be your will.

Electronic Wills

Nevada is the only state to authorize an "electronic will." This is a will that is created and stored exclusively in an electronic format. The will must use a distinctive electronic signature and at least one other form of identification of the will maker, such as a fingerprint, retinal scan, or voice or face recognition technology. While such technology is developing rapidly, there are currently no readily available or acceptable methods for making a trustworthy and valid electronic will. It seems that Nevada is laying the groundwork for a time when such wills become feasible to prepare. When that time arrives, other states are likely to follow Nevada's lead and allow electronic wills.

Oral Wills

An oral will, sometimes called a "nuncupative" will, is valid in only a few states. Generally, even where valid, oral wills are acceptable only if they're made under special circumstances, such as the will maker's danger of imminent death or while on active duty with the U.S. military.

Joint Wills

A joint will is one document made by two people to serve as the will of both. Each leaves everything to the other. Then the will goes on to specify what happens to the property when the second person dies. A joint will prevents the surviving person from changing his mind regarding what should happen to his property after the other person (usually, a spouse) dies.

A joint will is essentially a contract between the two makers. Both must consent for a revocation to be effective. Joint wills can tie up property for years, pending the second death, and the survivor cannot revise the will to reflect changing circumstances. For these reasons, I don't recommend joint wills. A couple can use two separate wills to accomplish most of the sensible goals of a joint will, without its limits and potential dangers. If the spouses' goal is to ensure that property will ultimately go to children of prior marriages, a marital property control trust is a far better way to achieve this goal. (See Chapter 14.)

SEE AN EXPERT

Getting help. Be sure to consult an attorney if you're considering a joint will.

Contracts to Make a Will

A contract to make a will—that is, an agreement to leave certain property to the other person who signs the contract—can be valid, but is usually not wise unless it is part of a thoughtfully prepared prenuptial agreement or living-together contract made between partners.

A typical instance of an unwise contract to make a will arises when someone provides a service—such as live-in nursing care—in return for an agreement that the person receiving the care will leave property to the caregiver. Tying up your property like this so you cannot change your will, even if circumstances change, isn't desirable for many reasons. Most lawyers prefer to establish a trust in these situations.

SEE AN EXPERT

Making promises binding. If you face a situation in which you want to guarantee now that someone will receive money from your estate, see a lawyer.

Living Wills

A "living will" is not a traditional will at all. Rather, a living will is a document in which you set out your desires regarding medical treatment in case you later become incapacitated and unable to communicate your wishes. Originally, living wills were used to state that someone wanted a natural death and didn't want life artificially prolonged by use of medical technology or procedures. Now, however, people frequently use living wills to describe all their wishes for health care, including artificial feeding, treatment for pain, and organ donation after death. Living wills, which may also be called health care directives, advance directives, or directives to physicians, are valid in all states and are legally binding on physicians.

You can also provide binding instructions regarding your health care by use of a durable power of attorney for health care, which is also valid in all states. This document lets you appoint someone who will have legal authority to make health care decisions for you if you cannot, and to enforce your treatment wishes. (See Chapter 14.)

Explanatory Letters

In addition to preparing your will, you may want to leave a letter explaining your motives and desires in leaving your property. At the beginning of your letter, you should expressly declare that it is separate from your will; this prevents confusion for those who are handling your affairs after death. While the letter has no legal or binding effect, it can give you some peace of mind while you live, and also help soothe potential slights or hurts of surviving family members or friends. (If you'd rather not write a letter, you can choose to make some short personal comments in your will itself. See Chapter 5.)

I wouldn't attempt to instruct you on how to express the feelings of your heart. What follows are some suggestions of topics you might wish to cover.

Explaining Why Gifts Were Made

You may have thought much about why you're leaving a specific item of property to a beneficiary. In your letter, you can set forth your thoughts. For example, you could write why you've left that boat to your old fishing buddy, or that necklace to your niece.

Explaining Disparities in Gifts

You may wish to explain your reasons for leaving more property to one person than another. This can be particularly valuable if you leave more property to one child than another. Ideally, while you live, you could call together those involved, explaining to them why you plan to leave your property as you do. However, as the ideal may not be (once again) feasible or prudent, explaining your reasons in a letter can be far preferable to silence and mystery. Among the common reasons some people decide to leave different amounts of property are:

- one child has already received more money from a parent than other children—say, for purchase of a house or to cover the costs of education, or
- one family member has greater need than others.

Expressing Positive Sentiments

You may wish to express loving emotions, gratitude, or other positive feelings when leaving a gift to a beneficiary. As for negative emotions, I suggest that you leave any you may have out of your will *and* your explanatory letter. An old maxim states, "Don't speak ill of the dead." The wise corollary is that the dead shouldn't speak ill of anybody else. Legally, of course, you can express whatever you like, except that if you libel someone, your estate would be responsible for any damages. (*Libel* means communicating a false written statement that may harm a person's reputation.)

Obviously, there are near-infinite reasons someone might want to express positive feelings in a letter, including:

- appreciating the service and care someone—a doctor, a car mechanic, a teacher, whoever— gave you
- appreciating the fun and love a friend provided, or
- expressing gratitude and respect for someone who aided you when you were in trouble.

Providing Care for Your Pet

In your explanatory letter, you can express feelings for your pet and leave any special instructions about how you would like it cared for. Along with this, it's important to use your will or a trust to make practical arrangements so your animals will have a place to go. This is discussed in more detail in Chapter 5.

Describing Personal Experiences and Values

Many people are interested in leaving behind more than just property. If you wish, you can also leave a statement about the experiences, values, and beliefs that have shaped your life. This kind of letter or document is often known as an "ethical will," and it can be of great worth to those who survive you. (Personally, I'm sad that I didn't think to urge my parents to prepare this kind of legacy before they died.)

While you could legally include an ethical will statement in your regular will—that is, the one you'll make with this book that leaves your property to others—I recommend that you include these sentiments in your explanatory letter or in a separate document. Trying to sum up what's in your soul may turn out to require many pages, and take considerable time. Better not to enmesh that profound searching with the task of preparing your conventional will. More practically speaking, you'll want to avoid including anything potentially confusing or ambiguous in your legal will.

As long as you don't contradict the provisions of your legal will, your options for expressing yourself are limited only by the time and energy you have for the project. You could do something as simple as use your explanatory letter to set out a concise description of your basic values. Or, if you feel inspired, you may leave something much more detailed for your loved ones. Many survivors are touched to learn about important life stories, memories, and events. You might also consider including photographs or other mementos with your letter. If writing things down seems like too much effort, you could use an audio or videotape to talk to those who are closest to you. A little thought will surely yield many creative ways to express yourself to those you care for.

RESOURCE

More information about ethical wills. If you want to go beyond writing down some of your experiences and values in your explanatory letter, there is a growing body of websites and literature that can help you explore different ways of making an ethical will. You might begin by visiting www.ethicalwill.com. The site offers some basic free information and sells ethical will-writing kits.

CAUTION

Trying to control behavior. For some, an ethical will means putting provisions in their legal will that attempt to reward beneficiaries for acting in certain ways—or to punish them if they don't. For example, a will writer might want to provide cash incentives to younger beneficiaries if they work for favorite causes. Usually, trying to establish this type of control over others is at best futile, and at worst destructive. If you weren't able to pass on your values and morals by example while you lived, it's very unlikely that you can do so through gifts of your property after your death. Moreover, the mechanics of imposing moral conditions on your gifts are inherently complicated. Among the issues that must be resolved are: Who is to determine whether the beneficiary is fulfilling your moral requirement? How is that to be determined? For how long must the beneficiary do what you want before they receive your gift? For all of these reasons, the will you make using this book cannot contain conditional gifts. (See Chapter 5 for more information about placing restrictions on gifts.)

What Happens to Your Property After You Die

After you die, what happens? Who knows? (Just kidding.) Well, you can know what happens to your property. It will be transferred as your will directs, and the other provisions of your will will be carried out. Here's the normal sequence of events:

1. Your executor locates your will, which you should have stored in a safe and accessible place.

2. If probate is required, the executor shepherds the estate through the probate court proceeding. Although probate can be a time consuming and tedious process, it rarely requires the legal expertise of a lawyer. Executors can legally handle it on their own. For detailed information for executors, read *The Executor's Guide*, by Mary Randolph (Nolo). Executors of estates in California have a step-by-step guide through probate with *How to Probate an Estate in California*, by Julia Nissley (Nolo).

3. The probate court officially gives the executor legal authority to conduct the estate's business in what's traditionally called "letters of administration." Other names can be used—for example, California calls this "letters testamentary."

4. If you have minor children and the other parent can't care for them, the probate court (normally) appoints the person you named in your will to be guardian for the children. (See Chapter 7 for how you can best control this.)

5. The executor manages your estate during the probate process, handling (usually without the need for court approval) any problems that arise and paying your debts, including any income, or estate taxes.

6. If a trust was created for your children by your will, money or property earmarked for that trust gets distributed to the designated trustee. (See Chapter 7 for information on creating a trust for your children.)

7. Once probate is completed, your property is distributed as your will directs. Completing probate generally takes at least four months and often as long as a year. Once the proceeding is completed, further creditor's claims against your estate aren't valid, assuming the creditor was properly notified of the probate proceeding.

Special Property Rules for Married People

Marriage is crucial to laws covering how you can leave your property. (Why don't they mention this in Hollywood romances or love songs?) There are two ways your marital status can affect how you leave property:

- First, your spouse may already own a share of some property you believe is yours alone.

- Second, your spouse may have the right to claim a share of your property after your death, whether you like it or not.

In both situations, state law determines what is yours to leave by will and what is not. This means that if you're married (this includes everyone who hasn't received a final decree of divorce or annulment), it's important that you understand the marital property laws of the state that's your permanent home, and any state where you own real estate. Real estate is always subject to the laws, including the marital ownership laws, of the state where it's located.

States can be divided into two types for the purpose of deciding what spouses own: community property states and common law states.

Community Property States	Common Law States
*Alaska	All other states
Arizona	(and the District of
California	Columbia) except
Idaho	Louisiana
Nevada	
New Mexico	
Texas	
Washington	
Wisconsin (called "marital property")	

*Only if the married couple makes a written agreement.

Same-Sex Couples

If you are in a registered domestic partnership or a civil union in Connecticut, Hawaii, Maine, New Hampshire, New Jersey, Oregon, Vermont, or Washington or married in Massachusetts, your state law grants a surviving partner or spouse inheritance rights similar to those granted by marriage in that state. The amount of the right of inheritance varies from about one-third to one-half of the estate, depending on the state. (In California, community property law provides that each partner owns half of all property obtained during the relationship, and that neither partner has a legal right to inherit any of the other's property.) However, you should not rely on your state's law (assuming it covers you) to transfer your property on your death to your partner. Make your own decisions about who gets what. Then prepare a will to ensure that your desires will be carried out. It's never wise to allow the state to do your financial planning, particularly not for a matter as important as who inherits your property.

CAUTION

Leave your partner at least half of your estate. In the common law states listed above, a surviving spouse who is left less than the statutory share can chose to take the higher share provided by law. If you leave your partner half or more of your estate, there'll be no problem about these laws. If you want to leave your partner less than half, talk with a knowledgeable lawyer and see if you're running any risks.

While marital property law issues are important, there is no reason to become anxious about them. Obviously, if you and your spouse plan to leave all of your property to each other, it doesn't matter who owns what. However, if you plan to leave some property to others, you should know which spouse owns what before you make your will. Otherwise, your wishes may be frustrated, at least in part. But here too, there's usually no significant problem with marital ownership laws. A spouse isn't likely to object to a few items of property being left to others by the other spouse, no matter what the legal rights are. So a daughter or son gets, say, some photos or antiques from a deceased spouse, when the surviving spouse legally owns half that property. It's surely rare that the surviving spouse insists on his or her legal rights and pulls back half the gift.

Attitudes and the applicable law can change drastically if a spouse wants to leave the other little or no property. Then who owns what becomes critical. What legal rights, if any, a surviving spouse has to any of a deceased spouse's property can also be crucial.

Do You Know Whether You're Married or Single?

Some people aren't absolutely certain whether they're married or not. Uncertainty can occur in three circumstances:

- **You have been told, have heard, or somehow believe you're divorced, but never received a final divorce decree to confirm it.** If you're in this situation, call the court clerk in the county where the divorce was supposed to have occurred and get the records. If you can't track down a final decree of divorce, it's best to assume you're still married.

- **You believe you're married by common law.** Most people aren't. Only the states listed below recognize some form of common law marriage.

    Alabama

    Colorado

    District of Columbia

    Georgia (if created before 1/1/97)

    Idaho (if created before 11/1/96)

    Iowa

    Kansas

    Montana

    New Hampshire (if a couple lives together at least three years, and one of them dies without a will)

    Ohio (if created before 10/10/91)

    Oklahoma

    Pennsylvania (if created before 1/1/05)

    Rhode Island

    South Carolina

    Texas

    Utah

Even in these states, merely living together isn't enough to create a common law marriage; you must hold yourselves out to the world as married.

- **You don't know whether your divorce is legal.** This is particularly true of Mexican and other out-of-country divorces where only one person participated. Don't rely on a foreign divorce. If you have any reason to think your former spouse might claim to be still married to you at your death, see a lawyer and get a divorce you know is valid. In the meantime, you carry the risk that if you die, your (would-be-ex) spouse may have a right to a portion of your property, no matter what your will provides. Pretty unpalatable, isn't it? So don't drag this one out.

RESOURCE

Prenuptial agreements can change every-thing. A valid prenuptial contract can change the rules about who owns what. If you have such a contract and are in doubt as to how its provisions affect your right to leave property in your will, see a lawyer. Also, spouses can agree during marriage to transfer ownership of property between them any way they want. For more information about prenups, see *Prenuptial Agreements: How to Write a Fair & Lasting Contract,* by Katherine E. Stoner and Shae Irving (Nolo).

SKIP AHEAD

Don't worry about this if you leave everything to your spouse. You don't need to pursue this subject any further if you and your spouse are leaving all of your property to each other. In that case, it doesn't make any difference whether property is separate or community.

Community Property States

The basic community property rule is simple: During a marriage, all property acquired by either spouse is owned in equal half shares by each spouse as community property, except for property received by one spouse as a gift or inheritance. This concept is derived from the ancient marriage laws of some European peoples, including the Visigoths, passing eventually to Spain, and through Spanish explorers and settlers to some Western states. More recently, it was also adopted by Wisconsin.

Anything that isn't community property is "separate property"—that is, property owned entirely by one spouse. For example, property owned before marriage usually remains separate property even after the marriage (some exceptions to this rule are described on the next page). Also, property can be given as separate property to one spouse by a will or gift.

In community property states, what you own typically consists of all of your separate property and one-half of the property owned as community property with your spouse. Together, this is the property you can leave in your will however you choose to. You do not have to leave your half interest in the community property to your spouse, although it's common to do so.

For many couples who have been married a number of years, the lion's share of property is community property; most or all property owned before marriage is long gone, and neither spouse has inherited or been given any substantial amount of separate property. Still, even if you believe this is your situation, I recommend that you take a moment to read the next few pages to be sure.

Community Property Defined

The following property is community property:

- All employment income received by either spouse during the course of the marriage. Generally, this refers only to the period when the parties are living together as husband and wife. From the time spouses permanently separate, newly acquired income and property are generally the separate property of the spouse receiving them.

- All property bought with employment income received by either spouse during the marriage (but not with income received after a permanent separation).

- All property which, despite originally being separate property, is transformed into community property under the laws of your state. This transformation can occur in several ways, including when one spouse gives it to the community (the couple)—for example, changing the deed of a separately owned home to community property. More commonly, separate property simply gets so mixed together with community property that it's no longer possible to tell it apart. Lawyers call this "commingling."

Separate or Community Property?		
Property	**Classification**	**Reason**
A computer your spouse inherited during marriage	Your spouse's separate property	Property inherited by one spouse alone is separate property
A car you owned before marriage	Your separate property	Property owned by one spouse before marriage is separate property
A boat, owned and registered in your name, which you bought during your marriage with your income	Community property	It was bought with community property income (income earned during the marriage)
A family home, the deed to which states that you and your wife own it as "husband and wife" and which was bought with your earnings	Community property	It was bought with community property income (income earned during the marriage) and is owned as "husband and wife"
A Leica 35mm SLR camera you received as a gift	Your separate property	Gifts made to one spouse are that spouse's separate property
A checking account owned by you and your spouse, into which you put a $5,000 inheritance 20 years ago	Community property	The $5,000 (which was your separate property) has become so mixed with community property funds that it has become community property

For example, if you receive $100 as a birthday present, it's your separate property. But if you deposit the money to the joint checking account you own with your spouse, it becomes impossible to distinguish it.

The one major exception to these rules is that all community property states allow spouses to treat income earned after marriage as separate property if they sign a written agreement to do so and then actually keep it separate, as in separate bank accounts. Most couples don't do this, but it does sometimes happen, as with a prenuptial agreement.

Separate Property Defined

All these are separate property:

- property owned by either spouse before marriage
- property one spouse receives after marriage by gift or inheritance, and
- property that the spouses agree, in a contract, to classify as separate.

These kinds of property remain separate property as long as they aren't mixed (commingled) with community property. As mentioned, if commingling occurs, separate property may turn into community property.

Community property states differ in how they classify certain types of property. One of the biggest differences is how the states treat income generated by separate property during a marriage. In California, Arizona, Nevada, New Mexico, and Washington, any income from separate property during a marriage is also separate property. In Texas and Idaho, it is considered community property. (Wisconsin's statutes on this point are confusing; if it matters to you, see a Wisconsin lawyer.)

Pensions and Community Property

Any property left in a pension plan is normally not transferred by your will; instead, you name a beneficiary to inherit any money due at your death. But when you're deciding on leaving gifts by your will, it may be important to you how the plan is legally characterized. Military and private employment pensions are community property— at least, the proportion of them attributable to earnings during the marriage. However, certain major federal pension programs, including Social Security and Railroad Retirement, aren't community property; under federal law, they are the separate property of the employee.

The table above lists some common examples of separate and community property.

Community Property Ownership Problems

Many, indeed most, married couples have little difficulty determining what is community property. But in some situations, that determination is neither obvious nor easy. If there's any confusion or uncertainty, it's best to resolve it while both spouses are still living. If you encounter any serious problems, you need to discuss and resolve

them. Then you should write out and sign a marital property agreement setting forth your determinations.

SEE AN EXPERT

See a lawyer if preparing a marital property agreement gets sticky. Some couples should see a lawyer before finalizing a marital property agreement. If there are serious disagreements over who owns what, it's sensible to get legal advice before resolving the conflict. You should also see a lawyer if the agreement gives one spouse significantly more than half the property acquired during a marriage. Judges have voided marital property agreements they deemed unfair, with one spouse taking advantage of the other.

Here are several potential problem areas regarding characterizing property:

Appreciated property. In most community property states, when the separate property of one spouse goes up in value, the appreciation is also separate property. However, if one spouse owns separate property before a marriage, but both spouses contribute to the costs for maintaining or improving it during the marriage, and the property has substantially appreciated in value, it can be difficult to determine what percentage of the current value of the property is separate property and what is community property.

The most common instance of this is a house originally owned by one spouse. Then for a length of time, say ten or 30 years, both spouses pay, from community funds, for the mortgage, insurance, and upkeep. Over the length of the marriage, the value of the house grows tremendously. How can the spouses determine what portion of the present value is community property? The best way is to agree on a division they decide is fair, and put this understanding in writing. If you can't do this on your own, see a lawyer. Resolving this issue is especially important if either of the spouses plans to leave a substantial interest in the house to someone other than the other spouse.

Businesses. Family-owned businesses can create difficult problems, especially if the business was owned in whole or part before marriage by one spouse. As with home ownership, the basic problem is to figure out whether the increased value is community or separate property. Even if the business didn't go up in value, the other spouse might have acquired an ownership interest by contributing community funds or labor to its operation.

Lawyers usually approach the problem like this: If both spouses work in the business, then any increase in value that the business undergoes (or, less likely, the maintenance of the pre-marriage value) is community property. However, if only the spouse who originally owned the business works in it, it is often not so clear whether the increase in (or maintenance of) its value was due to the work of that spouse while married, and is hence community property, or whether the business would have grown and prospered just as much anyway. Commonly, an increase in value of the business is due to both factors.

Trying to resolve what portion of the increase is due to each factor has enriched many divorce lawyers. If you and your spouse have any question over who owns what proportion of a business, try to resolve that issue, and write down your agreement.

SEE AN EXPERT

Leaving a family-owned business. If you plan to leave your share of the business to your spouse, or in a way your spouse approves of (in writing), you have no practical problem. However, if your view of who owns the business is different from that of your spouse, and you don't see eye to eye on your estate plans, it's important to get professional help. This may mean a family therapist as well as an attorney.

Monetary recovery for personal injuries. As a general matter, personal injury awards or settlements are the separate property of the spouse receiving them, but not always. In some community property states, this money is treated one way while the injured spouse is living and another way after death. Also, the determination as to whether it's separate or community property may depend on whether the injury was caused by the other spouse. In short, there is no easy way to characterize this type of property.

SEE AN EXPERT

Personal injury funds. If a significant amount of your property came from a personal injury settlement and you and your spouse don't agree about how you should leave it, see an experienced lawyer about the specifics of your state's law.

Borrowed funds. Generally, all community property is liable for debts incurred on behalf of the marriage. In addition, each spouse's one-half share of the community property is normally liable to pay that spouse's separate property debts.

A spouse's separate property is usually responsible for that spouse's separate debts—for example, if a spouse used a separate property business as collateral for a loan to expand the business. Unfortunately, it isn't always easy to determine whether a particular debt was incurred for the benefit of the community or for the benefit of only one spouse. Further, in some states such as California, one spouse's separate property may be liable for debts for food, shelter, and other common necessities of life incurred by the other spouse.

SEE AN EXPERT

What do you owe? If you're worried about what debts your property may be liable for, see a lawyer.

Inheritance Protection for Spouses in California, Idaho, Washington, and Wisconsin

In these four states—and in very limited circumstances—a surviving spouse may be entitled to inherit a portion of the deceased spouse's community or separate property. These laws are designed to prevent spouses from being either accidentally overlooked or deliberately deprived of their fair share of property.

To understand these rules, you need to know just a little bit about "quasi–community property." If you are married and acquire property in a common law state, and then move to California, Idaho, Washington, or Wisconsin, that property will be treated exactly like community property. This property is known as "quasi–community property," except in Wisconsin, where it's called "deferred marital property."

Here's a brief summary of the rules for the three community property states that offer statutory protection for surviving spouses.

California. If the deceased spouse made an estate plan before marriage and didn't include the surviving spouse in a will or trust, the surviving spouse can claim *all* of the community and quasi–community property, as well as a share of the deceased spouse's separate property. (California Prob. Code § 21610.)

Idaho. In some circumstances, if the deceased spouse gave away quasi–community property, or sold it for less than its value, the surviving spouse can demand that the property be returned to the deceased spouse's estate. The surviving spouse can then claim half of that property. (Idaho Code § 15-2-202 and following.)

Washington. If a spouse transferred quasi–community property for less than full value within three years of death, a surviving spouse may, under certain conditions, recover half of that property interest. (Wash. Rev. Code § 26.16.240.)

Wisconsin. Rather than take what the deceased spouse provided, the surviving spouse can elect to inherit up to one-half of what's called the "augmented deferred marital property estate." This is the total value of the deferred marital property of both spouses, including gifts of deferred marital property made by the deceased spouse during the two years before death. (Wis. Stat. § 861.02 and following.)

SEE AN EXPERT

Spousal protection laws are complicated. If you live in one of the states listed above and you wish to learn more about these spousal protection laws, see an experienced estate planning lawyer.

Common Law States

In common law states, there is no rule that property acquired during a marriage is owned by both spouses. To protect a spouse from being disinherited and winding up with nothing after the other spouse's death, common law states give a surviving spouse the right to claim a certain portion of the property the deceased spouse left.

Common law principles are derived from English law, where in feudal times the husband owned all marital property while a wife had few legal property ownership rights and couldn't leave property by will.

CAUTION

You can't disinherit your spouse. To avoid potential legal problems, leave your spouse at least 50% of your property. If you do this, common law spousal protection rules don't apply to you, and you can skip or skim this section. If you plan to leave a spouse less than 50% of your property, read this section carefully—and plan on seeing a lawyer.

Common Law States	
Alabama	Missouri
Alaska*	Montana
Arkansas	Nebraska
Colorado	New Hampshire
Connecticut	New Jersey
Delaware	New York
District of Columbia	North Carolina
Florida	North Dakota
Georgia	Ohio
Hawaii	Oklahoma
Illinois	Oregon
Indiana	Pennsylvania
Iowa	Rhode Island
Kansas	South Carolina
Kentucky	South Dakota
Maine	Tennessee
Maryland	Utah
Massachusetts	Vermont
Michigan	Virginia
Minnesota	West Virginia
Mississippi	Wyoming

*Property will be treated as community property if a married couple makes a written agreement to that effect.

(Louisiana has a system of law derived from France and is neither a common law nor community property state.)

A Smidgen of History

Hundreds of years ago, the English courts, confronted with the problem of a few people disinheriting their spouses, developed rules called "dower" and "curtesy." These are fancy words for the sensible concept that a surviving wife or husband who isn't adequately provided for in a spouse's will can claim a portion of the deceased spouse's property by operation of law. "Dower" refers to the rights acquired by a surviving wife, while "curtesy" means the rights acquired by a surviving husband.

When the United States was settled, most states adopted these concepts. To this day, all common law states still retain some version of dower and curtesy, although some have dropped the old terminology. Such protections aren't usually needed in community property states, because each spouse already owns one-half of all property acquired from the earnings of either during the marriage. Nevertheless, in very limited circumstances, a few community property states do provide extra protections for surviving spouses.

Who Owns What in Common Law States

In common law states, the property you own, whether you are married or single, consists of:

- everything held separately in your name if it has a title slip, deed, or other legal ownership document

- everything else you have purchased with your property or income, and

- your share of everything you own with a person other than your spouse.

Thus, in these states, the key to ownership for many types of valuable property is whose name is on the title. If you earn or inherit money to buy a house, and take title in both your name and your spouse's, you both own the house. If your spouse earns the money, but you take title in your name alone, you own it. If title is in her name, she owns it.

Preventing Injustice at Divorce

Despite the general common law rule that says that the person whose name is on the document owns the property, courts in most states will not allow a manifest injustice to occur at divorce. For example, under the "equitable distribution" divorce laws of most common law property states, a court has the power to divide property between the husband and wife in a manner the court thinks is fair (often, equally), no matter what the ownership documents say. However, the effect, if any, of equitable distribution laws on property a spouse leaves at death is, at present, unclear.

If an object—say, a new computer— has no title document, then the person whose income or property was used to pay for it owns it. If both spouses contributed, then ownership is shared.

EXAMPLE:

Wilfred and Jane, husband and wife, live in Kentucky, a common law property state. They have five children. Shortly after their marriage, Wilfred wrote an extremely popular computer program that helps doctors diagnose a variety of ills. Wilfred has received royalties averaging about $100,000 a year over a ten-year period. During the course of the marriage, Wilfred used the royalties to purchase a car, yacht, and mountain cabin, all registered in his name. The couple also own a house together. In addition, Wilfred owns a number of heirlooms received from his parents. Over the course of the marriage, Wilfred and Jane have maintained separate savings accounts. Jane's income (she works as a computer engineer) has gone into her account, and the balance of Wilfred's royalties

has been placed in his account, which now contains $75,000.

Wilfred's property (his estate) consists of the following:

- 100% of the car, yacht, and cabin, because title documents list all of this property in his name. Were there no such documents, Wilfred would still own them because they were purchased with his income.
- 100% of his savings account, because it is in his name alone.
- The family heirlooms.
- A 50% interest in the house. However, if the house were in Wilfred's name alone, it would be his property, even if purchased with money he earned during the marriage, or indeed even if purchased with Jane's money.

Family Protection in Common Law States

As I've said, if you're married and live in a common law state, you must leave your spouse at least half of your property to use a Nolo will. If you leave your spouse less, you risk running afoul of state law. All common law property states have laws that protect the surviving spouse from being completely or substantially disinherited. While many of these protective laws are similar, they differ in detail. In fact, no two states are exactly alike.

In most common law property states, a spouse is entitled by law to claim one-third of the deceased spouse's property no matter what the will provides. In a few, it's one-half or some other standard. This right is sometimes called "an elective share" or "a forced share."

Leaving Your Spouse Less Than Half

SEE AN EXPERT

Although few married people want to leave their spouse less than half their property, occasionally there are good reasons to do so, including:

- You are concerned about estate taxes. (If so, be sure to check out "Estate Taxes" in Chapter 14. You'll probably need planning beyond the scope of this book.)

- You are in a second or subsequent marriage and want to leave most or all of your property to children from a prior marriage. The sensible and legally secure way to achieve this is for you and your spouse to see a lawyer and sign an agreement specifically geared to your state's laws, stating that each of you may leave your property as you like.

- You just don't care for your spouse very much. In this case, get a divorce or see a lawyer.

Some states provide that all of the deceased spouse's property, including any that was transferred by means other than a will, is subject to the surviving spouse's claim. Other states take a different approach: they include not only all of the deceased spouse's property, but some or all of the separate property owned by the surviving spouse as well. (In these states, the total amount of property used to calculate the surviving spouse's share is called the "augmented estate.")

Furthermore, the exact amount of the spouse's minimum share often depends on whether or not there are minor children and whether or not the spouse has been provided for outside the will by trusts or other means.

In any common law state, you won't have any problem if you leave half or more of your property to your spouse. That is the reason for the rule in this book: *LEAVE YOUR SPOUSE AT LEAST HALF YOUR PROPERTY.* If you want to learn the precise rules for your state, say, to see if you could safely leave your spouse one-third instead of one-half of your property, see a lawyer.

In most states, a spouse can agree to give up (waive) the right to claim a share of the other spouse's estate. But in a few states there are at least some statutory restrictions on such waivers. If a waiver is permitted, it must be in writing. It can be done either before marriage, in a prenuptial agreement, or after marriage, in a postnuptial agreement. (It's generally considered gauche to bring up the subject during the wedding ceremony.) The effect of a valid waiver is that one spouse receives whatever property the other agreed to leave her or him, even if it's far less than the statutory amount.

Statutory inheritance rights are often waived in second or subsequent marriages. Especially if both spouses have a comfortable amount of their own property, neither may be concerned with inheriting from the other. And one or both spouses may want their property to go to other inheritors, particularly children from prior marriages.

Absent a valid spousal waiver, a surviving spouse has a choice: either take what the other spouse's will provides (called "taking under the will"), or reject the gift and instead claim the share allowed by state law. Taking the share permitted by law is called "taking against the will."

EXAMPLE:

Leonard's will leaves $50,000 to his second wife, June, and leaves all the rest of his property, totaling $400,000, to his two children from his first marriage. June can elect to take against the will and receive her statutory share of Leonard's estate, which will be far more than $50,000.

When a spouse decides to take against the will, the property that is taken must of necessity come out of what was left to others by the will. In other words, somebody else is going to get less. In the example above, the children will receive much less than Leonard intended. So keep in mind that if you don't provide your spouse with at least his or her statutory share under your state's laws, your gifts to others may be seriously jeopardized.

If You Move to Another State

What happens when a husband and wife acquire property in a noncommunity property state and then move to a community property state?

As discussed, California, Idaho, Washington, and Wisconsin (community property states) treat the earlier acquired property as if it had been acquired in a community property state. Thus, if you and your spouse moved from any noncommunity property state into California, Idaho, Washington, or Wisconsin, all of your property is treated according to community property rules. The legal jargon for this type of property is "quasi–community property," except in Wisconsin, where it's called "deferred marital property."

The other community property states don't recognize the quasi–community property concept and instead go by the rules of the state where the property was acquired. Arizona and Texas recognize quasi–community property for divorce purposes, but not for will purposes.

When couples move from a community property state to a common law state, each spouse generally retains a one-half interest in the property acquired while they were married in the community property state. However, the courts that have dealt with the problem haven't been totally consistent. Accordingly, if you have moved from a community property state to a common law state, and you and your spouse have any disagreement or confusion as to who owns what, check with a lawyer. ●

Taking Inventory of Your Property

Will writing is often viewed as a single process: deciding who gets what. But here we'll pull that process apart and first focus on the "what." In the next chapter, you'll concentrate on the "who" part of the equation—your beneficiaries.

This chapter explains how to fill out a worksheet on which you can list all your items of property. You can find a blank Property Worksheet in Appendix B or on the CD-ROM at the back of this book. Filling out this worksheet can help you jog your memory, to help you make sure you don't overlook any property.

Do you really need to take stock of what you own and make this kind of inventory? In any of the following situations, probably not:

- you have a small estate
- you keep all your property information in your head
- you plan to leave all your property to one person
- you'll leave your property to be shared by no more than a few beneficiaries, or
- you plan to make only one, or few, specific gifts and leave all the rest of your property to one person.

EXAMPLE:

Jane wants to leave all of her stained-glass supplies, tools, and equipment to her friend Alice, her car to her friend Amy, and everything else she owns (including stocks, jewelry, money market funds, and personal household possessions) to her sister Mary. Jane sensibly decides she doesn't need to make a written inventory of her property.

In sum, if for will purposes your property situation is simple and clear, you can skim this chapter and move quickly to the next one, where you'll focus on beneficiaries.

However, if you own many items of property, or wish to divide your property among a number of people and organizations, you'll probably want to make use of the worksheet to carefully list what you own and what you owe.

Remember, this worksheet is purely for your convenience. Make as much or as little use of it as you like. Don't worry if it gets a little messy, as long as you can read it when you begin to pin down your beneficiaries in the next chapter, and when you draft your will from Chapter 10 or 11.

One possible use of the worksheet can be to make a rough estimate of the current net value of your estate. It may be handy to have this estimate when you're deciding on individual gifts. Also, estimating your current net worth provides an indication of whether or not your estate will be liable for federal estate taxes when you die. Under current law, federal estate taxes start for a net estate worth $2 million to $3.5 million, depending on the year of death. (See Chapter 14.) Since all property you own is counted for estate tax purposes, the property worksheet asks you to list everything you own, whether it will be transferred by will or not. Don't get hung up by worries over the precise worth of any of your property. You're only making an estimate. Besides, for estate tax purposes, it's the net value of your property when you die that matters.

Getting Organized

As you complete this worksheet, it may occur to you that your property ownership documents and other important papers are scattered all over the place. Leaving this kind of mess at your death is almost guaranteed to make life difficult for your executor. Therefore, along with making your will, it's wise to adopt a coherent system to list and organize all your property. A convenient way to do this is to use *Get It Together: Organize Your Records So Your Family Won't Have To,* by Melanie Cullen with Shae Irving (Nolo).

List and Describe Your Property (Column 1)

The first column of the Assets section of the property worksheet is for listing each item of property—or, more specifically, each item you decide to list separately. There are no rules that require your property to be listed in any particular form or legal language, either here or in your will. The whole point is to be clear about what property you own, so that when your will takes effect, there is no question about what you meant.

> ⊘ **CAUTION**
>
> **Don't leave foreign property by your will.** Do not rely on a will from this book to leave foreign property, including real estate. Each country has its own laws and rules regarding leaving property, particularly real estate. So if you own foreign property, get some advice from a lawyer familiar with that country's laws.

Bank Accounts

You can list bank accounts by any means sufficient to identify them. If you have only one account, you can identify it by bank name: "Savings Account at Bay Savings Bank, Portland, Maine." If you have more than one account, list the account number: "Bank account #78-144212-8068 at Oceanside Savings, Market St. Branch, East Columbia, Missouri."

Money Market Accounts, Certificates of Deposit, and Stocks

These need to be listed clearly enough so there's no question what property is referred to:

- "The money market account #6D-32 2240001 at International Monetary Inc."
- "All stocks and any other assets in account #144-16-4124 at Smith Barney & Co., Mobile, Alabama"

- "Certificate of Deposit, No. 10235, Lighthouse Savings and Loan Association, Ventura, CA."

If you have taken possession of actual stock certificates, rather than leaving them with your broker, the way it's normally done, state where the certificates are located: "100 shares of General Motors common stock, kept in my desk drawer at my house at...."

Retirement Accounts

Here, you should list all money in individual retirement accounts—such as an IRA, Roth IRA, 401(k), or profit-sharing plan. Also note any vested rights to specific sums in a pension plan. Remember that these types of assets are primarily to be used for your retirement and may contain little or no money when you die.

Personal Possessions

For will-writing purposes, personal possessions can be divided between items of monetary or sentimental value, which you'll probably want to list individually, and items of lesser value, which can be listed as a group or unit.

Valuable Items. Examples of items that have significant monetary, personal, or sentimental value include:

- "My collection of 19th century American coins"
- "My 1986 Ferrari Automobile, License #123456"
- "My Tiffany lamp"
- "My gold earrings with the small rubies in them"
- "The Daumier print captioned 'Les beaux jours de la vie.'"

Less Valuable Items. If you're like most people, you have all sorts of minor personal items you don't want to bother itemizing. To deal with these, you can simply list all items in a certain category—for example, "all my tools" or "all my dolls" or "baseball cards" or "books" or "machines and equipment." Or you can simply include miscellaneous items as part of a general listing of household furnishings and possessions.

Personal Property

Your "personal property" consists of all your property except real estate. This includes your liquid assets, such as cash, checking, and savings accounts, cars, household furnishings, and business property (except business real estate). It also includes "intellectual property" like copyrights, patents or trademarks, and all other non–real estate possessions that you own.

Frequent Flyer Miles

Here's a new type of personal property that you may be able to leave to others—frequent flyer miles. Many major U.S. airlines allow you to leave your accumulated miles in your will. Some allow you to leave them to any beneficiary you name, while others limit your choice of beneficiaries. You should check with your airline to see what they allow. Though it's not legally required, it's a good idea to name the airline in your will and specifically state that you leave your frequent flyer miles with that airline to the beneficiary you name.

Household Furnishings and Possessions

Aside from valuable or valued items already listed, other household furnishings and possessions—from your clothes to the washer-dryer—can be listed generally: "All my other household furnishings and possessions at 12 High Street, Chicago, Illinois."

Business Interests

This category includes all business interests except any business real estate, which is dealt with under the real estate section below.

Solely owned businesses can be listed simply by name:

- "The Funjimaya Restaurant"
- "The King of Hearts Bakery"

Your ownership of a shared business can be listed like this:

- "All my interest in the Ben-Dee partnership"
- "All my shares of X Corporation"
- "All my interest in the BJA Limited Liability Company."

SEE AN EXPERT

Leaving an interest in a shared business. The fact that you own an interest in a shared-ownership business doesn't automatically mean you can leave your interest to whomever you want. First, the co-owners, partners, or corporate shareholders may have ownership, buy-out, and/or management rights that must be considered. Second, there's always the practical problem of trying to insure continuity, or survival, of the business, which often takes far more planning than deciding who to leave ownership to. If you have problems with any of these matters, see a lawyer.

Patents, Copyrights, and Royalties

Another type of business ownership is a patent or copyright or a share of one.

A copyright can be identified by reference to the title of the copyrighted material:

- "The copyright to the lyrics and music of the song 'I Feel So Insufficient'"
- "My 50% interest in the copyright of the book *Great Times: How to Throw a Party*."

A patent is best identified by the patent number, issued by the patent office, and the title: "Patent #2,886,421, 'Three-Way Mirror and Portable Traffic Light.'"

You can list a trademark or service mark separately on the worksheet, but these are usually integral parts of a business. (The name of a product is, or can be, a trademark; legally, it can be owned and licensed independent of the business. The name of the business itself is a service mark.) An ownership interest in a trademark is normally left as part of that business. Leaving a trademark separate from the business it defines would be at best confusing and at worst create all sorts of litigation risks. An interest in a service mark cannot be left separate from the business.

Real Estate

To describe real estate (called "real property" in legalese), simply list its address or location. This is normally the street address, or condominium apartment number. If there's no post office address, as is the case if you own undeveloped land, simply describe the property in normal language—for example, "my 120 acres in Lincoln County near the town of Douglas, Indiana." You don't need to use the legal description from the deed.

Occasionally, the term "real estate" is used to include items that are properly classified as personal property. For instance, farms are often sold with tools and animals. If you intend to leave personal property together with real estate, state generally what the personal property consists of. It's best to specify the large ticket items (such as a tractor or cattle) and refer generally to the rest of the items as "personal property." And of course, be sure what you specify here doesn't contradict anything you wrote in the personal property section of the worksheet.

EXAMPLE 1:

"My 240-acre truck farm in Whitman County with all tools, animals, machines, and other personal property found there at my death, except for the two bulls."

EXAMPLE 2:

"My fishing cabin on the Wild River in Maine and all the fishing gear, furniture, tools, and other personal property I keep there."

State How Your Property Is Owned (Column 2)

Obviously, it's important to know how you own property. First, you may share ownership with others. Second, even for property you own outright, you may have arranged to transfer certain items by methods other than a will, something you surely want to keep in mind when leaving will gifts.

Below is a very basic summary of the major types of property ownership and transfer methods and the abbreviations you can use to note them on the worksheet. If you have questions about any of them, refer to Chapter 3, Special Property Rules for Married People, or Chapter 14, Estate Planning.

For any property that you own with another person, you need to list (or determine) exactly what share of it you own, so you know exactly what you can transfer by will. Or, to reverse the point, it's important that you understand what property isn't eligible to be included in your will because it's owned in part by someone else.

You'll probably be able to quickly determine the legal categories your property falls into. However, occasionally, to be sure about the ownership status of a particular piece of property, you may have to do some work. For example, you may have to dig out the deed to your house or your stock certificates to clarify whether you own property in joint tenancy or not. Never guess! If you're not sure how you own an item of property, take the time to find out. Do it even if it means you have to check records at the county land records office or do similar detective work.

If you live in a community property state and are married, you may have more difficult problems concerning property ownership, as discussed in Chapter 3. Be sure to resolve them. For example, if you're unsure whether a $10,000 bank account is community property or your separate property, bear in mind that it matters a great deal how you and your spouse characterize it, and be sure to put your agreement in writing.

SEE AN EXPERT

Get help if you're unsure. If your conclusions about your gifts or the value of your estate depend heavily on characterizations of property about which you're uncertain, you should seek advice from a lawyer or accountant. Otherwise, you may end up leaving property you don't own, or fail to leave property that you do.

Property You Can Leave by Will

There are three categories of property that you can legally leave by your will. On the worksheet, you can identify these types of property by the abbreviations given below, or simple use a **W** to indicate the property can be transferred by will.

Sole Ownership (S.O.). Property you own solely and outright. This generally includes all property in your name in common law property states and all your separate property in community property states. (See Chapter 3.)

Tenancy in Common (T.C.). Property you own with someone that isn't in joint tenancy or tenancy by the entirety. If the ownership document doesn't specify a type of shared ownership, it's tenancy

in common. You can leave your portion of such property, unless you're restricted by a contract such as a partnership agreement.

Community Property (C.P.). In community property states, most or all property acquired during a marriage. You can leave your one-half share of community property to whomever you want to have it. (See Chapter 3.) The other half of the community property already belongs to your spouse, and you have no power to leave it in your will.

Property You Cannot Leave by Will

The following types of property cannot usually be left by your will.

Joint Tenancy (J.T.) and Tenancy by the Entirety (T.E.). Property where the ownership deed specifies that it is held in joint tenancy (often abbreviated as "JTWROS," meaning "joint tenancy with right of survivorship") or tenancy by the entirety (a form of joint tenancy for spouses). You cannot normally transfer this property by will because the share of the first joint tenant to die automatically goes to the surviving owners. Joint tenancy and tenancy by the entirety must be spelled out in an ownership document.

In the rare case of simultaneous death of all joint tenants, or both tenants by the entirety, the property is divided into as many shares as there are joint tenants. Then each joint tenant's estate receives one share. So, if you want to be extra thorough, you can make provisions in your will for what happens to your share of joint tenancy or tenancy by the entirety property if you and the other joint tenants die simultaneously. In this case, you can leave your share of the property, like any other gift, to whomever you want. (See Chapter 5.)

Community Property With Right of Survivorship. A handful of states—Alaska, Arizona, California, Nevada, Texas, and Wisconsin—expressly permit spouses to hold property "as community property with right of survivorship." In other words, in these states spouses can obtain the benefit of joint tenancy while owning community property. With this form of ownership, a surviving spouse automatically receives a deceased spouse's share of community property outside of probate.

Living Trust Property (L.T.). Property that you have transferred to a living trust. This property cannot be transferred by will unless you terminate the living trust.

Insurance, Pensions, and Retirement Accounts. (I/P). Insurance policies, pensions, and other retirement benefits, such as a traditional or Roth IRA, profit-sharing plan, or 401(k) plan, with a named beneficiary. You can't leave these types of property by a will.

For estate tax purposes, the value of a life insurance policy owned by the deceased is the face value (the proceeds) of that policy. This can be important when estimating the size of an estate for tax purposes.

Bank Account Trusts (B.A.T.). Bank trust accounts, usually called "Pay-on-Death Accounts" or sometimes "Totten Trusts," where you have named beneficiaries to take the funds when you die. You can't leave these funds by your will unless you terminate the trust account.

Securities Registered in Transfer-on-Death Form. All states except Texas allow securities—stocks and bonds—to be held in transfer-on-death form, where named beneficiaries receive the securities at the owner's death. Securities held in this form can't be left by will.

Transfer-on-Death Deeds. In some states, you can prepare and record a deed now that will transfer your real estate when you die. In the deed, you name the beneficiary or beneficiaries to receive the property outside of probate. The deed is revocable until your death. The states that allow this are Arizona, Arkansas, Colorado, Kansas, Missouri, New Mexico, Nevada, Ohio, and Wisconsin.

TIP

Special rules for Washington residents. Washington has a law called the "superwill statute" that changes some of the rules above. If you live in Washington, you can leave the following types of property in your will:

- your share of joint tenancy bank accounts
- pay-on-death bank accounts
- property in your living trust, and
- money in individual retirement accounts (but not in 401(k) plans).

If you set up one of these devices or accounts and then later use your will to change the beneficiary, the property goes to the person you name in your will. However, if you designate a new beneficiary after you make your will—for example, by updating the paperwork for a pay-on-death bank account or amending your living trust—the gift in the will has no effect. (Wash. Rev. Code Ann. § 11.11.020.)

List Your Percentage of Shared Property (Column 3)

In this third column, list the percentage of each item of shared property you own. You should have just figured this out as part of filling in Column 2. People who own property as tenants in common should be particularly careful, however. Since you can own any percentage of that property—from 1% to 99%—it's important that you know what portion is yours. Also, this information is necessary to determine the net value of your estate for estate tax purposes.

If the property is community property or a tenancy by the entirety, the ownership is automatically 50-50. If it's held in joint tenancy, all joint tenants own equal shares. Thus, if there are two joint tenants, the ownership is 50%; if there are three, each owns one-third, and so on.

Estimate the Net Value of Your Property (Column 4)

In this last column, enter an estimate of the net value of each item of property, which means your equity in your share of the property. "Equity" is the market value of your share, less your share of any encumbrances on it, such as a mortgage on a house or the loan amount due on a car. Doing this can clarify the value of what you have to leave, which may be helpful when deciding on gifts. And, as I've said, it also provides an indication of whether or not your estate is likely to be subject to death taxes, especially federal estate taxes.

EXAMPLE:

You own a house with a market value of $250,000 as tenants in common with your brother. You each own half. Compute the value of your share by first subtracting the amount of any mortgages, deeds of trust, liens, past due taxes, etc., from the market value to arrive at the total equity in the property. If there's a $100,000 mortgage and no other debts, the total equity is $150,000. Because you own half of the property, it follows that your share is worth $75,000.

As already stated, making rough estimates of the value of your property and debts is fine. There's no need to burden yourself with seeking precise figures. The worth of the gifts you leave, and any death taxes your estate will have to pay, will be based on the net value of all your property when you die, not its current worth. For example, if you think your solely owned house is worth roughly $200,000 (net), your car $5,000, and your stamp collection would fetch $12,000 if you put an ad in a philatelist's journal, use those numbers. If these items are owned as community property with your spouse, or in joint tenancy, divide the amounts in half to determine the value of your share.

I can't think of a reason why you might need an appraiser to give you a valuation of any of your property at this stage. (Appraisals may be necessary for tax and probate purposes after you die.) At most, take a few minutes to investigate what any particular item of property is worth. ●

Your Beneficiaries

Now it's time to focus on your beneficiaries —the people and, possibly, organizations who will receive property under your will. You may already know exactly who your beneficiaries are, and what they'll receive. Fine. But even if you do, you can likely benefit from reading this chapter to make sure that you haven't overlooked any important beneficiary concerns.

Deciding who is to receive your property is the heart of preparing your will. Normally, it involves making personal decisions, not legal ones. For most people, it's satisfying to leave gifts to those they care about, and to contemplate the help those gifts can bring. And, of course, it can be very satisfying to know you've arranged to leave items you cherish to people who'll value them as you do.

Exploring the Meanings of Giving

What does, or can, gift-giving involve? What types of gifts can there be? Why are creative faculties called "gifts"? These questions, and a myriad of other interesting aspects of gifts, are brilliantly explored in *The Gift: Imagination and the Erotic Life of Property*, by Lewis Hyde (Vintage). This strikingly original book examines gifts in many cultures, from our market-driven one to those where gift-giving is the basic mode of transaction. Subjects covered range from myths to marriage (why is it traditionally said in western societies that a woman is "given" in marriage?), from poetry to Indian potlatches. It's a book that has a permanent place on my most-treasured-books shelf.

With very few restrictions, you can will your property however you choose. Most people simply leave their worldly goods to family, friends, and perhaps some charities. You can leave property to be shared by beneficiaries. For instance, you can leave a stock account to be shared by three children, each to get one-third of its worth on your death, rather than having to leave individual stocks in the account to different children. (Of course, you can do the latter if you want to.)

More inventive gifts are also possible. If you wish, you can leave some money to friends to throw a party on your behalf, or to sponsor a series of jazz (or classical or western) concerts. An anonymous benefactor of the college I went to earned my lifelong gratitude by endowing the milk supply in the dining hall, so milk lovers could always have as much as we wanted. (Continuing endowments, however, are beyond what you can accomplish with a will from this book.)

This chapter provides a worksheet on which you can record all your beneficiaries and what property you want to leave them. As with all the worksheets in this book, this one is designed to assist you, not inflict unnecessary paperwork. Adapt the worksheet to your needs. You may well not want to bother listing beneficiary information; if you want to leave all property to your spouse, or your children if your spouse doesn't survive you, you'll surely remember this when preparing your will. But if you have more complex beneficiary intentions, you may find the worksheet a helpful tool. But before we get to it, let's look deeper into what the term "beneficiaries" can cover.

Types of Beneficiaries

You'll probably name several different kinds of beneficiaries in your will. To help you keep them straight, let's define each briefly.

Primary Beneficiaries: Your first choices to receive specific gifts of property—that is, property identified in your will. If you leave specific items of property to several different people or organizations, you have several primary beneficiaries.

Beneficiary Complexities

For many people, choosing beneficiaries is clear and easy. Others, however, face uncertainties or complications. For example, one or both people in a second or subsequent marriage may have children from earlier relationships. I know several couples who have "his, hers, and our kids." Some have his, her, and our property as well. Deciding how to divide property between the children (and possibly others) can be difficult. Plus, there are often other concerns. For instance, after a spouse dies, what happens if the surviving spouse needs the deceased spouse's property to maintain his or her lifestyle? Or perhaps the couple shared ownership of a house or condominium. Can the surviving spouse continue to live there, while preserving the deceased spouse's share for children of prior marriages? Estate planning for second or subsequent marriages is discussed further in Chapter 14.

Single people can have different, but equally important concerns. A single parent of a minor child or children will naturally be concerned about who will raise the children if she or he cannot. (See Chapter 7.) Also, a single person may not be sure who to name as his or her executor, the person responsible for handling and distributing the single person's property after he or she dies. (See Chapter 6.)

Whatever difficulties you may face deciding on who to give what, it's crucial to understand that these are personal decisions only you can make. There's no legal formula that can resolve your mind for you. All a lawyer could possibly contribute would be to act as a high-paid therapist substitute, facilitating your decision-making process. If you find that naming your beneficiaries raises problems, remember you can take time to work things through. Making a will should never be a hurried process.

EXAMPLE:

Ken leaves his house, car, and bank accounts to his wife, Gertrude. He leaves his art collection to the local museum. He leaves his books to the public library. Finally, he wants his daughter, Leslie, to inherit a 60% interest in his vacation home and his son, Peter, to inherit a 40% share. All of these people and organizations are Ken's primary beneficiaries.

Beneficiaries of Shared Gifts: Two or more beneficiaries who each receive a share of the same item(s) of property.

EXAMPLE:

Harriet includes the following clause in her will: "I leave my house at 42 Woden Road, Richmond, Virginia, equally to Ben Davis and Susie Davis Appledorn."

Alternate Beneficiaries: People or organizations you name to receive a specific gift if the primary beneficiary doesn't receive it. An alternate inherits because the primary beneficiary predeceases you or doesn't survive you by the number of days required by the will.

EXAMPLE:

Lily's will requires all her beneficiaries to survive her by 45 days. Here's a provision naming an alternate: "I leave my stock account with Slick Brokerage Co. to Cindy Padrewski, or, if she does not survive me, to Nicholas Maes."

You can also name more than one alternate to receive a specific gift if the primary beneficiary does not receive it.

EXAMPLE:

"I leave all my shares of Zeta Corporation to my cousin Sean O'Reilly, or, if he does not survive me, to his daughters Barbara O'Reilly and Moira O'Reilly Covenelli in equal shares."

Residuary Beneficiary: The person or organization named to receive the "residue" of your estate. The residue, or residuary estate, is what remains of your property after all specific gifts are made and debts, taxes, probate, and attorney fees are paid.

EXAMPLE:

"I leave my residuary estate to Caleb Hamilton."

Some will writers make few or even no specific gifts and simply leave the bulk, or all, of their property through the residue. You can name more than one residuary beneficiary to share in the residue as you provide.

EXAMPLE:

"I leave 40% of my residuary estate to Feliz Noreno, 40% to Juan Locas, and 20% to the Salvation Army of Chicago, Illinois."

Alternate Residuary Beneficiary: A person or organization you name to receive your residue if the residuary beneficiary does not receive it.

EXAMPLE:

"I leave my residuary estate to Caleb Hamilton, or, if he does not survive me, to his son Billy Ray Hamilton."

You can name two or more alternate residuary beneficiaries to share the residue in whatever proportion or manner you choose.

EXAMPLE:

"I leave my residuary estate to Leona Da Britta, or, if she does not survive me, to Marcello Da Britta and Caroline Da Britta in equal shares."

Putting Restrictions on Beneficiaries

Some people want to leave gifts with strings attached. However, the will forms in this book don't allow you to impose controls over your gifts, with the important exception of property left to minor or young adult beneficiaries. This section explains some restrictions you *cannot* accomplish with this book.

"Life Estate" Gifts

Life estates are gifts where a beneficiary gets only the income or use of property during his or her life. You specify someone else to inherit the property when the life beneficiary dies. Leaving a life estate is sometimes desired for estate tax reasons, or in some second or subsequent marriages. Life estates are normally created by a trust (what I call a "property control trust"), which can be included in a will.

EXAMPLE:

Marilyn James is married to Martin Smith. Marilyn has two grown children from her first marriage. Marilyn's major asset is the house she owns, which she and Martin have lived in for ten years. In Marilyn's will, she creates a trust leaving the house to Martin in a life estate and then to her children. This means Martin has the right to use the house during his lifetime, but upon his death the life estate terminates and the house goes to Marilyn's children.

Drafting a property control trust may seem easy at first glance, but it isn't. Here are only a few of the questions that might arise:

- Could a surviving spouse with a "life estate" interest in a house sell the house and buy another one?
- Could he rent the house?

- Suppose a surviving spouse has massive medical bills. Can she borrow against the house (pledging it as security) to pay them?
- What right do the will writer's children have to find out what the surviving spouse is doing regarding the house?

Technical IRS requirements must also be met, and a mistake in complying with them could result in undesirable tax consequences. All these problems should be resolved by the terms of the trust. Since a trust cannot be changed or amended once the will writer dies, and may last for many years, a poorly drafted trust can cause all sorts of problems down the road.

TIP

Trusts for disabled children. Many Americans have a disabled child or other loved one who requires long-term support and medical assistance from government programs. Unfortunately, money and property left directly to people with disabilities may disqualify them from government assistance. *Special Needs Trusts: Protect Your Child's Financial Future,* by Stephen Elias (Nolo) provides a solution. Using the book's clear explanations and instructions, you can draft a special needs trust for your child to provide for him or her without jeopardizing public benefits.

SEE AN EXPERT

Other property control trusts. Other property control trusts are discussed in depth in *Plan Your Estate,* by Denis Clifford and Cora Jordan (Nolo), but you'll still need a lawyer to prepare one. If you do decide you want to establish a property control trust, don't just turn the whole matter over to the lawyer. Carefully sketch out the substance of what you want and the contingencies you're worried about before you see the lawyer.

Conditional Gifts

You cannot make a conditional gift using this book. For example, you cannot leave money to your nephew, Ed, if he goes to veterinary school,

but, if he doesn't, to your niece Polly. The reason Nolo's wills don't allow conditional gifts is that most conditional gifts create far more problems than they solve. To continue the example of Ed, the potential animal doctor, here are just a few problems inherent in this approach: How soon must Ed go to veterinary school? What happens if he applies in good faith but fails to get in? Who decides if he's really studying? What happens to the money before Ed goes to veterinary school?

SEE AN EXPERT

See a lawyer and set up a trust if you want to make a conditional gift. If you want to impose conditions on a gift, someone must be responsible for being sure the conditions are fulfilled. The best way to do this is by leaving the property in a trust, managed by a trustee. Creating this kind of trust requires the assistance of a lawyer.

Deciding How to Leave Your Property

This section explores issues you should think about as you map out the beneficiary portions of your will.

Leaving Everything (or Almost Everything) to Your Mate

For some people, choosing beneficiaries is simple. A common example is a member of a couple, married or not, who wants to leave everything to his or her mate. (Form 1 of this book's wills is specifically designed for a spouse who wants to leave most, or all, property to the other spouse.)

But even if you want to leave all, or most, of your property to your spouse, you still should consider who you want to name as your alternate beneficiaries. If you want more than one alternate—for example, your three children—do you want them to share the property equally or unequally? In addition, if you want to leave a few gifts to beneficiaries other than your spouse—perhaps some cash to a favorite nephew or some jewelry to an old friend—these beneficiaries and the specific property they are to receive must be spelled out in your will.

Leaving Everything to Several Beneficiaries

Another common situation exists when you want to leave all, or the bulk, of your property to a couple or a few beneficiaries, specifying the percentages or fractions of each one's share. For instance:

- "I leave all my property to be shared equally between my two children, Soshana Bix and Verdette Bix."
- "I leave my property as follows: 45% to Ron Sampson, 40% to Holly Sampson Buren, and 15% to Mark Greenstein."

When all property is shared this way, there is no need to list property that each beneficiary receives. It's up to the beneficiaries to divide the property so that each receives the share specified in the will. They can hang onto the property together, or sell it and divide the proceeds. (Issues raised by shared gifts are discussed in "Naming Beneficiaries to Share Gifts," below.)

Leaving Specific Gifts

If you're like many people, you'll want to leave a number of gifts to different primary beneficiaries in your will. To accomplish this with a will from this book, just identify each beneficiary and what property he or she receives. The property must be described with sufficient clarity so that there's no doubt what you're referring to. No special legalese is required. The descriptions you listed on the property worksheet in the last chapter (if you did so) should work just fine.

Minors or Young Adults as Beneficiaries

Minor children are children under 18. They can be named as any type of beneficiary and can own property—but an adult must manage it for them. If you name a minor, whether your own child or another's, as any type of beneficiary, you'll need to arrange for adult management for any property the child or children could inherit. You can take care of this in your will. (See Chapter 7.)

This book defines a young adult beneficiary as someone from 18 to 35. Although such beneficiaries are, legally, adults, you may not want them to inherit property outright. With the wills in this book, you can arrange for mature adult supervision of the property.

Organizations as Beneficiaries

An organization is simply some form of legal entity. It can range from a tax-exempt charity to what's called an "unincorporated association," such as a labor union. You can leave property to any organization you consider worthy, whether a charity or a public or private organization—for example, the Old Forge Public Library, the American Red Cross, the Greenview Battered Women's Shelter, or the University of Oregon.

Most organizations named as beneficiaries in a will are tax-exempt charities, which means the IRS has legally approved their tax-free status. However, the organization you name need not be tax-exempt, unless you wish your estate to qualify for a charitable estate tax deduction for that gift. Few readers of this book need be concerned with that.

Forgiving Debts

One type of gift you can make in your will is to forgive a debt—that is, release a person who owes you money from that obligation. Any debt, written or oral, can be forgiven. To forgive debts you'll need to use Chapter 11 to draft a customized will rather than using a fill-in-the-blanks will from Chapter 10.

> **! CAUTION**
> **Your powers of debt forgiveness may be limited.** If you're married and forgiving a debt, be sure you have full power to do so. If the debt was incurred while you were married, you may have the right to forgive only half the debt (especially in community property states) unless your spouse agrees in writing to allow you to forgive his or her share of the debt as well.

Explaining Your Intentions

Forgiving a debt may come as a pleasant surprise to someone living with the expectation that it must be repaid. Your will can contain a brief explanation stating your intention, but you may wish to explain your reasoning beyond this short statement. If so, write your explanation in a brief letter. (See Chapter 2 for more information about writing a separate letter to accompany your will.)

Leaving Property to Beneficiaries Outside the U.S.

There is no problem with leaving property to beneficiaries who live outside the United States. You can leave that property to anyone you want to, wherever they live. It will be your executor's responsibility to see that the property is delivered to the beneficiary.

Property that is physically located outside the U.S.—the obvious example being foreign real estate—must be transferred according to the law of the country where it's located, and so cannot safely be left by a will from this book.

Leaving Property to a Married Person

When you leave property to someone who's married, the property belongs to that person individually. For example, if your will states "I leave my antique clock to Mary Kestor," her husband has no rights to the clock. Mary would be entitled to keep it in the event of divorce and can leave it in her will to whomever she chooses. If you want to emphasize your intent, you can say: "I leave my antique clock to Mary Kestor as her separate property."

By contrast, if you wish to make a gift to a married couple, simply make it in both their names. For example: "I leave my silver bowl to Edna and Fred Whitman." Again, you can provide emphasis by stating: "I leave my silver bowl to Stan Petrewski and Odile St. Germain as husband and wife."

Adopted and Out-of-Wedlock Children

You should name all your children in your will, and either provide for them or disinherit them. It's a bad idea to leave property to "my children" instead of listing them by name. Courts confronted with a gift to "children" may have to decide if that term was meant to include stepchildren or any children born out of wedlock. (Interestingly, the concept of an "illegitimate" child is far from universal. For instance, Celtic law didn't distinguish between one's children—the father acknowledged them all.)

While most states consider adopted people, whether they were minors or adults when adopted, as "children" when the term is used in a will, the rule for out-of-wedlock children isn't nearly so clear. Basically, for inheritance purposes, states recognize an out-of-wedlock child as a child of the mother unless the child was formally released by the mother for adoption. However, an out-of-wedlock child isn't normally a child of the father for inheritance purposes unless the father legally acknowledged the child as his. But a number of special circumstances and exceptions to this rule can cause a different outcome. In any case, the point is not to risk being caught up in these rules and exceptions, but rather to state precisely who your children are.

Children Conceived After a Parent Dies

Rapidly advancing medical technology now makes it possible for a child to be conceived after the biological mother or father dies. (In legal terms, these are known as "posthumously conceived" children.) If sperm or embryos are frozen before a father's death and later used to begin a pregnancy, a child could be born to a father who has been dead for years. Similarly, a fertilized embryo could be carried by another woman well after the embryo donor's death.

Complications from this development have already made it to courts in a handful of states, with inconsistent results. For example, a Massachusetts court ruled that twins conceived through artificial insemination using a late husband's sperm could be entitled to inherit from his estate under the state's intestacy laws. However, in similar circumstances, an Arizona court ruled that its inheritance laws excluded a child conceived after a father's death.

The rights of a posthumously conceived child may be important for reasons other than inheritance— for instance, the surviving parent may want the baby to qualify for government or other benefits that come only with being the child of the deceased parent.

California has taken the lead in adopting laws governing children conceived after a parent's death. Specifically, California law provides that a child conceived after death will be deemed to be the child of the deceased person and born during his or her lifetime if it is proved by clear and convincing evidence that:

- the decedent specified in writing that his or her genetic material should be used for posthumous conception of a child
- the writing is signed by the decedent and at least one witness
- the person designated by the decedent to use the genetic material was the spouse or registered domestic partner of the decedent (or another person specifically named in the document)
- written notice was given to the decedent's executor, within four months of the decedent's death, that the decedent's genetic material was available for posthumous conception, and
- the child was conceived within two years of the date of issuance of decedent's death certificate.

(Cal. Prob. Code, § 249.5.)

Clearly, this is a rapidly changing area of law, as well as technology. If you are planning for a posthumously conceived child, you'll want to consider what his or her property rights will be. You'll need to know your state's law (if any) on the subject, as well as figure out what you think is best. It's essential that you consult a knowledgeable estate planning lawyer to discuss these matters.

Providing for Pets

Legally, pets are property. Many pet owners, of course, disagree. They feel a bond with their animals and want to be sure that when they die, their pets will get good care and a good home. The easiest way to do this is to make an arrangement with a friend or family member to take care of your pet. Then, in your will, you leave your pet to that person, along with some money for the expense of your pet's feeding and care.

In most states, you can establish a trust for your pet. The trust is a legally independent entity, managed by a trustee you name. You also define the terms of the trust—how your pet is to be cared for—in the trust document. Pet trusts can be desirable for people who feel they'd prefer not to leave their pet outright to someone. But creating a pet trust is more costly and complicated than simply leaving your pet outright.

States That Allow Trusts for Pets

Alaska	Nebraska
Arizona	Nevada
California	New Hampshire
Colorado	New Jersey
District of Columbia	New Mexico
Florida	New York
Illinois	North Carolina
Iowa	Oregon
Kansas	Pennsylvania
Maine	Tennessee
Massachusetts	Utah
Michigan	Washington
Missouri	Wyoming
Montana	

SEE AN EXPERT

You'll need an attorney to prepare a pet trust. You cannot prepare a pet trust on your own. You'll need to hire an attorney to get the document drafted.

RESOURCE

More information. For a more detailed discussion of providing for pets, see *Every Dog's Legal Guide: A Must-Have Book for Your Owner*, by Mary Randolph (Nolo).

Naming Beneficiaries to Share Gifts

What happens if you want to leave one item, or several, to be shared by more than one beneficiary? For example, suppose you wish to leave your house or your antique music box or your wonderful '55 T-Bird to be shared by your three children. It's certainly legal to do this, but any shared gift raises some issues you need to resolve.

Possible Conflicts Among Beneficiaries

When two or more beneficiaries inherit property together, they all must agree what to do with that property, or there's trouble. Often, they all want to sell the property and divide the profits, in the proportions the will specifies. No problem. Or the beneficiaries may all agree to maintain the property together. Again, no problem. But what if the beneficiaries disagree about how to use the gift? Suppose a house is left to three children, and two want to sell it but the other doesn't. Or suppose you leave a stock account to be shared equally by two beneficiaries. One wants to sell certain stock, the other wants to hold it. Who prevails?

With a will from this book, it's up to the beneficiaries of a shared gift to work out such problems. (The only exception is property left to all your minor children in a family pot trust, where the trustee controls.) If they can't resolve any conflicts, a legal proceeding may be required. Generally, any co-owner has the legal right to get a court order to have the property sold and the profits distributed in the shares the will specified.

In theory, you could put provisions in your will governing possible conflicts between beneficiaries of a shared gift. With the gift of a house, for example, you could provide that it cannot be sold unless all three of your children agree. But if there's disagreement, problems will likely follow. If two want to sell the house, but one doesn't, who must maintain the house? Can the child who wants to keep the house live in it? If she does, must she pay the others any rent? How would rent be set? What happens if one child dies?

It's often wise to discuss shared gifts with the proposed beneficiaries. If they agree on what to do with the gift, theoretical problems are not likely to become real ones.

SEE AN EXPERT

Heading off conflict. If you think serious problems are likely to arise among shared-gift beneficiaries, consider making a new gift plan. If that isn't feasible, see a lawyer to draft specific will provisions covering what happens if there's a conflict.

Ownership Shares

When you make a shared gift, you must decide what share of the property each beneficiary receives. If you don't specify shares or percentages, the will forms in this book state that each beneficiary will receive an equal share. For example, if you simply leave two stock accounts to your four children, and don't state how they are to be shared, each child would receive a one-quarter interest in the accounts.

If you want a gift to be shared equally, it's better to state that expressly. The provision in the will forms is a safety net, to make sure the terms of a shared gift are clear even if you fail to define them.

Alternate Beneficiaries

Using this book's forms, you can leave a shared gift by one of two methods. Which method to use depends on how you want to handle alternate beneficiaries for the gift. (General considerations of alternate beneficiaries are discussed below.)

Here are your two choices:

- **If you want the survivors to serve as alternates,** name all the primary beneficiaries for a shared gift in a single specific gift paragraph in your will.

- **If you want to name alternates for each beneficiary,** divide the gift into percentages or fractions, and use a separate specific gift paragraph for each primary beneficiary.

These choices can seem a bit confusing at first glance. Here's some more explanation to help you understand each option.

Survivors as alternates. Many parents of young children, leaving them a shared gift, definitely want to provide that if one child does not survive them, the others receive the portion that would have gone to the deceased child. If you want the surviving primary beneficiaries to share the portion of any primary beneficiary who doesn't survive you, use a single paragraph. The will forms provide that surviving beneficiaries of a shared gift left in a single paragraph inherit any deceased beneficiary's share, in equal shares.

EXAMPLE 1:

Amelia wants to leave her book copyrights equally to her four children. If any child doesn't survive her, she wants that child's share to go equally to the survivors. She enters her decision in her will as follows:

"I leave all my book copyrights to my children, Salman Swift, Elisa Swift, John Swift-Cohn, and Grant Swift."

If one of Amelia's children dies before she does, each of the three survivors will inherit a one-third share of the copyrights.

EXAMPLE 2:

Carl wants to leave his boat to his niece and two nephews. He wants the niece to receive a one-half interest in the boat, and the nephews one-quarter each. If any of these beneficiaries does not survive Carl, he wants the others to split that interest equally. Carl's will provides:

"I leave a 50% interest in my boat to Juliette Alegretti, 25% to Sonny Alegretti, and 25% to Alfredo Alegretti II."

EXAMPLE 3:

Jack uses a single paragraph of the Specific Gift clause to leave land in Texas to be shared equally by his grandchildren Tessa, Torcio, and Alexos. Tessa dies before Jack does. When Jack dies, the land will go to Torcio and Alexos in equal shares (assuming, of course, that Jack doesn't revise his will after Tessa dies).

If, using this method, you also name an alternate, that person would receive the gift only if all the primary beneficiaries failed to survive you.

EXAMPLE:

Mariel wants to leave a stock account to her two children; if one of them dies before Mariel does, she wants the other one to inherit the entire account. If both children don't survive her, she wants the account to go to her favorite charity. The clause in her will looks like this:

"I leave my Schwab stock account, No. 88800-34, to Allison Gimbel and Rachel Gimbel, in equal shares or, if none of them survive me, to the San Francisco Society for the Prevention of Cruelty to Animals."

Separate alternates for each primary beneficiary.
You may want to name different alternates for each cobeneficiary—perhaps each beneficiary's spouse or children. If so, use a separate paragraph to list each primary beneficiary and that beneficiary's alternates.

EXAMPLE 1:

Ming leaves his house to his three children. Ben-wa gets 30%, Susan gets 30%, and Ho Mein gets 40%. He names each child's spouse as the alternate beneficiary for that child. This part of his will looks like this:

"I leave a 30% interest in my house at 631 South Maple, Galesburg, Illinois, to Ben-wa Lee or, if he does not survive me, to Carol Lee."

"I leave a 30% interest in my house at 631 South Maple, Galesburg, Illinois, to Susan Lee, or, if she does not survive me, to Yo-Hing Chan.

"I leave a 40% interest in my house at 631 South Maple, Galesburg, Illinois, to Ho Mein Lee or, if she does not survive me, to Matt Weigant."

EXAMPLE 2:

Mike leaves his house to his two adult sons, Anthony and Travis, in equal shares. If one son does not survive him, he wants that son's share to go to that son's child or children. To accomplish his goal, Mike uses two separate specific gift paragraphs, as follows:

"I leave a 40% interest in my house at… to Anthony Radinsky or, if he does not survive me … to Jessica Radinsky and Tricia Radinsky, in equal shares.

"I leave a 40% interest in my house at… to Travis Radinsky or, if he does not survive me… to Jason Radinsky. "

EXAMPLE 3:

Walter leaves his house equally to his two children, Butterfly and Apollo (Walter was once a hippie). He uses two separate gift paragraphs, leaving 50% of the house to Butterfly and 50% to Apollo. Walter names Butterfly's three children, John, Susan, and Kelly, as her alternate beneficiaries, and Apollo's one child, Harmony, as his alternate beneficiary.

EXAMPLE 4:

Mike wants to leave his cabin to his two sons, Anthony and Travis, and his sister, Virginia. He wants each son to receive a 40% share and his sister a 20% share of the cabin. In the event one son does not survive him, he wants that son's share to go to that son's child or children. If his sister predeceases him, Mike wants that 20% share to pass to her son, Malcolm. To accomplish his goal, Mike uses three separate specific gifts paragraphs, as follows:

40% share in cabin:
   Primary beneficiary: Anthony
   Alternate beneficiaries: Anthony's children, Jessica and Tricia, equally

40% share in cabin:
    Primary beneficiary: Travis

    Alternate beneficiary: Travis's son, Jason

20% share in cabin:
    Primary beneficiary: Virginia

    Alternate beneficiary: Virginia's son, Malcolm

Naming Alternate Beneficiaries

What happens if a person named in your will to receive a specific gift does not survive you? Who gets the property? Should you address this contingency in your will? For most people, the answer is a definite "yes." They name one or more alternate beneficiaries, to receive specific gifts left to each primary beneficiary, if that beneficiary predeceases them. Doing this is sensible for a number of reasons. Perhaps you've made some gifts to older people, or relatives in poor health who may not survive you. Or you don't want the bother of redoing your will if the unlikely occurs and a younger beneficiary dies before you. Or you're concerned that you might not have time, before your own death, to revise your will if a beneficiary unexpectedly dies.

On the other hand, some people don't want to contemplate their beneficiaries dying before they do, and choose not to name alternate beneficiaries. This decision is more sensible if the beneficiaries are healthy and considerably younger than the will writer than if they are elderly, or in ill health. Also, some people figure that if a beneficiary does die before they do, they'll probably have time enough to make a new will that names a new beneficiary.

Finally, there's another reason why you may choose not to name an alternate beneficiary for a specific gift. All the will forms in this book state that if a primary beneficiary fails to survive you by the period defined in the will (the usual period is 45 days), and you haven't named an alternate beneficiary, the gift goes to your residuary beneficiary. If your residuary beneficiary is the person you want to receive a particular gift if the primary beneficiary dies, you've already, in effect, named an alternate beneficiary for that gift; you wouldn't need to do it a second time.

EXAMPLE:

Betsy McCray leaves $30,000 to her friend Daniel Carlan. She doesn't name an alternate beneficiary for this gift. Her will names her daughter, Kendall, as her residuary beneficiary, and her other daughter, Sara, as her alternate residuary beneficiary. If Daniel does not survive her, Betsy wants Kendall or, next, Sara, to have the $30,000, received as part of the residuary estate.

If you don't want your residuary beneficiary to be the first in line to inherit a specific gift should the primary beneficiary for it fail to survive you, you can name an alternate beneficiary for each gift.

There are different considerations for naming alternate beneficiaries for a shared gift than for a gift to a single beneficiary. Let's examine each separately.

Alternate Beneficiaries for Gifts to One Person

To name one or more alternate beneficiaries for a gift left to a single beneficiary, simply list the alternate's name, or names, in your will after naming the primary beneficiary.

EXAMPLE:

Sally decides to leave her antique piano to her brother Tim Jestunson. In case Tim fails to survive her, Sally wants her friend Ruth Jones as the alternate beneficiary. She enters this information in the Specific Gifts part of her will as follows:

    "I leave my antique piano to Tim Jestunson, or, if he does not survive me, to Ruth Jones."

There's certainly no rule regarding who you should name as alternates for specific gifts. That's entirely up to you. The possibilities are as wide open as with primary beneficiaries, ranging from mates to charities, in any combination you choose.

If you name more than one alternate beneficiary for a specific gift, you should state the percentage or proportion of the gift each alternate beneficiary will receive. If you don't, they will receive equal shares, under the terms of the will.

EXAMPLE:

Brian's will leaves his home to Ruth Abrams. If Ruth doesn't survive him, his will provides that the alternate beneficiaries are Ruth's children, in equal shares. Here's how the clause would look in Brian's will.

"I leave my home at 2307 Butterfly Lane, Bayview, California, to Ruth Abrams, or, if she does not survive me, to Jacob Abrams and Susan Abrams, in equal shares."

Some parents leave the bulk of their property to their children. As an alternate beneficiary for one child, these people name their other child or children. Other parents designate grandchildren as alternate beneficiaries.

A specific gift left to one primary beneficiary and more than one alternate beneficiary raises issues for any shared gifts: potential conflicts among the alternate beneficiaries, if they inherit, and defining each one's share. (See "Naming Beneficiaries to Share Gifts," above.)

Alternate Beneficiaries for Shared Gifts

When it comes to shared gifts, naming alternate beneficiaries is more complicated. Your options are discussed in detail above, in "Naming Beneficiaries to Share Gifts."

Other Levels of Contingencies

What about naming another level, or layer, of alternate beneficiaries, in case the primary beneficiary and alternate both die before you do? With two exceptions discussed below, this book allows you to name primary beneficiaries and alternates and that's it. There are several sensible reasons for this:

1. It's a highly remote possibility that the beneficiary and alternate will both predecease you.

2. If this actually happens, you can revise your will.

3. Even if you did not revise your will, the property left to these beneficiaries would still pass under your will, and go to your residuary beneficiary.

4. In theory, you could create three—or for that matter, 30—layers of alternate beneficiaries for specific gifts. But the complexities involved in will drafting increase drastically with each additional layer of alternate beneficiaries.

Now that you know the general rule, here are the two exceptions:

Shared Gifts. You can provide another level of alternate beneficiaries for a shared gift where the surviving primary beneficiaries are the first alternates. But pondering the possibility that all primary beneficiaries of a shared gift may predecease you is surely a grim notion. Further, it's so unlikely that many people don't trouble themselves over such a remote contingency. But if you are concerned about it, in a single specific gift paragraph leaving a shared gift, after naming the primary beneficiaries, you provide that if they do not survive you, the person you name in the alternate blank will inherit the gift.

EXAMPLE:

Leo plans to leave his valuable patent to his children, Caesar, Doreen, and Ginger, in equal shares. A mathematician who worries about possibilities, however unlikely, Leo is comforted by making arrangements for who will receive the patent if all three of his children die before he does. In that case, he wants the property to go to Ginger's children, Angelique and Sharon, in equal shares. He enters this information in his will as follows:

"I leave my patent, #2,458,877 (anhydrous use of the chemical…in the production of…) to Caesar Aadler, Doreen Aadler, and Ginger Aadler-Wilson, in equal shares, or, if they do not survive me, to Angelique Aadler-Wilson and Sharon Aadler-Wilson, in equal shares."

Residuary Beneficiaries. You can, if you wish, add a second level of alternate beneficiaries for your residuary beneficiary. (Residuary beneficiaries are discussed below.) By preparing a will from Chapter 11, you can name both an alternate residuary beneficiary and also an alternate for this alternate, thus giving you three levels of protection.

SEE AN EXPERT

Naming further levels of alternate beneficiaries. The wills in this book should meet most people's needs for naming alternate beneficiaries. If you want to add additional levels of alternates, see a lawyer.

Naming Residuary Beneficiaries

It's vital that you name a residuary beneficiary. Your residuary estate (residue) consists of all property subject to your will that is not left by specific gifts. Your residue includes property you overlooked when making your will and property that came into your hands after you made your will. Your residue does *not* include property that passes to people outside of your will under other arrangements you made while you were alive, such as putting the property in a living trust, setting up a pay-on-death bank account, or holding title in joint tenancy.

Naming More Than One Residuary Beneficiary

You can, if you wish, name more than one residuary beneficiary. For example, you can leave your residue to be shared equally between two people. Or you could name a number of different individuals and organizations to share the residue in the proportions set out in your will.

Naming an Alternate Residuary Beneficiary

It's particularly important to name an alternate residuary beneficiary. You want to be sure you have a backup, in case your first choice for residuary beneficiary fails to survive you. Your residuary is your last "fail safe" option. If a specific gift can't be made, because the beneficiary and alternate beneficiary (if you named one) die before you do, that gift becomes part of your residue. If your residuary beneficiary also predeceases you, and you didn't name an alternate residuary beneficiary, your will would be out of options, and your residue would have to be distributed according to state law.

If you leave your residue to be shared by beneficiaries, you can name different alternates for each residuary beneficiary. For example, if you leave your residue 40% to Alice and 60% to Laura Sue, you can specify that the alternate residuary beneficiary for Alice is Pilar, and the alternate residuary beneficiaries for Laura Sue are Desireé and Manuel. Here's how such a clause would look in your will:

"I leave my residuary estate, that is, the rest of my property not otherwise specifically and validly disposed of by this will or in any other manner, including lapsed or failed gifts, to the following beneficiaries in the following shares:

Residuary Beneficiaries	Percent Each Receives
"Alice McDonnough	*40%*
"Laura Sue Noble	*60%*

"If Alice McDonnough does not survive me, her share of the residue shall go to Pilar Vargos.

"If Laura Sue Noble does not survive me, her share of the residue shall go to Desireé Coline and Manuel Perez, in equal shares."

Creating a Second Level of Alternate Residuary Beneficiaries

If you want to create a third level of beneficiaries for your residue—that is, alternates for your alternates—you need to use a residuary clause from Chapter 11. Simply write in exactly what you want.

EXAMPLE:

Jo names her husband Alberto as her residuary beneficiary. She names their two children, Rudolfo and Sophia, as the alternate residuary beneficiaries, to share equally. She then names alternates for each of her alternates. The alternates for Rudolfo are his three children, Luke, Mary, and Andy. The alternate for Sophia is her mate Tyrone.

If Alberto and Rudolfo die before Jo does (and she does not amend her will), half of her residuary property will go in three equal shares to Rudolfo's children, Luke, Mary, and Andy. Sophia will inherit the other half.

As you can see from this example, the chance of the second-level alternate residuary beneficiaries inheriting property is very slim. Most people, frankly, don't bother worrying about such remote possibilities. But if you do want to go this far, you can.

Explaining Your Gifts

Some people include personal comments in their wills, usually explaining why they left the gifts they did. I know of wills in which the writers expressed at some length their love for a mate, children, and friends. As I stated in Chapter 2, I believe that it is preferable to make your comments in a separate letter accompanying your will.

Whether in a will or out, comments are not, and are not intended to be, legally binding. While some lawyers insist that all comments must be made outside of a will, so there's no chance anyone could claim they were intended to have legal effect, I think that's a bit too cautious. If for some reason you want to include comments in your will instead of writing a separate letter, Nolo relies on your intelligence and ability to get the job done right. If you do want to make comments (either in your will or outside of it), just follow these straightforward rules, and you should encounter no problems:

1. Be sure your words can't be construed as making or modifying gifts left by your will. Common sense works fine here to ensure that you don't in any way modify the substance of your will by your comments.

2. Use a will only for short comments. If you want to explain your gifts or motivations at length, use a separate letter. It's awkward, if not confusing, to have paragraphs of non-binding commentary in a will.

The beneficiary clauses in the fill-in-the-blanks will forms in Chapter 10 do not contain additional lines for making comments. If you're filling in the forms by hand, you'll need to attach an extra page or pages to your draft. If you're using a word processor, just type in your comments after the relevant gift clause. Here's an example.

I leave _____ *$10,000* _____
to _my veterinarian, Dr. Surehands, for all her_
kind and competent treatment of my pets over
the years *or, if* _she_ _does_ *not survive me,*
to _my husband_ _____.

Another common reason for including comments in a will is to explain to children why property is left to them in unequal portions. There can be a number of reasons: the special health or educational needs of one child, the relative affluence and stability of another, the fact that one child has previously been given money, or estrangement between the parent and child.

But a child who receives less property may conclude that you cared for him or her less. Or, at least, a parent could worry that this might result. To deal with such concerns, you may wish to explain your reasons for leaving your property unequally. For example:

I leave my residuary estate, that is, the rest of my property not otherwise specifically and validly disposed of by this will or in any other manner,
to _40% each to my son Charles and my_
daughter Diane and 20% to my son Tim *or,*
if _any of them does_ *not survive me, to* _their_
share shall be divided equally between the
survivors. I love all my children deeply and
equally. I give 20% to Tim because he received
family funds to go through medical school, so it
is fair that my other two children receive more
of my property now.

Making Harsh Comments in a Will

Short of libel, the scope of your remarks is limited only by your imagination.

Some famous people wrote wills with some biting words. Benjamin Franklin's will left his son William, who was sympathetic to England during our Revolution, only some land in Nova Scotia and stated, "The fact he acted against me in the late war, which is of public notoriety, will account for my leaving him no more of an estate that he endeavored to deprive me of." And then there was the German poet Heinrich Heine, who wrote a will leaving his property to his wife on the condition that she remarry, so that "there will be at least one man to regret my death." William Shakespeare cryptically left his wife his "second best bed," a gift that has intrigued scholars for centuries.

! CAUTION

Be careful about making insults in your will. If you libel someone in your will, your estate can be liable for damages. If you want to say something nasty, check it out with a lawyer who knows libel law.

Survivorship Periods

A survivorship period requires that a beneficiary must survive you by a specified time period to inherit. One reason for imposing survivorship periods is to avoid double probate costs and possible double estate taxes. If a person to whom you leave property dies soon after you do, the property will be included in his estate. The result is that the property you had hoped the person would use and enjoy merely raises the dollar value of his estate, possibly increasing probate fees and taxes. Also, this property now passes under the terms of your beneficiary's will, rather than being left to the alternate beneficiary you chose. To avoid this, most wills set a specific time period by which a beneficiary must survive the will writer.

EXAMPLE:

"I leave my 1955 T-Bird to my best friend Anthony Blaine, or, if he doesn't survive me by 45 days*, to my cousin, Jacques de Paris."*

The basic, fill-in-the-blanks wills in Chapter 10 impose a 45-day survivorship period on all your beneficiaries, except alternate residuary beneficiaries. No survivorship period is required for these beneficiaries because normally there's no backup for them. Better to let them inherit, even if they die shortly after you do, than let your property pass under state law. The basic wills require beneficiaries to "survive" you, and then define "survive" to mean "be alive or in existence as an organization on the 45th day" after your death.

In a customized Chapter 11 will, you can select any reasonable survivorship period you want, or none at all, or stay with the 45-day period. My preference is for relatively short periods, 45 to 90 days, to be sure you don't tie property up beyond the time in which it otherwise might be transferred.

Simultaneous Death

Worries about simultaneous deaths often trouble will writers. The first, and by far the most common, worry is what happens if both spouses, or mates, are killed in a common disaster. Second is what happens if all joint tenants die simultaneously.

Spouses or Mates

Many couples, married or not, who leave each other property wonder what would happen to it if they were to die together. If a survivorship period is used, the property left to the other spouse or mate will pass to the alternate beneficiary or alternate residuary beneficiary.

EXAMPLE:

Martha and George, a married couple, die in a plane wreck. Both their wills contain 45-day survivorship periods. Thus George's property, which he willed entirely to Martha, doesn't go to her because she didn't survive him by the set time. Instead, George's property goes to whomever he named as alternate for Martha. This same process is repeated for Martha's property; it goes not to George's estate but to her alternate beneficiaries.

But if a spouse decides for some reason not to include a survivorship requirement in the will, property of that spouse might go to the other, even if this spouse survived by only a few seconds. This could result in the property being inherited by the momentarily surviving spouse's beneficiaries, which might not be what the will writer wanted.

To prevent this, or if you simply want the assurance of using a simultaneous death clause even if you use a survivorship provision, you can include a "Simultaneous Death" clause in your will. To do this, you must prepare your will from Chapter 11. This clause provides that for purposes of interpreting your will, you are presumed to have outlived your spouse, if you both die simultaneously. I've included the option of a simultaneous death clause because I've learned that some people want to address this concern specifically.

You may wonder how a simultaneous death clause can work for both spouses' wills. That is, how can a husband be presumed to have survived his wife for purposes of his will, but the reverse be presumed for her will? On a legalistic level, the answer is because each will is interpreted independently of the other. On the real level, it's because doing it this way works to get the results people want. In the famous words of Justice Holmes, "The life of the law has not been logic, it has been experience."

Simultaneous Death of Joint Tenants

What happens if people (married or not) who own joint tenancy property die simultaneously? While unlikely, this is not impossible, and some people understandably are concerned with it. The answer is the property is divided into as many equal shares as there are joint tenants. Then a share is left to each owner's estate.

EXAMPLE:

Jim and Mary Smith, owners of a house in joint tenancy, die together. A half-interest in the joint tenancy property is included in Jim Smith's estate. The other half-interest is included in Mary Smith's estate.

Unless you specify differently, under the wills in this book your share of any joint tenancy property which passes under your will because of simultaneous death is part of your residue, and goes to your residuary beneficiary. However, you can specifically name a primary beneficiary for your share. You need a will from Chapter 11 to accomplish this. Here's an example:

"If I have any interest in joint tenancy property subject to this will, I leave that interest to Tyler Geise or, if he does not survive me, to Richard Ossawa and Lois J. Wright, in equal shares."

If you have more than one joint tenancy property, and you want to name different will beneficiaries for each property, you'll have to adapt this clause. Use separate paragraphs describing each specific joint tenancy property and naming beneficiaries for it.

EXAMPLE:

Matt and Ji-Li own most of their assets in joint tenancy. If they die simultaneously, each wants his or her half of their joint tenancy assets distributed to a number of different beneficiaries. Matt prepares the following clause for his will:

"If I have any interest in joint tenancy property subject to this will, I leave that property as follows:

I leave my interest in the house at 553 Carbory Lane, Millwod, Michigan, equally to my two children, Nannette Yung-Johnson and Carol Yung-Johnson;

I leave my interest in the stock account #232323232 with Lazard Freres to my Alma Mater, the University of Michigan;

I leave my interest in the CTP Limited Partnership to the Sierra Club."

Do remember that if one joint tenant does survive the others, that person receives all the joint tenancy property, no matter what your will says. Your will affects joint tenancy property *only* if all the joint tenants die simultaneously.

Using the Beneficiary Worksheet

If you want to make a list of your beneficiaries, you can use the Beneficiary Worksheet in Appendix B or on the CD-ROM. If you already completed the Property Worksheet, start with that list.

First, identify each item of your property that you want to leave as a distinct gift. Then list a beneficiary or beneficiaries for each item. If the names are extremely common or there may otherwise be confusion as to who you mean, use middle names. If you want to leave some property to be shared, state what portion or percentage each beneficiary receives. Normally, you don't need to list beneficiaries' addresses; they're not included in your will. But if you think your executor might have a hard time locating a beneficiary, you might note on the worksheet how that beneficiary could likely be found. And, obviously, you should then give the worksheet, and any future updates, to your executor.

After naming your primary beneficiary or beneficiaries for each specific gift, you can put down your choice for an alternate or alternates for that gift.

After you go through the first two sections of the worksheet and make all specific gifts and forgive debts (if desired), use Section 3 to name your residuary beneficiary and alternate residuary beneficiary.

If You've Got a Simple Beneficiary Situation

If you plan to leave all of your property to one person, or to several to share, you can simply list your choice(s) in Section 3 of the worksheet as your residuary beneficiary or beneficiaries. Then, when you complete your will, you won't make any specific gifts at all. All your property will pass under the residuary clause.

Minor or Young Adult Beneficiaries

If you want to leave property to a minor (a child under 18) as any type of beneficiary, you simply list the minor's name here. You'll need to impose some form of adult supervision over that gift, but you don't need to concern yourself with that now. You'll handle that matter in Chapter 7, Children.

Similarly, you can impose mature supervision over gifts you leave to young adults under age 35 by use of a child's trust. Again, how you can do this is explained in Chapter 7.

Disinheritance

Disinheritance is not a subject that concerns most people preparing a will. The word "disinheritance" has harsh, perhaps sad, overtones, since it means you've decided to exclude from your will a family member or other person involved with your life. But, sad or not, it's certainly been known to happen. You can disinherit anyone you want to, except for your spouse in many states. (And in Florida, you must leave your house to your spouse or minor child.) Also, if you've made a valid contract to leave someone some property in your will, you can't negate that contract simply by disinheriting the person in your will. Here are the general rules regarding disinheritance.

> ### Leaving Someone a Token Amount
>
> Some people wonder if they should leave a minimal amount, perhaps one dollar, to relatives or other people they fear may contest their will. This is not a good idea. Will contests are very rare, but leaving one dollar to someone doesn't prevent that person from contesting your will. Also, leaving some beneficiaries a token amount causes needless work for your executor. Each beneficiary under a will is expected to sign a receipt for the amount delivered. Why burden your executor with obtaining a receipt for a trifle that you didn't have to leave in the first place?

Your Spouse

In the great majority of states—those that follow the common-law property ownership system—you cannot fully disinherit a spouse. These states' laws allow a surviving spouse to claim a portion of a deceased spouse's estate, no matter what the deceased spouse's will provides. In community property states, your spouse usually has no legal right to any of your half of the community property, or to any of your separate property. (See Chapter 3 for in-depth information about spousal property rights.)

Your Children

To an outsider, it may seem poignant that a parent would want to disinherit a child, but nevertheless, it happens. If you want to disinherit a child, your intent to do so must be explicitly stated in your will. You cannot disinherit a child simply by failing to mention that child in your will. Legal rules protect children, particularly children born after the date of the will, from being accidentally disinherited, which means being not mentioned in your will. If a child isn't mentioned in your will, the law may presume that the omission was just an oversight. In that case the omitted child (in legalese, a "pretermitted heir") is entitled to some of your property anyway. How much depends on whether you have a surviving spouse and how many other children you have.

To help you make sure your will and property won't become enmeshed in an overlooked child problem, list all your living children in your will, whether natural, adopted, or born out of wedlock. If you leave some property to each child, even only as an alternate or alternate residuary beneficiary, you won't have any problem with state inheritance laws. However, as a backup measure, the wills in this book state that if you list a child but don't leave him or her property in any way, your failure to do so is intentional—that is, you intended to disinherit the child. But don't rely solely on this backup provision. If you decide to disinherit any of your children, state it expressly, in a will prepared from Chapter 11.

Your Grandchildren

Grandchildren don't have any legal right to inherit if their parent (your child) is still alive. So there's no need to expressly disinherit such grandchildren, even if you don't want them to inherit any of your property. But in many states, children of a deceased child do have a statutory right to inherit from a grandparent, if such children aren't provided for or disinherited in the grandparent's will.

That is why the will forms require you to list all children of a deceased child. If you have any such grandchildren, either leave them some property, as any type of beneficiary, or expressly disinherit any you want to.

A Former Spouse

It isn't necessary to specifically disinherit a former spouse. Simply leaving this person out of your new will achieves the same result. If you want to emphasize your feelings, you can specifically state in your new will that your former spouse is to receive nothing from your estate. (But watch out for libel laws.)

> **CAUTION**
>
> **Make a new will after a divorce.** In several states, a final judgment of divorce (or annulment) has no effect on any gift made by your will to your former spouse; in other states it revokes such a gift. And in a few others, divorce revokes the entire will. Therefore, after a divorce make a new will.

Other People

With the exception of your spouse and "overlooked" children or grandchildren, you can disinherit anyone you want to, including other relatives, simply by not naming them in the will. Actually, the word "disinherit" isn't correct here, since no one but a spouse or children has any inherent right to your property.

Still, if for some reason you want to state in your will that a certain person is to receive nothing from you, you certainly can. For instance, perhaps you're concerned that someone might claim you promised to leave them property. You could use a specific disinheritance clause to show you didn't forget to leave that person something, but consciously chose not to, believing they weren't entitled to anything.

If you want to explicitly state in your will that someone is not to receive any of your property, you need to use Clause e from Chapter 11.

No-Contest Clauses

A no-contest clause automatically disinherits anyone who unsuccessfully challenges your will. The purpose of a no-contest clause is to discourage any beneficiary from challenging your will in court. The beneficiary risks losing all inheritance rights under your will if the lawsuit is lost. If you believe there's any likelihood that someone may challenge your will, or if you just want to be very cautious, you can include the no-contest clause (Clause x) in a will prepared from Chapter 11.

SEE AN EXPERT

Anticipating trouble. Generally, courts enforce no-contest clauses. However, if you believe there's any reasonable chance someone will contest your will, you should see a lawyer. You may be able to take action now to be sure your executor will be best prepared to defeat any lawsuit.

Property You No Longer Own at Your Death

A will isn't binding during your life. Before you die, you can give away or sell any property mentioned in your will. Even if the will is never amended or rewritten to recognize that you no longer own particular pieces of property, the gift or sale is valid.

But if you do dispose of property, you may cause a discrepancy between what your will provides and the amount or type of property actually left in your estate. What happens if, at your death, your will leaves people property that you no longer own?

Specific Items

If you've left someone a specific piece of property in your will—say, a particular Tiffany lamp—but you no longer own that property when you die, that beneficiary is out of luck. Lawyers call this "ademption." People who don't inherit the property in question are often heard to use an earthier term.

Insufficient Liquid Assets to Pay Cash Gifts

If you've left cash gifts and there aren't enough cash resources to fully pay them, this necessitates what's called an "abatement." While not common, this problem is certainly not unheard of. Unless you include specific instructions in your will about what to do in the event of a cash shortfall, state law provides the rules for how your executor must conduct abatement proceedings. Some states require that property first be taken from the residue and sold so that cash gifts can be paid; others first require a pro-rata reduction of cash gifts, if possible without the sale of specific objects of property. The details of how different states reduce gifts vary too much to be covered here.

This book's fill-in-the-blanks wills (in Chapter 10) don't include abatement instructions. This means any abatement would be carried out according to the laws of the state where the will is probated. If you prepare your will from the clauses in Chapter 11, however, you can choose from two different abatement clauses (or ignore the matter). One option provides for pro rata reduction of all cash gifts if there isn't enough money to pay them in full. The other option provides that shortfalls in specific cash gifts are to be made up from the residue. If you choose the residue option, and there's a shortage of cash available to pay all cash gifts, the people who receive your residue will lose out first. If selling property from the residue doesn't raise enough cash, your executor is directed to abate in the fairest way possible, consistent with state law.

If you don't include either clause in a Chapter 11 will, any necessary abatement will be conducted in accordance with your state's statutes.

EXAMPLE 1, PRO RATA OPTION:

Roberta leaves cash gifts of $20,000 each to Kate, John, and Marri. When she dies, there's only $30,000 cash in her estate. The three beneficiaries each receive $10,000.

EXAMPLE 2, RESIDUARY OPTION:

Paul leaves $20,000 each to Steve, Stephanie, Barbara, and Jack. When he dies, there's only $40,000 cash in his estate. However, Paul's estate also contains a house that is left to the residuary beneficiary. To give each beneficiary the full amount of their cash gifts, the house must be sold. The residuary beneficiary takes what's left over after all cash gifts are paid.

> **CAUTION**
>
> **Keep your will up to date.** What happens if you leave more property in your will than is actually available can be a complex matter. However, the overall point is simple. Don't leave more than you own, after what you owe and what your estate will likely need to pay in tax is subtracted. Make a new will whenever changes in what you own disrupt your gift-leaving plan.

Choosing Your Executor

Now it's time to decide who you want to serve as your executor. As you know by now, your executor is the person you name in your will to take on an important job: handling your property during probate and distributing it as your will directs. You should also choose an alternate executor, in case for any reason your original choice can't serve.

Most wills must go through probate, the process in which a will is submitted to a court, debts paid, and property distributed as the will directs. The probate court supervises the executor's handling of the estate. If, however, your will is exempt from probate (see Chapter 14), your executor will pay your debts and distribute your property without any court supervision.

To help with this job, your executor has the authority to hire professionals who will be paid out of the estate's assets—a lawyer to handle the probate court process and an accountant to prepare the necessary tax forms.

Terminology

Some states use the term "personal representative" instead of executor. But "executor" works in all states. If someone dies without a will or makes a will but forgets to name an executor, the person appointed by the court to take this position is called the "administrator."

Responsibilities of an Executor

Your executor's powers and responsibilities are, in general terms, defined by state law. In addition, all the will forms in this book contain a standard clause defining and granting extensive specific powers to the executor. (Texas has a special clause. See Clause 7 in Chapter 10, or Clause q in Chapter 11.)

When you read the "Executor's Powers" clause, the duties may seem so awesome and burdensome that you doubt anyone would want the job, let alone be able to manage it. Fortunately, in reality, an executor's job is not usually very hard, though it takes some time. Normally, it's the probate attorney (in truth, mostly her secretary and staff) who handles the legal details. With a well-drafted will, the legal matters are almost always routine. Usually, the executor just checks in with the probate attorney occasionally, signs legal papers, pays your final bills and any death taxes (using estate funds), and makes sure your property actually goes to the people and organizations named in the will.

The reason so many specific powers are listed in the Executor's Powers clause is that occasionally a financial institution—a bank, title company, or stock brokerage company, for example—insists that a precise clause authorize the executor to do some act involving that institution. Rather than making it necessary for your executor to argue with the institution, it's safer, although unfortunately wordier, to include specific authorization for the types of issues that may come up.

Typical Duties of an Executor

An executor typically must:

- obtain your original will
- get certified copies of your death certificate
- locate will beneficiaries
- examine and inventory your safe deposit boxes
- collect your mail
- cancel credit cards and subscriptions
- notify the Social Security Administration and other benefit plan administrators of your death and collect any benefits due
- learn about your property, which may involve examining bankbooks, deeds, insurance policies, tax returns, and many other records

- get bank accounts covered by the will released, and

- hire a probate lawyer, if necessary.

Hiring a Lawyer: The Executor's Choice

You can't require your executor to hire a particular attorney to handle the probate of your will. It's up to the executor to decide how to handle probate. (In California, the executor can handle probate without an attorney by using *How to Probate an Estate in California*, by Julia Nissley, Nolo.) Normally, although the executor is responsible for overseeing the probate process, most of the work is done by a lawyer. If, in your will, you state a preference for a particular attorney, presumably the executor will follow that request but is not legally bound to do so.

In addition to these practical tasks, your executor—or the lawyer hired to handle the probate court proceeding—will also have to:

- file court papers to start the probate process and obtain legal authority to act as your executor

- sensibly manage your assets during the probate process, which commonly takes six months to a year

- handle court-supervised probate matters, which include transferring property to your beneficiaries and making sure your final debts and taxes are paid, and

- have final income tax forms prepared for you, and, if necessary, have estate tax returns for your estate prepared and filed.

Legally, your executor is what's called a "fiduciary," which means he or she must act in good faith. Your executor cannot unfairly profit from financial transactions from the estate, like buying estate property at less than market rates, or otherwise take advantage of his position. Realistically, if your executor does a competent,

honest job, as you obviously believe she or he will, the fiduciary duty standard will be met.

RESOURCE
More information about the executor's job. For a thorough explanation of an executor's duties, see *The Executor's Guide: Settling a Loved One's Estate or Trust*, by Mary Randolph (Nolo). The book explains in depth the legal, financial, and practical matters that an executor may have to handle after a death. It also offers tips on things you can do ahead of time to make your executor's job easier.

The Executor's Fee

Your executor is legally entitled to be paid, from your estate, for doing that job. The fee scale varies from state to state, ranging from a fixed percentage of the probate estate (the total value of the property passing through probate) to "reasonable compensation." In reality, an executor often waives the fees, especially if he inherits most of the estate anyway. You might want to discuss the question of fees with the person you choose to be your executor, to be sure the two of you are in agreement.

Posting a Bond

Many probate courts require an executor to post a bond—an insurance policy that protects beneficiaries if the executor is dishonest or incompetent—unless you expressly waived this requirement in your will. If you've chosen an executor you trust, there's no reason to require in your will that your executor put up a bond to insure that all duties are properly carried out. The cost of buying the bond—normally, about 10% of its face amount—must be paid out of your estate. Obviously, this means one or more of your beneficiaries will receive less than if a bond hadn't been bought.

All wills in this book provide that no bond is required of any executor. There may, however, be some unusual personal reason why you want your executor to post a bond. The most likely reason is that you don't have anyone you fully trust to serve as your executor, so you've had to settle for the best you can get. You may decide it's worth the cost of a bond to your inheritors to be sure there's financial recourse if the executor proves untrustworthy or acts improperly.

If you decide to require your executor to post a bond, you'll need a will from Chapter 11. You can delete the standard "no-bond" clause and substitute one requiring a bond.

How to Choose Your Executor

The most important criterion in naming an executor is trust; choose someone you have complete faith in. For many people, the choice of executor is obvious—their spouse or mate. Others select a best friend, grown child, or other close relative. If no obvious person comes to mind, work through your possible selections, using your common sense to make the wisest choice. Keep in mind that human concerns are usually more important than technical expertise.

Factors to Consider

First, if possible, your executor (or at least one of them, if you appoint coexecutors) should reside in your state, or at least fairly close to where you live. Because of paperwork and other administrative responsibilities, which may include making one or more appearances in court, it's best not to name someone who lives far away from your property and the probate proceeding (which generally takes place in the county where you were living before your death).

However, given the choice between someone you completely trust who lives far away and someone nearby about whom you have doubts, definitely choose the person you trust.

Many states impose requirements on out-of-state executors, such as requiring the executor to appoint an "agent"—a person who lives in the state and is available to accept legal papers ("service of process"). Your executor, working with the probate lawyer if need be, can readily handle such matters. (See the chart below for a complete list of restrictions.)

Many people name as executor someone who benefits substantially under the will. This makes sense, because an executor who has an interest in how your property is distributed is likely to do a conscientious job. Often this person is a mate, an adult child, or other close family member.

You also want to be sure to name someone who's willing to do the job. Obviously, you should discuss this with the person of your choice before finalizing your decision. Someone who is named as an executor in a will is always free to decline to serve; the job can't be forced on anyone.

Finally, you want to name someone who's healthy and likely to be around after your death. Of course, there are no guarantees here, and if your choice for executor dies before you do, you may want to revise your will and name someone else. (See Chapter 13, Changing or Revoking Your Will.) To be more secure, you should always select at least one alternate executor to serve if your first choice cannot.

Restrictions on Out-of-State Executors

Alabama	Nonresident can be appointed executor only if already serving as executor of same estate in another state. (Ala.Code § 43-2-22)	Iowa	Nonresident can serve as executor only if resident appointed coexecutor, unless court allows nonresident to serve alone. (Iowa Code § 633.64)
Arkansas	Nonresident executor must appoint an agent who lives in county where will is probated. (Ark. Code Ann. § 28-48-101(b)(6))	Kansas	Nonresident executor must appoint an agent who lives in county where will is probated. (Kan. Stat. Ann. § 59-1706)
Connecticut	Nonresident executor must appoint in-state probate court judge as agent to accept legal papers. (Conn. Gen. Stat. Ann. § 52-60)	Kentucky	Nonresident can be appointed executor only if he or she is related to person making will by blood, marriage, or adoption. (Ky. Rev. Stat. Ann. § 395.005)
Delaware	Nonresident must appoint county register of wills as agent to accept legal papers. (Del. Code Ann. tit. 12 § 1506)	Maryland	Nonresident executor must publish notices in a newspaper and appoint an in-state agent to accept legal papers. (Md. Code Ann. [Estates & Trusts] § 5-503)
District of Columbia	Nonresident executor must designate probate register as agent. (D.C. Code Ann. § 20-303)	Massachusetts	Nonresident executor must appoint an in-state agent to accept legal papers. (Mass. Gen. Laws ch. 195, § 8)
Florida	Nonresident can be appointed executor only if he or she is related to person making will by blood, marriage, or adoption. (Fla. Stat. Ann. § 733.304)	Missouri	Nonresident must appoint an in-state agent to accept legal papers. (Mo. Rev. Stat. § 473.117)
Illinois	Nonresident executor may be required to post bond, even if will expressly states bond not required. (755 Ill. Comp. Stat. § 5/6-13)	Nevada	Nonresident can serve as executor only if resident appointed coexecutor. (Nev. Rev. Stat. Ann. § 139.010)
Indiana	Nonresident can serve as executor if resident appointed coexecutor and nonresident posts a bond. Nonresident can serve alone if he or she posts a bond, files a written notice of acceptance, and appoints an in-state agent to accept legal papers. (Ind. Code Ann. § 29-1-10-1)	New Hampshire	Nonresident executor must appoint an in-state agent to accept legal papers. (N.H. Rev. Stat. Ann. § 553:5)

Restrictions on Out-of-State Executors (continued)			
New Jersey	Nonresident must post bond unless will waives requirement. (N.J. Stat. Ann. § 3B:15-1)	Texas	Nonresident executor must appoint an in-state agent to accept legal papers. (Tex. Prob. Code Ann. § 78)
North Carolina	Nonresident executor must appoint an in-state agent to accept legal papers. (N.C. Gen. Stat. § 28A-4-2)	Vermont	Nonresident executor can be appointed only with court approval; court must approve nonresident executor upon request of surviving spouse, adult children, parents, or guardian of minor children. Nonresident executor must appoint an in-state agent to accept legal papers. (Vt. Stat. Ann. tit. 14, § 904)
Ohio	Nonresident can be appointed executor only if he or she is related to person making will by blood, marriage, or adoption—or if he or she lives in a state that permits nonresidents to serve. (Ohio Rev. Code Ann. § 2109.21)	Virginia	Nonresident executor must post a bond and appoint an in-state agent to accept legal papers. Bond not required if resident appointed coexecutor. (Va. Code Ann. § 26-59)
Oklahoma	Nonresident executor must appoint an in-state agent to accept legal papers. (Okla. Stat. Ann. tit. 58, § 162)	Washington	Nonresident executor must appoint an agent who lives in county where will is probated. (Wash. Rev. Code Ann. § 11.36.010)
Pennsylvania	Nonresident can serve as executor only with permission of probate register. (20 Pa. Cons. State. Ann. § 3157)	Wisconsin	Nonresident executor must appoint an in-state agent to accept legal papers. Nonresident executor can be removed or refused appointment solely on grounds of residency. (Wis. Stat. § 856.23)
Rhode Island	Nonresident executor must be approved by a judge, and must appoint an in-state agent to accept legal papers. (R.I. Gen. Laws §§ 33-8-7 and 33-18-9)	Wyoming	Nonresident executor must appoint an in-state agent to accept legal papers. (Wyo. Stat. § 2-11-301)
Tennessee	Nonresident can serve as executor if related by blood or marriage to person making will or if approved by a judge. Nonresident can also serve if resident appointed coexecutor. (Tenn. Code Ann. § 35-50-107)		

If Your Executor's Name Changes

A few readers of prior editions of this book have asked, "My executor, who is my daughter, has married and changed her last name. Do I need to change my will?"

This concern can be handled easily. The safest method is to prepare an amendment to your will, called a codicil, setting forth your daughter's new name. (See Chapter 13.) But even if you don't do that, a probate court would surely (well, as sure as you can be with law and judges) interpret your choice for executor to mean your daughter, since you used her legal name as it existed when you wrote your will.

Naming More Than One Executor

Legally, you can name as many executors as you want. But if you want to name more than one, think carefully about your motivation.

When you name more than one executor, you must decide whether each has authority to act independently for your estate, or if all executors must agree in writing before any action can be taken. The wills in this book allow coexecutors to act independently. If all executors must agree, problems can arise. Some may be practical. Getting two or more people to sign every probate court document can delay the process, perhaps considerably. But more important, what happens if all the executors don't agree? Answering this question helps focus on your motivation for wanting shared executors.

Some parents want to name all of their children as executors as a symbolic act of equal love, so they don't seem to be favoring any child. The parents believe the children will get along fine regarding their will and property. In these circumstances, the parents authorize any child to act for the estate, so that probate and other matters may be handled as efficiently as possible.

Similarly, a parent may name two or more children as executors for convenience, so that if one or more is temporarily unavailable there will be no delays in the executor's work. Again, any of the executors can act for the estate.

A quite different motivation enters the picture if you believe that more than one executor is needed so they can keep an eye on each other. In other words, you aren't really sure there's one person you fully trust to do the executor's job. For instance, you may worry that there is no one child who will divide family heirlooms fairly, no matter what your will provides.

Naming two or more children as executors and requiring them all to agree doesn't necessarily mean you regard any child as malicious. You're just recognizing that family property, particularly treasured items (whether monetarily valuable or not), can be invested with intense memories and desires—indeed, a range of emotions. So to minimize squabbles or resentments over property, you want to have two or three kids as executors, to police each other. It's fine if this works, but what if it doesn't? Then there's a serious legal conflict, and a court proceeding may be necessary to resolve it.

My point here is that naming more than one executor is far from a guarantee that personal conflicts will be controlled. If you suspect there may be any conflicts between coexecutors (or between any beneficiaries and your executors), it's best to face that problem squarely now, rather than push it off to coexecutors and hope they can resolve whatever comes up. Perhaps focused discussion among family members on who really wants what could help. Or perhaps it's wisest to select the person you think will serve best as executor, and leave it at that. Or you can try to leave your gifts so specifically that there's no room for argument over what you intended. Then, if you also want to name more than one executor, you can go ahead and take your chances.

If you do choose to name more than one executor, you'll need to use the "assemble-the-clauses" will of Chapter 11 rather than a simpler fill-in-the-blank will from Chapter 10.

SEE AN EXPERT

If you sense trouble, see a lawyer. If you want to require that it takes more than one of your executors to act for your estate, this indicates that you don't trust each to act alone. Have a lawyer prepare a detailed executors' clause to handle your particular needs and desires.

Naming a Corporate Executor

Is it a good idea to name a corporate executor, such as a bank or trust company? I strongly recommend against it in almost all circumstances. Your executor is your personal representative in the distribution of your property after your death. You want someone human, with genuine concern, not an institution, to do the job. If your most trusted friend is your banker, name him as executor, but not the bank itself.

However, special circumstances may compel you to choose a corporate or professional executor. For example, if you're actively involved in running a business, and your executor will be responsible for continuing that business at least for a while, you'll want someone with business acumen or experience. If you can't find any person you know and trust to take on this major responsibility, you'll have to select a professional management firm. Banks often provide this service. Also, some private trust companies specialize in managing trusts. A private trust company could provide you—and your trust—with more sophisticated and personal attention than a bank. Another option is to name a trusted person and a professional management company as coexecutors.

Also, if there's simply no one you trust at all to serve as your executor, selecting an institution is preferable to failing to name an executor. But a real problem here, as with naming an institutional executor for any reason, can be finding an institution willing to take on the job. Sure, you can find one if you've got plenty of money, but if you have a more modest estate, many financial institutions may not think they'd make enough to bother serving as your executor.

> ### Naming Your Executor to Act in Other Capacities
>
> It's fine, if you want, to appoint your executor to handle other legal tasks for your estate or your family. Indeed, it's often desirable to place decision-making authority in one person in order to avoid risks of conflict, as well us cut down on duplicating information. For example, if you create a trust for your minor child, you may well want your executor to be the trustee of that trust. Or, if you decide to prepare durable powers of attorney (see Chapter 14), you may name your executor as your "attorney-in-fact" to make financial and health care decisions for you if you become incapacitated.

Naming an Alternate Executor

It's important to name an alternate executor. Clearly, your executor performs a vital job, and in case the person you selected is unable to do the work, you want to be sure someone you've chosen can. If you name coexecutors, the alternate won't serve unless all the coexecutors can't. If none of your choices can serve, a probate court will appoint someone, following the priority list set out by state law, which considers closest relatives first.

Naming an Executor for Another State

Your estate will go through probate in the courts of your home state, normally in the county where you were residing before your death. But if you owned real estate in another state, a separate probate court proceeding will probably be necessary there, too.

You may want to name an "ancillary executor"—someone specifically authorized to act for your estate in that other state—if:

- the other state places restrictions on nonresident executors, or
- it would be more convenient or efficient to appoint an executor who lives in that state.

For instance, if you're living in Nebraska when you die, but own real estate in Maine, there will probably be probate proceedings in both states. A Nebraska resident could serve as executor in Maine, but if you know someone who lives in Maine who will do the job, it can make matters more efficient to name that person as your ancillary executor for that state.

You can name an ancillary executor in the "assemble-the-clauses" will of Chapter 11.

Executor Worksheet

If you wish, you can list the name and address of your choice for your executor and alternate executor on the tear-out Executor Worksheet in Appendix B or on the CD-ROM at the back of the book.

Children

Read this chapter only if you're concerned with children—your own or another's—to whom you want to leave property.

In the context of making your will, the word "children" has two meanings. The first is "minors" —those who are not yet legal adults. That is, they are under age 18. The bulk of this chapter addresses concerns of parents with minor children. The second meaning of children is offspring of any age. Parents obviously can have "children" who are themselves adults.

Parents of *minor children* have two concerns: who will raise the children if the parents can't, and who will supervise property the parents (or others) leave for the children? Parents of *adult children* can leave property to them just as to any other adult. However, if you have young adult children, you may not want them to receive their property outright until they've reached an age when they can (hopefully) manage money sensibly. So you, too, may arrange for the supervision of property you leave them. This chapter explains how you can use your will to impose mature adult control over property you leave to minor or young adult beneficiaries.

For this chapter, I provided a worksheet for listing the person you want to be responsible for raising your minor children if you can't. That worksheet also has a space for writing out the reasons for your choice. Additionally, there are various worksheets you can use to record information regarding how you want an adult of your choosing to manage property you leave to children. As with all worksheets in this book, these are provided for your assistance—as tools that may be useful, not as mandatory paperwork.

REMINDER

Posthumously conceived children. If you're considering the possibility of having a child after your death by using frozen genetic material, be sure to read the discussion of this subject in Chapter 5.

Providing for Your Minor Children

Most parents of minor children are extremely, and understandably, concerned about what will happen to their children if disaster strikes and the parents die unexpectedly. Indeed, selecting a legal and personally appropriate method for handling this grim possibility is the major reason many younger parents write wills. If both parents are raising the children, the major concern usually is providing for the children in case of the simultaneous death of the parents. If only one parent is involved—because the other parent is deceased, has abandoned the child, or is unavailable for some other reason—the single parent is similarly anxious to arrange for someone to care for the child if that parent dies.

Providing for your minor children if you die involves two distinct concerns:

Providing personal care. Who will raise the children if you can't? In legal terms, this means choosing a personal guardian for each child.

Providing financial care. How can you best provide financial support for your children? Here, you will consider what property will be available, and who will handle and supervise it for their benefit.

Custody of Your Minor Child

If two biological or adoptive parents are willing and able to care for their child, and one dies, the other normally has the legal right to assume sole custody. ("Adoptive" parents are people who have legally adopted a child, not those functioning informally as stepparents.) This is true whether the parents are married, divorced, or never married, as long as both parents are involved in raising their children. But what happens if both parents die? Or suppose there's only one parent in the picture, and that parent dies?

If there's no parent available who's able to do the job, some other adult must become the minor child's legal guardian and take custody of the child. Obviously, it's desirable for you, as a parent, to nominate the person you want to serve as personal guardian for your children if one is needed. You can also nominate an alternate personal guardian, in case the first choice can't serve. These choices must be stated in your will. In almost all states, you cannot use another estate planning document, such as a living trust, for this purpose.

If both you and the other parent die, the person named as a minor's personal guardian in your wills doesn't become the legal guardian until formally appointed by a court. If no one contests your choice, a court will almost certainly confirm this person. However, a judge who is convinced it's in the best interests of the child has the authority to name someone else as guardian. Children aren't property, and naming a personal guardian in a will doesn't have the same automatically binding effect as a provision leaving a lamp to a beneficiary.

A court rarely rejects an unopposed nominee. It will do so only if there are grave and provable reasons to reject the proposed guardian, such as alcoholism or a serious criminal background. A responsible parent won't, of course, select a guardian with such problems.

Minors Who Don't Need Guardians

"Emancipated minors" are minors who have achieved legal adult status. They do not require adult personal guardians. The rules for emancipation are governed by your state's laws; typical grounds are marriage, military service, or the fact that a 16- or 17-year-old is living independently with the authority of a court "emancipation" order. Emancipation is uncommon. You cannot emancipate your child in your will.

Making Your Choice

You may have already decided who you want to name as your child's personal guardian. But for some parents, deciding on a personal guardian is the toughest decision they face when writing their wills. From your perspective, there may be no ideal person. Whether choosing a personal guardian is simple, difficult, or wrenching, it's entirely a personal decision. All I can tell you, if you find the decision difficult, is that you're not alone.

Of course, you need to remember the obvious: You can't draft someone to parent your kids. Be sure any person you name is ready, willing, and able to do the job. If at all possible, both parents should appoint the same person in their wills.

You should also name an alternate personal guardian, in case your first choice can't serve. If you've chosen one member of a couple to be personal guardian, it can be sensible to name the other as alternate.

If you are ready to name your children's personal guardian and alternate guardian, proceed to "Worksheet: Personal Guardians." If, however, you have any doubts or questions, read the following material before making your choices. Perhaps you and the child's other parent are separated or divorced, and you believe someone else would be a better choice to raise the child. Or perhaps you and the other parent want to name different personal guardians for different children.

Naming More Than One Person as Guardian

Normally, it's not wise to name more than one person to serve as guardian for your children. Naming multiple guardians raises the possibility that they may disagree about the best way to raise a child, resulting in conflict and perhaps even requiring court intervention. However, there is one situation in which naming two guardians makes good sense: when you want to name a couple to care for your children together.

If you know a couple—for example, your sister and her husband—who are willing and able to take good care of your children, it's fine to name them both. If needed, the couple will act as your children's surrogate parents. Both of them will be allowed to do things for your children that require legal authority, such as picking up your children from school, authorizing field trips, or taking them to the doctor.

Keep in mind, however, that if you name a couple as guardians, they must be able to agree on what's best for your children. Any severe difference of opinion between them could require court intervention—something difficult for the couple and, worse, distressing to your kids. Also, if you name a couple that parts ways while you are still alive, you should revise your will to name one or the other to care for your children, or to choose a different couple to act as guardians.

The main point is that you must choose carefully when naming a couple as personal guardians for your children. Select a couple that can make joint decisions without conflict, has a unified parenting style, and is likely to stay together a long time. If you have any reservations about the longevity of the couple's relationship or any concerns about either person's parenting style, you may be better off just naming one of them—for example, name just your sister. If you like, you can explain the reasons for your choice in your will.

If You Don't Want the Other Parent to Have Custody

Even if you do not want the other parent to obtain custody of your child if you die, if that parent seeks custody, he or she will usually—but not always—be granted it. In an age when many parents live separately, predicaments like the following are, sadly, common:

"I have custody of my three children. I don't want my ex-husband, who I believe is emotionally destructive, to get custody of our children if I die. Can I choose another guardian?"

"I have legal custody of my daughter and I've remarried. My present wife is a much better mother to my daughter than my ex-wife, who never cared for her properly. What can I do to make sure my present wife gets custody if I die?"

"I live with a man who's been a good parent to my children for six years. My mother doesn't like him because we aren't married, and she would try to get custody of the kids if I die. What can I do to see that my mate gets custody?"

There's no definitive answer to these types of questions. The personal guardian you name in your will can seek custody of the children even if the other parent is alive. However, if you die while the child is still a minor and the other parent disputes your choice in court, the judge will very likely grant custody to the other natural parent, unless this parent:

- has abandoned the child, or
- would be harmful to the child.

Abandonment. Abandonment normally means not providing for or visiting a child for an extended period. It must be declared in a formal court proceeding, where a judge finds that a parent has substantially failed to contact or support a child for an extended period of time, usually (depending on state law) at least a year or two. Abandonment can be declared at a guardianship hearing if, after your death, the other parent, who hasn't visited or supported the child for an extended period, contests your choice in your will of someone else to serve as guardian.

Harm to the child. It's usually difficult to prove that a parent would be harmful to a child, absent serious problems such as alcohol abuse, mental illness, or a history of cruel treatment of the child. The fact that you don't like or respect the other parent is never enough, by itself, to deny custody. But if you honestly believe the other natural parent would harm your children, is incapable of properly caring for them, or simply won't assume the responsibility, here's how to proceed:

Step 1: Name the person you want to be your child's personal guardian in your will.

Step 2: Explain, in your will, why you're making your choice. (For this, you'll need to use a customized will from Chapter 11.)

EXAMPLE:

Liz, the custodial parent of Samantha, has married Rick, who has raised Samantha with her since the child was a year old. Samantha's biological father (Liz's ex) has no interest in Samantha and hasn't taken care of her for years. So Liz specifies in her will that if she dies, she wants Rick to be appointed guardian of Samantha. She includes a paragraph that gives the date Rick began caring for Samantha, describes how he has functioned as a parent, and states that Samantha's father has neither taken any interest in the child nor paid any child support for nine years.

This statement in the will can be very helpful to Rick's efforts to be appointed personal guardian if Liz dies before Samantha reaches 18. Unlike a biological or adoptive parent, a stepparent isn't legally presumed to be the best guardian for a child. However, unless Samantha's biological father contests Liz's choice of Rick as guardian, it will probably be honored. And even if the biological father does seek custody, it may well not be granted to him. Rick can file a custody suit, asserting that the ex-husband legally abandoned Samantha, and use Liz's will as evidence that granting Rick custody will be in Samantha's best interest.

SEE AN EXPERT

Anticipating a custody fight. If there's a disputed custody proceeding after your death, a judge has wide discretion in deciding how much weight, if any, to give to written statements you made before you died about your child's custody. Technically, these statements are "hearsay" and they may not be admitted to a court as legal evidence. Of course, a judge must read these statements to decide if they are hearsay, and since this judge is usually the same one who decides the custody issue, she'll have learned what you want to convey. If you think there's any reasonable possibility the other parent, or any relative or "friend," will contest your nomination for your children's personal guardian, discuss your situation with a lawyer who specializes in family law. A knowledgeable lawyer can help you prepare your best case in advance.

If You Name Your Same-Sex Partner as Guardian

If you coparent your children with a same-sex partner, you probably want to nominate your partner as the personal guardian of your children. The likelihood of the nomination being respected will depend on where you live and what the legal relationship is between you and your partner and between your partner and your children.

If your children have another legal parent, perhaps from a prior relationship, the court will choose that parent over your partner unless you provide a good reason not to.

If you live in any of the states that recognize same-sex marriage, domestic partnership, or civil unions, and your children were born after you and your partner entered into a legal relationship under the laws of that state, then you and your partner are both legal parents under state law and there's no reason a court in your state wouldn't respect your partner's legal right to continue parenting your children after your death, with or without a nomination in your will. (Of course, you should always make the nomination and explain your reasons for it, as discussed below.)

It's likely that courts in other states would also respect the legal relationship between your partner and the children, but it's not quite as secure. For this reason, many attorneys recommend that even if you are married, registered, or have entered into a civil union, you still use an adoption to secure the legal relationship between a non-biological parent and a child born to that parent's partner. An adoption decree may be more acceptable to another state than a legal relationship based solely on your state's law, which may not be recognized in some other states.

If you live in a state that doesn't offer any legal relationship for same-sex couples, then the court will make the final decision about who will care for your children. The court will consider your choice for personal guardian, but it may not understand or fully respect your relationship with your partner. For these reasons, take advantage of the opportunity to fully explain to the court why you named your partner to care for your children. You might say, for example, *"I name my life-partner Ruth Williams as the personal guardian for our son Matthew Price because we conceived and raised him together and she is his only other parent."* Or, *"I name my domestic partner Richard Bennett as personal guardian for our daughter Jane Bennett-Hines because he is her other legal parent, as recognized by the state of California."* Read more about explaining your choice in the next section.

RESOURCE

Learn more about same-sex families. For a detailed discussion of parenting issues for same-sex couples, see *A Legal Guide for Lesbian & Gay Couples,* by Denis Clifford, Frederick Hertz, and Emily Doskow (Nolo).

> ### How Your Will Works to Name a Personal Guardian
>
> The wills in this book provide that "If a personal guardian is needed" the person you've named is to serve. With most parents, a personal guardian will be needed only if neither parent is alive. But if you nominate someone other than the other parent as personal guardian and explain in your will why you did, it shows that in your opinion, a personal guardian is needed. If you die while the child is still a minor, the person you named as guardian would file a court proceeding seeking judicial appointment as guardian. Then it would be up to a court to decide.

Explaining Your Choice

Let's look a little deeper into how you might explain your choice for personal guardian if you don't want the other parent to assume that responsibility. The same concerns apply to a parent who doesn't want the next-of-kin, such as a grandparent or sister, to obtain custody if no parent is available. First, let's look at what you might want to cover in the explanation you include in your will.

When appointing a child's personal guardian, courts in all states seek to act in the child's best interests. In making this determination, the courts commonly consider a number of factors, so you might wish to cover them in your explanation:

- who the parents nominated as the personal guardian
- whether the proposed personal guardian will provide the greatest stability and continuity of care for the child
- who will best be able to meet the child's needs, whatever they happen to be
- the quality of the relationships between the child and the adults being considered for guardian

- the child's preferences, to the extent they can be gleaned, and
- the moral fitness and conduct of the proposed guardians.

Here's an example of an explanation in a will of a parent's choice for guardians:

> *"I have nominated my companion, Peter Norris, to be the guardian of my son, Marty, because I know he would be the best guardian for him. For the past six years Peter has functioned as Marty's parent, living with us, helping to provide and care for him, and loving him. Marty loves Peter and regards him as his father. They spend much time together. Peter is loving and conscientious. Marty hardly knows his biological father, Tom Delaney, who hasn't seen him for four years. Tom Delaney has rarely contributed to Marty's support or taken any interest in him."*

To include an explanation of your reasoning, you need a customized clause from Chapter 11.

Naming Different Personal Guardians for Different Children

In your will, you can name different personal guardians for different children. This can be desirable, especially if all children don't share the same two biological parents.

EXAMPLE:

> Melissa has a 15-year-old daughter, Irene, from a first marriage, and two-year-old twins from her second marriage to Alfonso. Irene's father abandoned her years ago. Irene doesn't get along well with Alfonso.
>
> Melissa uses her will to name her friend Nancy, who is close to Irene, to be Irene's personal guardian, should something happen to her while Irene is still a minor. When it comes to the twins, their father, Alfonso, would of course have custody of them if Melissa died. Similarly, Melissa would have custody of the twins if Alfonso died. Melissa and Alfonso both name Alfonso's mother, Ellie, as personal guardian for the twins, to serve if both parents die simultaneously. Ellie, who already often cares for the twins, is not particularly close to Irene, and wouldn't want the additional responsibility of caring for her.

To name different personal guardians for different children, you need a customized clause from Chapter 11.

Worksheet: Personal Guardians

Okay, enough background. On the Personal Guardian Worksheet (in Appendix B or on the CD-ROM), you can record your choices for personal guardian of your children. Remember, you don't need to name the other parent if it's fine with you if the other parent gets custody if you die. Rather, you're naming a personal guardian to serve only if both parents die. As discussed above, if you want someone to serve instead of the other parent, you should explain why in your will.

Management of Your Children's Property

As discussed in Chapter 5, you can leave gifts to any of your children, whether minors or adults, as any type of beneficiary—primary, alternate, residuary, or alternate residuary. For instance, it's common to name one's spouse as the primary beneficiary of major items, or everything, with the couple's children as alternate beneficiaries. Or a divorced parent may leave a few small gifts to friends as primary beneficiaries and leave the bulk of her estate equally to her three children as her residuary beneficiaries. If you filled out the beneficiary worksheet discussed in Chapter 5, you've already listed what you want to leave to each of your children.

Be sure you cover all your children in your will. Leave property to each of your children, as any type of beneficiary, except for any of them you explicitly disinherit. Revise your will if you have a new child, or a child dies. You can prepare a new will or add an amendment (called a "codicil") to your existing will. (See Chapter 13.)

It's important to understand that minors cannot legally own property outright, free of supervision, beyond a minimal amount—in the $2,500 to $5,000 range, depending on the state. An adult must be legally responsible for managing any significant amount of property owned by a minor child. Therefore, a vital part of preparing your will is arranging for responsible supervision of any property your minor children might own. This includes all property you leave them, and any other property they might acquire, whether by gift, their own work, or some other source, that doesn't come with a built-in adult supervisor. This section shows your options for arranging such supervision.

No supervision is legally required for gifts received by any child over 18. However, many parents don't want to risk allowing their children to receive substantial amounts of property outright while they're comparatively young. So you can also, in your will, impose supervision over gifts you leave to your children who are younger than 35.

This book provides a choice of three methods which you can use in your will to provide for adult supervision for gifts to your children. These methods are:

- name a "custodian" to manage the property as authorized by a specific law of your state, called the "Uniform Transfers to Minors Act"
- create a "family pot trust" that will hold property left to all your children, or
- create a "child's trust" for each child.

All of these methods are safe, efficient, and easy

Leaving Property to Your Spouse for the Benefit of Your Children

Many parents simply leave property outright to the other parent, with an understanding that it is to be used for their children's benefit. This approach makes sense if the parents trust each other, but it doesn't work well if the other parent is out of the picture or financially imprudent. Also, leaving property to the other parent won't handle the adult supervision problem if both parents die simultaneously. Thus, if you named your minor or young adult children as alternate beneficiaries for property left first to your spouse, you need to provide a method in your will for adult supervision of any property your children might inherit.

to put in place. This section provides a summary of each method and some suggestions to help you decide which is best for you and yours. The following sections explain how to include each method.

Use only one method with a basic will. If you use one of the basic wills from Chapter 10, you must use only one of these three possible methods for leaving property to your minor (or young adult) children. Each basic will form contains the following clauses:

- Gifts Under the Uniform Transfers to Minors Act
- Family Pot Trust
- Child's Trust

Select whichever one of these three methods you prefer, and delete the other two sections from your will.

However, a few people may want to use more than one method in their will. For instance, a person with a 23-year-old child from a first marriage and three minor children from a later marriage may want to use a child's trust for property left to her 23-year-old and a family pot trust for her three young children. If you want to do this, you must prepare a customized will from Chapter 11.

Whatever method or methods you select, you should also appoint an adult "property guardian" for your minor children in your will, to cover property they may receive by other means. Appointment of a property guardian is covered later in this chapter.

SEE AN EXPERT

Special problems involving children. You need a lawyer's advice, if you have:

- a child with a physical or mental disability who may need ongoing care for life, or
- children from a former marriage, unless you want to leave them property outright. If you want to provide for your spouse and also protect the right of your own children to ultimately inherit your property, you need a property control trust.

The Uniform Transfers to Minors Act

All states except South Carolina and Vermont have adopted the Uniform Transfers to Minors Act, called the "UTMA." (See list below.) Uniform laws, as the name states, are standardized laws created by a legal commission. However, when a state legislature adopts a uniform law, it can make changes in the "uniform" version.

The UTMA authorizes you to appoint an adult "custodian" and "alternate custodian" in your will to supervise property you leave to a minor. The custodianship ends, and any remaining property must be turned over to the child outright, at the age the UTMA specifies. In most states, this is either 18 or 21. There are a couple of exceptions: in six states, you can extend the age up to 25, and in a few other states, you can vary the age between 18 and 21.

The authority of the custodian to supervise the gift is defined in the UTMA, and is very broad. Basically, the custodian has complete discretion to control and use the property as she determines is in the children's interest. Normally, no court supervision is required.

Whether or not it's sensible for you to use the UTMA usually depends on the age at which the custodianship ends, the value of the property, and possibly on how many children you have. A family pot trust is preferable if you want to keep property together for all your kids.

- **States that permit the property to be turned over when the child becomes 21 or older.** In these states, using the UTMA provides dual benefits. First, should you die before the child reaches 21 (or up to 25 in six states), the custodian can manage the property free of court supervision. Second, the child doesn't receive what remains of the gift at least until age 21, the normal age for completing, or nearly completing, college. So, in these states, using the UTMA is often sensible for gifts primarily intended for college education, that is, gifts worth up to about $100,000—or even $150,000. Depending on the college the child attends, that much can easily be expended for the child's education and living needs. (Ain't that amazing?) Because there isn't likely to be much left by the time the child becomes 21, there's little sense in tying up the property beyond that age.

- **States that require the property to be turned over to the child at 18.** In these states, the benefit of using the UTMA is solely that the custodian is free from court supervision should you die while the child is a minor. Because any remaining property must be turned over to the child at 18, using the UTMA makes sense only if you're comfortable with the idea of the child gaining control over the property at that relatively young age. Most parents want to impose management on large gifts, worth over $50,000, until the child is well over 18.

States That Have Adopted the Uniform Transfers to Minors Act

State	Gift Must Be Released When Minor Reaches Age:	State	Gift Must Be Released When Minor Reaches Age:
Alabama	21	New Mexico	21
Alaska	18 (can be extended up to 25)	New York	21
Arizona	21	New Jersey	21 (can be reduced to no lower than 18)
Arkansas	21 (can be reduced to no lower than 18)	North Dakota	21
California	18 (can be extended up to 25)	Ohio	21
Colorados	21	Oklahoma	18
Connecticut	21	Oregon	21 (can be extended up to 25)
Delaware	21	Pennsylvania	21 (can be extended up to 25)
District of Columbia	18	Rhode Island	21
Florida	21	South Dakota	18
Georgia	21	Tennessee	21 (can be extended up to 25)
Hawaii	21	Texas	21
Idaho	21	Utah	21
Illinois	21	Virginia	18 (can be etxended up to 21)
Indiana	21	Washington	21
Iowa	21	West Virginia	21
Kansas	21	Wisconsin	21
Kentucky	18	Wyoming	21
Maine	18 (can be extended up to 25)		
Maryland	21		
Massachusetts	21		
Michigan	21		
Minnesota	21		
Mississippi	21		
Missouri	21		
Montana	21		
Nebraska	21		
Nevada	18 (can be extended up to 25)		
New Hampshire	21		
New Jersey	21 (can be reduced to no lower than 18)		

States That Have Not Adopted the UTMA

At present, the UTMA has not been adopted in South Carolina or Vermont.

Even if you live in one of these states, it is theoretically possible for you to use the UTMA in your will, if the minor, custodian, or gift property itself resides in an UTMA state when you die. But for most parents, all these are, and will likely remain, in the state where they live. Even if one of them is now in an UTMA state, you don't know where it will be when you die. Committing yourself to this kind of updating is an unnecessary burden, since you can easily use a child's trust instead.

The Family Pot Trust

This book's family pot trust is a legal structure, valid in all states, that you can establish in your will in order to manage property you leave to all of your minor children. Normally, one pot trust is established for all your children, no matter what their ages. However, it is possible to establish a pot trust for minor children, and another type of trust, a "child's trust," for young adult children.

What's a Trust?

A trust is a legal entity you can create as part of your will. In the trust, you name:

- the beneficiaries—the people for whose benefit the trust property must be used

- the trustee who will manage the trust property, and a successor trustee in case your first choice can't serve, and

- the property that will go in the trust.

Your will sets out the trustee's duties and powers and the beneficiaries' rights. During the existence of the trust, the trustee must file annual state and federal tax returns for the trust. The trustee isn't normally subject to court supervision.

With a family pot trust, all property left to all the trust beneficiaries—your children—goes into one trust. You name one adult as trustee, to manage the property for the benefit of all the children. The trustee does not have to spend the same amount of trust funds for each child. For example, if there are three children and one of them needs an expensive medical procedure, most or even all of the trust property could be spent on that child, even though the other children would receive little or nothing. While this potential result might seem unfair, it in fact mirrors the reality of many families. Parents rarely divide money absolutely equally between their children. The child or children who have more needs get more spent on them. And of course, over time, which child needs more is likely to change.

So the point of a pot trust is to have all property left to the children be available for any child's needs, as the trustee decides. This is exactly what cannot be done with gifts left under the UTMA (or, as you'll see, with a child's trust). Using those devices, distinct property is set aside for each child. One child's property cannot legally be used for needs of another child of the family, no matter how dire and pressing those needs are.

Another advantage of a pot trust is that the property in it does not have to be divided. Often, especially with younger children, it's not desirable to sell a family home or business, which might be required if you created a separate trust, with distinct property, for each child.

As a general rule, a pot trust makes sense only when your children are young and grouped fairly close in age. The pot trust in this book's wills lasts until the youngest child reaches 18. Then the trustee divides up the remaining property equally between the children. You cannot vary this age. If you do not want property turned over to your children when the youngest turns 18—say you want each child to be 30 before receiving property—a pot trust is not for you. You need to use a child's trust, or perhaps an UTMA custodianship, for each child.

If there is a significant age gap between your children, the oldest children may have to wait many years past the time they become adults before they receive their share of the property. For instance, if two of your children are ages two and four and another child is 30, the 30-year-old might have to wait until age 46 to receive his or her share of the property left in a pot trust. In this case, you might well want to use a pot trust only for your younger children. The pot trust option is available to you as long as you have two or more minor children, even if one or more of your other children are adults.

If you decide to use a pot trust, you may want to revise your will when your children get older. For instance, if your children are now ages four, four (the twins) and two, a pot trust could be very sensible. But when they become 19, 19, and 17, you would create a new plan, perhaps a separate child's trust for each child.

The Child's Trust

A child's trust is valid in all states. The main advantage of a child's trust over the UTMA or a pot trust is that it allows you to specify the exact age each child must reach before receiving outright the property you left him or her in your will.

Many parents don't want to risk having large amounts of property turned over to their children when they reach 18 and become legal adults, or even when they're 21 or 25. By creating a child's trust in a will, a parent can provide that property is supervised for the benefit of a child until she reaches an age when she can (the parent hopes) sensibly manage money.

Although the child's trusts in this book are designed primarily to manage property inherited by minors, they can also be used to impose age controls on property left to young adult children.

The child's trusts in the will forms in this book state that each child's trust ends when that child becomes 35, unless you have specified a different age, between 18 and 35, for that trust to end. We at Nolo selected 35 as the absolute cut-off age for each child to receive his or her trust property because these trusts are not intended for the lifetime management of property. Age 35 seemed like the most sensible dividing line between "young adults" and "fully mature adults" (or youth and middle age).

SEE AN EXPERT

Extending the age of a child's trust. If you want a child's trust to last beyond age 35, review your situation with a lawyer and evaluate why you want

to choose an older age. If your children aren't able to manage money by age 35, they may never be, and you'll need a more sophisticated trust.

If you die before a child has reached the age you've specified for him or her to receive trust property outright (or age 35, if you didn't specify), the trust becomes operational. The trustee manages the trust property and can spend it for the beneficiary's "health, support, maintenance, and education." The trustee is given broad discretion to interpret these terms.

Generally, a child's trust is desirable if the property you leave is worth a good deal, and you don't want the minor to receive it at age 18 or 21 (or 25 in the few states offering that option). Using the pot trust or UTMA, you're stuck with one of these age limits. Also, as discussed, if your children vary widely in age, a pot trust will make the older children wait until the youngest turns 18 for trust property to be distributed.

What Happens If Property Management for a Minor Is Never Needed?

If you set up an UTMA custodianship or a trust for property you leave a minor, the device will become operational only if it's needed. If a child is over the age you've specified for him or her to receive property outright, the management provisions in your will for that child become irrelevant.

For instance, suppose you leave your wife your property, with your 15-year-old daughter as the alternate beneficiary. You arrange for a child's trust to be created if your daughter inherits, to last until she reaches 25. If she doesn't receive property from your will, because your spouse survives you, no child's trust will be established for her. Similarly, if she does receive property but is over 25, the child's trust would not be necessary, and your will provisions for it would be ignored.

Comparing Property Management Methods		
	UTMA Custodianship	**Child's Trust**	**Family Pot Trust**
Legally permitted?	Yes, in all states except South Carolina and Vermont	Yes, in all states	Yes, in all states
Appropriate amount of property	• If age for release of gift is 18 in your state, use for gifts under $50,000 • If age for release is 21 or older, sensible for gifts up to $150,000, especially if to be used for college expenses	• Good for gifts of any amount if UTMA age for release of gift in your state is 18, or if UTMA isn't available in your state • Good for gifts in excess of $100,000 to $150,000 if UTMA applies in your state and age for release of gift is 21 or older	Any amount
Paperwork	No trust tax returns required, but minor must file a yearly return based on money actually received	Trustee must file yearly income tax returns for trust Income tax rate higher than individual for most income retained by trust Trustee must do accounting when property turned over to child	Trustee must file yearly income tax returns for trust Income tax rate higher than individual for most income retained by trust Trustee must do accounting when property turned over to children
Court supervision	None	None	None
Termination	Custodian must turn over property to child at age specified by statute, usually 18 or 21	You specify the age at which the child gets control of the trust property, up to age 35	When youngest child reaches 18, trustee must turn property over to beneficiaries
Uses of property	Custodian has broad statutory power to use property for child's living expenses, health care, and education	In wills in this book, trustee has power to use trust property for that child's living expenses, health care, and education	In wills in this book, trustee may use any trust property for any of the trust beneficiaries' living expenses, health care, and education

Life Insurance or Retirement Plans Left to Minors

For many parents, a major source of funds left to children is a life insurance policy, or perhaps a retirement plan, such as a 401(k) plan, naming the children as beneficiaries. You don't leave these benefits directly through your will. Instead, you name the children as beneficiaries on the forms provided by your insurance company or benefit plan administrator.

If you want the insurance proceeds or retirement benefits for a particular child to be managed by an adult, and you live in a state that has adopted the UTMA, you can name a custodian to manage any of this property the child receives while a minor. Instruct your insurance agent or retirement plan administrator to give you any necessary forms.

Another option is to create a living trust and name the trust (technically, the trustee of the trust) as the beneficiary of the insurance policy. Then, in the trust, you name your children as beneficiaries of any insurance proceeds received by the trust, and create child's trusts for that money.

If your state hasn't adopted the UTMA, ask your insurance company or retirement plan administrator whether it will allow a trust created for a child in your will to be named as a beneficiary, or alternate beneficiary, for the policy or plan. Some insurance companies won't do this, arguing that the trust won't exist (meaning become operational) until you die. If this can't be arranged, you can still name your minor children in your will as beneficiaries (or alternates) for the policy or plan. Any funds they receive from it while minors would be managed by the person you appoint as their property guardian.

Using More Than One Type of Trust

As discussed, it is conceivable, though unlikely, that you might want to create a family pot trust for young children, and a separate child's trust for a young adult child. You can only do this by preparing a will from Chapter 11 and including clauses for both kinds of trusts. You cannot use a basic will from Chapter 10 for this purpose. Obviously, there must be no doubt which of your property goes where—that is, what goes into the family pot trust and what goes into a child's trust.

Using two types of trusts can be tricky. For instance, the responsibilities of a trustee under a pot trust are different than those of a trustee under a child's trust. If you name the same person as trustee, you're requiring them to wear two trustee hats and keep two separate types of records. If you choose two different people as trustee, you want to be as sure as you can that they won't clash. Even though they're managing different portions of your property, it's not prudent to risk a conflict between trustees. For these reasons, I don't recommend using two different types of trust. But if you feel you must do it, you can.

SEE AN EXPERT

Other types of trusts for children. In some situations, you might want a different kind of child's trust than the two this book provides. Consult a lawyer if you want to:

- place extensive controls over the use of property in the trust—for example, you want real estate managed in a certain way
- create a trust to continue after a child becomes 35, or for a child already over 35
- create a trust where property is distributed to each child in installments—say, one-third when the child reaches 25 and the final third at age 35. You can get fancier still, giving the trustee discretion over how much to distribute, and when, or trying to define how a child demonstrates fiscal responsibility and thereby becomes entitled to receive trust property.

How to Use the Uniform Transfers to Minors Act in Your Will

If you've decided to use the UTMA for gifts to one or more of your minor children, here's how to accomplish that in your will.

You can name UTMA custodians for as many children as you wish. In addition, you can name different custodians for different children. When preparing your will, you'll first list all gifts you leave, including gifts to your minor or young adult children. Then you'll complete a separate UTMA clause for each child.

Choosing the Custodian

You can name any adult you choose as custodian or alternate custodian. The custodian must be a person, not an institution. You can name only one custodian and one alternate custodian per clause. You cannot name cocustodians or alternate cocustodians.

By law, no bond is required, and the custodian is entitled to reasonable compensation from the gift property. Of course, it isn't mandatory that the custodian take compensation. Commonly, when the custodian is a parent or close relative or friend, the custodian chooses not to be paid. Custodians have a right to hire experts, if necessary, and pay them from custodial property.

When selecting a custodian for gifts left to your own child, it is normally a good idea to name the person who will most likely be taking care of the child after your death, assuming the person is competent to manage property. This is usually the other parent, if living. The logical choice for alternate custodian under this arrangement would be the person you've named as your child's personal guardian.

However, if you leave gifts to your children as alternate beneficiaries—for instance, only if your spouse doesn't survive you—obviously you can't name that spouse as the custodian. In this case, the sensible choice for custodian would be your choice for the child's personal guardian; name the alternate personal guardian as the alternate custodian.

You aren't required to name the child's personal guardian or alternate personal guardian as custodian or alternate custodian. It's usually sensible to do so, but there are instances when the personal guardian simply doesn't have sufficient experience and skills to manage property prudently. In this situation, choose someone better qualified. But try to minimize the possibility of conflict between the care provider and the financial supervisor by selecting someone who gets along with your choice for personal guardian.

You'll probably want the same adult to serve as custodian for property left to all your children, but sometimes there are good reasons to name different custodians for different children. This is often the case when children don't share the same two parents.

EXAMPLE:

Joan, a single parent, has two children, Don, age 14, and Mavis, age three. She leaves each child $50,000 in her will, under the California Uniform Transfers to Minors Act, and specifies that each child will receive his or her property at age 25. Don is close to Joan's brother Bill, who agrees to serve, if necessary, as custodian for the gift to Don. But Bill doesn't want the additional responsibility of supervising Joan's gift to Mavis, should Joan die before Mavis is 25. So Joan names a friend, Melissa, who's willing to do the job as Mavis's custodian.

Choosing the Age at Which the Custodianship Ends

In most UTMA states, the minor must by law receive what remains of the gift at either 18 or 21. As noted earlier, a few states use a different approach. They establish an age at which the minor is to receive the property outright, but let you change it within a set range.

If you live in one of these "flexible age" states and want to vary the age at which the minor will receive the gift, you must prepare a will from Chapter 11. The fill-in-the-blanks wills in Chapter 10 don't permit you to vary the age.

States That Let You Change the Age at Which a Minor Receives Property		
	Unless you change it, minor will receive property at age:	You can change the age to:
Alaska	18	19 to 25
Arkansas	21	20 to 18
California	18	19 to 25
Maine	18	19 to 21
Nevada	18	19 to 25
New Jersey	21	20 to 18
North Carolina	21	20 to 18
Oregon	21	22 to 25
Pennsylvania	21	22 to 25
Tennessee	21	22 to 25
Virginia	18	19 to 21

Worksheet: UTMA Custodians

On the UTMA Custodians Worksheet in Appendix B, or on the CD-ROM, you can list all the pertinent information for each UTMA custodian you'll name in your will. As with all worksheets in this book, its use is optional. You'll need a separate entry for each custodian. Transfer this information to your will when you prepare it.

How to Create a Family Pot Trust or Child's Trust

Here we'll focus on both types of trusts you can use when leaving property to minor children. The child's trust, as mentioned above, can also be used for property left to young adults under 35.

Choosing the Trustee

The same concerns arise whether you're choosing a trustee for a family pot trust or child's trust. Legally, you can name any adult you want to serve as trustee. As discussed, if feasible, you should name the person you've chosen as personal guardian. Your choice of trustee is legally binding. You also name a successor trustee to act if the initial trustee can't serve.

One Trustee or Different Trustees

There is only one trustee for a pot trust; you cannot name cotrustees. And normally, the same person is named to serve as trustee for all child's trusts you create in your will, no matter how many. The will forms in this book require that you name a single trustee and successor trustee for each child's trust you create in your will. If you like, however, you may name a different trustee for each child's trust.

EXAMPLE:

Lori, a single parent, makes a will and names Sid as personal guardian of her 16-year-old son, Joe, and Eileen as personal guardian of her four-year-old daughter, Cheri. Sid and Eileen are also both willing and competent to manage the property Lori leaves in child's trusts for each of her children. So Lori names Sid as trustee of Joe's trust, and Eileen as trustee of Cheri's.

Remember that with a basic will from Chapter 10, you can use only one method for leaving property to your minor children. You have the choice of using either a child's trust, or a family pot trust, or the Uniform Transfers to Minors Act. With a basic trust you must use a single trustee for a family pot trust or all child's trusts you create. If you want to name different trustees, or successor trustees, for different child's trusts, you'll need to prepare your will from Chapter 11. You cannot use a basic will from Chapter 10 for this purpose.

Similarly, if you want to use more than one method for leaving property to your children—say a pot trust for young ones and a child's trust for an older one—you must prepare a will from Chapter 11.

What the Trustee Does

The job of a trustee can involve work, of course, especially if trust property must be managed for many years. A trust with complicated assets or very large amounts of money can require a substantial amount of work. The trustee's core responsibility is to act honestly and manage the trust or property competently. Common trustee responsibilities are:

- investing the trust principal conservatively
- using the income (and the principal, if necessary) to pay for the children's living expenses, health care, and education, and
- maintaining trust financial records and filing an annual trust income tax return.

If you pick someone with integrity and common sense, your children's property will probably be in good hands. If necessary, the trustee can pay for help to handle the more technical aspects of financial management. For instance, where large amounts are involved, it's routine for the trustee to turn tax and accounting duties over to an accountant.

The family pot and child's trust forms in the wills in this book provide that a trustee is entitled to "reasonable compensation" for services. Since a trustee of a family pot or child's trust will have an ongoing responsibility, some compensation seems fair. However, in practice, many trustees decline payment, preferring to maximize trust assets for the child.

SEE AN EXPERT

Trustee compensation. If you don't want to give the trustee the right to be paid, see a lawyer.

Naming the Other Parent as Trustee

If both parents are involved in raising the children, and one or both establish a pot trust or child's trust in a will, the other parent is usually named as trustee. However, this isn't legally required. Particularly if the parents are separated or divorced, one parent may decide that some other adult is better suited to managing the child's trust property. For example, if you name a personal guardian for the children to take precedence over the other parent, you'll probably want to name that person as trustee.

If you name the other parent as trustee, it's usually sensible to name the person you've chosen as the child's personal guardian as the successor trustee. That way if both parents die and the personal guardian must actually raise the children, that person will handle the children's property, too. But here, too, you can split these duties if you believe the personal guardian simply isn't able to manage money well.

Where Should the Trustee Live?

It's preferable—but not legally required—that the trustee and successor trustee live in the same state as the children. There are inherent personal and practical problems in managing property for a child who lives far away. Also, a few state courts may require an out-of-state trustee to post a bond. However, if the trustee lives nearby, that is usually close enough for practical purposes. For example, a trustee in Manhattan could most likely suitably manage trust property of children who lived in nearby New Jersey or Connecticut, especially if he was in close personal touch with the kids. But do think twice about naming that New York trustee for a minor who lives in Los Angeles. Not only is such a trustee likely to face logistical problems managing trust assets, she will probably not be in close enough personal contact with the minor to do the best job.

Naming an Institution as Trustee

What about naming a bank or other financial institution as trustee? It's legal, but I recommend against it, except as a last resort. Most banks won't act as trustees for accounts they consider too small to be worth the bother; as a rough rule, this means accounts worth less than $250,000. And even for larger estates, they charge hefty fees for every little act. In addition, it's my experience that banks are simply too impersonal to properly meet your own children's needs. Far better, I believe, to name a human being you trust.

Creating a Family Pot Trust

If you've decided you want to create a family pot trust for your children, here's how you'll accomplish that in your will.

Setting Up the Trust

First, list all gifts you leave, including gifts to your minor children in any beneficiary capacity. Then complete a separate pot trust clause, where you list all your children who are beneficiaries of the pot trust. Don't list the age any child must reach for the trust to end; under the terms of the trust, it must end when the youngest child reaches 18. Then you name the trustee and successor trustee for the pot trust.

EXAMPLE:

[First, complete the specific gift clause:]

"*I leave my house and all my money market and stock accounts to   my spouse, Ginger Gilliman , or, if she does not survive me, to   my children Sheila Thorzacky, Thadeus   Thorzacky, and Nina Thorzacky, in equal shares .*"

[Then, later, the pot trust clause:]

"***Family Pot Trust.*** *All property I leave by this will to the children listed in Section A below shall be held for them in a single trust, the family pot trust.*

"***A. Trust Beneficiaries***
Sheila Thorzacky
Thadeus Thorzacky
Nina Thorzacky

"***B. Trustee of the Family Pot Trust.*** *The trustee shall be   Barbara Gilliman , or if she cannot serve as trustee, the trustee shall be   Fred Thorzacky .*"

No bond shall be required of any trustee.

Worksheet: Family Pot Trust

On the Family Pot Trust Worksheet in Appendix B or on the CD-ROM, you can list all pertinent information for your trust. As with all worksheets in this book, the use of this worksheet is optional.

Creating a Child's Trust

If you've decided to create a child's trust, or more than one, in your will, here's how to go about it.

Setting Up the Trust

First, in your will, you list all gifts you want to leave, including gifts to your minor or young adult children, as any type of beneficiary. Then, to create a child's trust, in a separate clause, enter the name of each child for whom you want to create a trust. A separate trust is created for each child listed if at your death that child receives property under your will and has not reached the age you set for the trust to end. Next, list the age that each child must be to receive the trust property outright. Finally, complete the child's trust clause by naming the trustee and successor trustee.

EXAMPLE:

[First, the specific gift clause:]

"I leave my house equally to my son Mordecai Klein and my daughter Esther Klein, or, if either fails to survive me by 45 days, to the other."

[Then, the child's trust clause:]

"All property I leave in this will to a child listed in Section A below shall be held for that child in a separate trust.

*"**A. Trust Beneficiaries and Age Limits.** Each child's trust shall end when the beneficiary becomes 35, except as otherwise specified in this section.*

Trust for	Shall end at age
Mordecai Klein	30
Esther Klein	30

*"**B. Trustees.** The trustee of each child's trust shall be Howard Smellzier or, if he cannot serve as trustee, the trustee shall be Hilde Smellzier .*"

No bond shall be required of any trustee.

Worksheet: Child's Trust

On the Child's Trust Worksheet in Appendix B or on the CD-ROM, you can set out all the information you'll need to create one or more child's trusts in your will. As with all worksheets in this book, the use of this worksheet is optional.

Choosing a Property Guardian

You should definitely name a property guardian and alternate property guardian in your will. A property guardian named in a will manages all property of your minor children that doesn't come with built-in adult supervision. This can include property you left your minor children for which you didn't establish a trust or UTMA custodianship, or property they receive from other sources. As I've said, minors cannot legally control property of significant value—about $2,500 to $5,000, depending on state law. A property guardian manages property of the minor child until the child becomes 18, when the property is turned over outright to the child.

In a few states, the personal guardian may sometimes be called by a different name, such as "property custodian." However, using the phrase "property guardian" in your will makes your intent clear and suffices in all states.

The nomination of a property guardian is legally binding—with the usual lawyer's caveat that nothing that enters the judiciary is ever absolutely certain. If the need for a property guardian arises a substantial time after a parent dies, that parent's nomination of a property guardian may not be binding on a court. Still, it's often persuasive, and it won't hurt.

Don't rely on the property guardian any more than you must for supervising property you leave your children. A property guardian is a backup, in case some property a minor child receives doesn't have a more desirable form of adult management.

Why Not Name Only a Property Guardian?

Why not eliminate more complicated UTMA or child's trust methods and rely solely on the property guardian? Because this method has serious drawbacks. In many states, a property guardian must make frequent, burdensome reports to a court, which usually means paying a lawyer to get the job done. In addition, state law often imposes restrictions and controls on how a property guardian can spend children's property.

By contrast, a trustee of a family pot trust or child's trust or a custodian under the Uniform Transfers to Minors Act is generally free of court supervision and reporting requirements, and has considerable power to use money for living expenses, health needs, and education. Also, a property guardian must turn property over to the minor when she becomes a legal adult at age 18. Again, in contrast, an UTMA custodianship (in most states) or a child's trust allows you to require adult supervision until the beneficiary is older than 18.

If you fail to name a property guardian, and one is needed, a guardian will be selected by a judge, who could be more concerned with ensuring a crony a fee than with watching out for your children's best interests. (Quite a while ago, when I lawyered in Manhattan, a scandal arose over such behavior.)

Making the Choice

Most married people name the other parent as property guardian. Absent an appointment by a will, a surviving parent doesn't automatically become the property guardian for property the deceased spouse left to a child, though in practice this is often what results. Still, if this is what you want, it's best to state it expressly in your will.

Legally, you can name whomever you want as your children's property guardian and alternate property guardian. You don't have to name the other parent. Your choice of property guardian will be binding whether or not you select the other parent. For single parents, the sensible choices for property guardian and alternate can be the persons named as the children's personal guardian and alternate personal guardian. However, if you think your choice for personal guardian is not a good money manager, you can name someone else.

You can also appoint different property guardians for different children if you want to. To accomplish this, you'll need to prepare your will from Chapter 11.

Worksheet: Child's Property Guardian

You can list the pertinent information concerning your choices for property guardian and alternate on the Child's Property Guardian Worksheet in Appendix B or on the CD-ROM.

Leaving Property to the Children of Others

You may want to leave gifts to minors or young adults who aren't your own children—grandchildren, nieces or nephews, grandnieces or grandnephews, or the child of a close friend. You can, of course, leave gifts to any children, including any minors, you choose to. If you leave gifts to others' minor or young adult children, you can choose among the methods discussed below to provide adult supervision for those gifts.

You can impose control over gifts you leave to anyone under 35 by use of a child's trust. And most states allow you to appoint a custodian under the Uniform Transfers to Minors Act. At the risk of being a bit repetitive, this section briefly discusses methods for leaving gifts to others' children.

Leaving a Gift to the Child's Parent

Using this method, you rely on the parent to use a gift left in your will for the benefit of the child. The parent is under no legal obligation to do so, only a moral one. The advantage of this method is that no formal supervision of the gift is required. No records need be maintained, no tax forms filed. This strategy can make sense for money you want used for college expenses, if you completely trust the parent.

Using the Uniform Transfers to Minors Act (UTMA)

You can use the UTMA, which has been adopted in all states except South Carolina and Vermont, for gifts left to minors in your will. See the UTMA chart earlier in this chapter for each state's rules for the age a child must reach to receive an UTMA gift.

You must complete a separate will clause for each child for whom you name a custodian under the UTMA. In that clause, you appoint a custodian and alternate custodian to supervise gifts you've left to a minor. In some states, the gift must be turned over by the custodian to the child at age 18. In most states, the age for release of the gift is 21, or up to 25 in Alaska, California, Nevada, Oregon, Pennsylvania, or Tennessee.

You can appoint whomever you want as custodian and alternate custodian of each child's gifts. Often it's sensible to appoint the child's parent.

EXAMPLE:

John, an elderly widower, wants to leave $75,000 to his 12-year-old niece Sally in his will. He decides to name her mother, Mary, as the custodian, and her father, Ben, as alternate custodian. In his will, John first provides that he leaves $75,000 to Sally Earners. Then he completes a Uniform Transfers to Minors Act clause as follows:

"All property left by this will to Sally Earners shall be given to Mary Earners as custodian for Sally Earners under the Uniform Transfers to Minors Act of Minnesota. If Mary Earners cannot serve as custodian, Ben Earners shall serve as custodian."

You don't have to appoint the same custodian and alternate custodian for all gifts you leave to others' children under the Act. For instance, if you leave gifts to three grandchildren, each with different parents, you might sensibly decide to appoint each child's mother as his or her custodian, and each child's father as alternate custodian.

Using a Child's Trust

A child's trust created in your will can be used to impose control over gifts you leave to any minor or young adult. The will forms in this book allow you to select any age between 18 and 35 for each child to receive trust property outright. Since these trusts are primarily designed for minor children, and not for lifelong management of property, they aren't suitable to tie up property after a beneficiary becomes 35.

When you create a child's trust, you name a trustee and successor trustee to manage each child's trust property. You can name whomever you want for this job. Often it's sensible to name a child's parent to serve. It's preferable to name a trustee, and successor trustee, who reside in the same state, or at least the same part of the country, as the child.

If you prepare a fill-in-the-blanks will from Chapter 10, the same persons must serve as trustee and successor trustee for every child's trust you create in your will. If you want to name different trustees for different children, you'll need to prepare your will from Chapter 11.

Leaving a Gift Outright to a Child

Simply leaving property to a minor will almost surely require court proceedings to appoint a property guardian to supervise the gift, if it's worth more than a few thousand dollars. Generally, this is undesirable, especially because, unlike a parent, you can't even appoint a property guardian for the child in your will.

Worksheet: Property Management for Gifts to Others' Children

You can record your decisions regarding leaving gifts in your will to other people's children on the Gifts Left to Others' Children Worksheet in Appendix B or on the CD-ROM. On the form you can list each child you want to leave property to, the age that child is to receive the property (if you have the option to choose an age), the method used to transfer the property (either a child's trust or the UTMA), and the adult property manager for that gift. If you use a child's trust, the adult will be called the trustee; under the UTMA, the adult will be called a custodian.

Debts and Taxes

Liabilities for debts and taxes have a way of lingering on, even after your death. One of your executor's responsibilities will be to make sure all your outstanding debts are satisfied before any of your property is put in the hands of your beneficiaries. So one aspect of preparing your will is to take stock of what you estimate, or guess, your liabilities will be at your death. If it seems that your last debts and taxes could be substantial, it's sensible to provide, in your will, how they should be paid. This chapter looks at types of debts you may have, whether it's prudent to bother about them in your will, and your options if you choose to deal with them.

Before you start worrying about last debts or taxes, let me assure you that most people face no significant problems here. They may die owing some money—last bills, say, for utilities and perhaps some credit card debt—but nothing major. Similarly, most readers' property will not be liable for death taxes. Federal estate taxes apply only to estates in excess of $2 million or $3.5 million, depending on the year of death. (See Chapter 14.) A number of states impose estate taxes, and a few impose a traditional inheritance tax as well. However, the impact of state estate tax is rarely severe. Most estates are too small to be subject to state estate tax, and even when the tax is due, it's usually a minor sum. A few states impose heftier estate taxes, however, so it may pay to learn a little about your state's rules. (State estate taxes are discussed in Chapter 14.)

You may, however, conclude that it's likely you will die with significant debts. A frequent culprit here is those nasty, high-interest credit cards. When you leave this credit-happy world, you may well go out with a sizable amount of debt—personal loans, court judgments against you, and perhaps income taxes. Whether such debts pass to the beneficiary along with property left to him or her, or must somehow be paid out of the estate, depends upon how the debt is characterized.

Finally, there are several expenses incurred after you die—including costs of funeral, burial, and probate—which may take your survivors by surprise if you do not plan ahead for paying them. Funeral and burial, for example, may cost several thousand dollars. But they can be much less costly, especially if you've done some planning and make it clear you don't want costly funeral or memorial services. In addition, probate and estate administration fees often cost thousands of dollars.

When to Bother About Last Debts and Taxes

Typically, you do not need to concern yourself with debts or taxes if:

- your debts and expenses are likely to be negligible or represent only a small fraction of your estate, or
- you are leaving all your property to your spouse or to a few beneficiaries to share without divvying it up in specific gifts. Your debts and taxes will be borne equally by the beneficiaries.

You may need to be concerned about how to cover your debts and estate taxes when your will-making plan involves dividing up your property among a number of beneficiaries, because you may want to ensure that certain beneficiaries receive property but not be obligated to pay any portion of your debts or taxes. And you need to plan even more carefully if debts or taxes payable by your estate are likely to cut significantly into gifts left to individuals and charitable institutions. The danger, of course, is that the people whose gifts are used to pay debts and expenses may be the very people who you would have preferred to inherit your property free and clear.

EXAMPLE:

Ruth has $40,000 in a money market account and several valuable musical instruments, also worth $40,000. She makes a will leaving the money market account to her daughter and the instruments to her musician son, but does not specify how her debts and expenses should be paid. Due to medical bills and a personal loan from a friend, Ruth dies owing $35,000. After Ruth's death, her executor decides to pay debts out of liquid assets—that is, the money market account. As a result, the executor pays the $35,000 out of that account, leaving the daughter with only $5,000. The son receives the $40,000 worth of musical instruments. This imbalance is not what Ruth desired.

This book's wills provide that your executor decides how debts and taxes are paid, unless you've specified what should be done. Leaving payment decisions up to your executor is much less likely to work well if your debts and taxes are substantial and could significantly affect your gifts. For example, suppose your gifts are all tangible property of some kind, with very little cash or liquid assets. If there are major debts to be paid, do you want your executor to sell items left to a particular beneficiary? Suppose you've died owing a personal loan to a finance company that has a lien against all your property. Do you want your executor (or even the finance company) to decide which assets must be used? The point is simple: If debts, taxes, or both could disrupt your beneficiary plan, better for you to face that problem now, and specify in your will how you want these bills paid.

There is no one way to determine what is a "substantial" or "significant" amount of debt. It all depends on your specific beneficiary plan and your debts. With a small estate, debts of $20,000 may be substantial. By contrast, suppose you have an estate worth $540,000, with $300,000 cash, and leave the cash to be divided equally among several beneficiaries. If the estate has only $5,000 in debts, it may be fair and sensible for the executor to decide to pay the debts solely from the cash gifts,

so you might not bother with specifying a payment method.

Who Pays Debts After Your Death?

There are two basic types of debts—secured and unsecured—that you may be concerned with when making a will.

Unsecured Debts

Unsecured debts are debts that are not tied to specific property. They are the most common types of debts. Ordinary examples are medical bills, most credit card bills, utility bills, and probate fees. These debts and expenses must be paid from your estate as your executor decides, unless you leave other specific instructions in your will. By contrast, federal student loans can be cancelled if the borrower dies.

Secured Debts

Secured debts are debts owed on specific property that must be paid before that property belongs to its owner free and clear. The most common example is a mortgage on a house. Another common type of secured debt occurs when a major asset such as a car, appliance, or a business is paid for over a period of time. Usually, the lender of credit retains some measure of legal ownership in the asset—termed a "security interest"—until it is paid off.

Yet another common type of secured debt occurs when a lender, as a condition of the loan, takes a security interest in property already owned by the borrower. For instance, most finance companies require borrowers to pledge "all their personal property" as security for a loan.

Other types of secured debts include tax liens and assessments that are owed on real estate, and in some instances, liens or legal claims on personal property and real estate created as a result of litigation or home repair. For example, someone who prevailed against you in a lawsuit can file a lien against your house for the amount of the judgment.

If you leave property in your will that is subject to a secured debt, the debt legally passes with the property. So the beneficiary is responsible for the debt, unless you've specified resources to pay it in your will.

EXAMPLE 1:

Sonny and Cati, a married couple, owe $78,000 in property tax payments on their real estate holdings. In separate wills, Sonny and Cati leave their real estate to each other and name their children as alternate beneficiaries to take the real estate in equal shares. Sonny and Cati make no special provision for payment of their real estate debts. They die in a car crash. The children get the property, and also the responsibility for paying the $78,000 in past due taxes.

EXAMPLE 2:

Nanette leaves her mortgaged house to her partner, Jan. When Nanette dies, the amount owing on the mortgage is $86,300. Nanette's will also specifies that Jan shall receive the house free of the mortgage, and identifies funds to be used to pay it.

EXAMPLE 3:

Phil drives a late-model luxury sedan. Although the car is registered in Phil's name, the bank holds legal title pending Phil's payment of the outstanding $75,000 car note. Phil prepares a will from this book, leaving the car to his longtime companion Paula. The car note is a secured debt and will pass to Paula with the car.

EXAMPLE 4:

Carla borrowed $10,000 from a finance company to pay her income taxes. To get the money, she signed an agreement pledging "all her property" as collateral for repayment. Carla has a daughter, Juliet, and a son, Mark. Carla leaves Juliet a precious dollhouse collection that has been passed down through the family for five generations and leaves Mark the rest of her property, that is, her residue. She specified that her debts be paid from her residue.

When Carla dies, she still owes $9,000 on the loan. The $9,000 debt is legally payable out of any and all property in Carla's estate. But only if the residue totals less than $9,000 can the finance company go after the dollhouse collection.

When the Debt Exceeds the Property's Value

Because an item of property is usually worth more than any debt secured by it, an inheritor who does not want to owe money can sell the property, pay off the debt, and pocket the difference. However, at times, relying on this approach is not satisfactory. For example, if you leave your daughter your car, with high monthly payments, they might be more than she could manage. Thus, generally, if you think a particular beneficiary will need assistance with paying a debt owed on property, try to leave that beneficiary enough money or assets to pay the debt.

Choosing Specific Assets to Pay Debts

The fill-in-the-blanks wills in Chapter 10 do not allow you to specify how your executor is to pay debts and taxes. Under these wills, your executor decides which of your assets shall be used to pay unsecured debts and taxes, except as otherwise required by state law. As I've said above, secured debts pass with the specific item of property they're attached to. With a Chapter 10 will, you are relying on your executor to make the best decision regarding payment of unsecured debts and taxes. You could leave a separate nonbinding letter to your executor listing your preferences. But if you want to undertake this much direction, perhaps you should go all the way and specify in your will itself what assets are to be used to pay what debts.

With a will prepared from Chapter 11, however, you can direct your executor to use particular assets to pay particular debts and expenses. For example, you can direct that a mortgage be paid off from set assets, so the beneficiary receives the real estate free and clear. You don't have to use such a clause, however. The Chapter 11 wills direct that your executor will pay your debts and taxes as he or she decides is best, unless you provide otherwise in your will.

Tips on Choosing Assets

If you decide to select specific assets to pay your debts and expenses, here are some tips on what assets to choose.

Select liquid assets over nonliquid assets. Liquid assets are those easily converted into cash at full value, such as bank and deposit accounts, money market accounts, stocks, and bonds. On the other hand, tangible assets such as motor vehicles, planes, jewelry, stamp and coin collections, electronic items, and musical instruments must be sold to raise the necessary cash. Hurried sales seldom bring in anywhere near the property's full value, which means the net worth of your estate will be reduced.

EXAMPLE:

Harry writes mystery books for a living. He has never produced a blockbuster but owns 15 copyrights, which produce royalties of about $70,000 a year. During his life, Harry has traveled widely and collected artifacts from around the world. They have a value of $300,000 if sold carefully to knowledgeable collectors. Harry makes a will leaving his copyrights and his cash assets of $210,000 to his wife and the artifacts to his children. He also designates that the artifacts should be used to pay his debts and expenses—which total $150,000 at death.

Harry's executor, who is not a collector and has little time or inclination to sell the artifacts one by one, sells them in bulk for $140,000— less than half of their true value. The remaining $10,000 comes from the cash his wife would have received. Harry's children receive nothing.

Avoid designating property you have left to specific beneficiaries. It is important to review your specific gifts before you designate assets to pay debts and expenses. If possible, designate liquid assets that have not been left to specific beneficiaries. In other words, choose liquid assets that will be part of your residue. Only as a last resort should you earmark a tangible item left in a specific gift.

One exception to this general recommendation occurs if you believe you are unlikely to owe much when you die, and that probate expenses for your estate will be low. In that case, it can make sense for you to designate a substantial liquid asset left as a specific gift to also pay debts and expenses. You might also want to leave a separate note to the beneficiary to explain why you did this.

CAUTION

Describe property consistently. Property both left as a specific gift and listed as a source for paying your debts should be described in exactly the same words in both will clauses to avoid confusion.

How Specific Assets Are Used to Pay Debts

If you direct your executor to use specific assets to pay identified debts, the first question after your death is whether those assets are sufficient to cover all your debts. If so, no problem. Your executor pays the bills and distributes any remaining cash to the appropriate beneficiary.

If, however, the source you specify is insufficient to pay all your bills, your executor will still face the problem of which property to use to make up the difference (again, unless state law requires a set priority of payment, which isn't likely). For this reason, it is often wise to list several resources and specify the order in which they should be used. Also, make sure that they are worth more than what is likely to be required.

EXAMPLE 1:

Ella, a widow, makes a will that contains the following bequests:

"I leave my house at 1111 Soto Street in Albany, New York, to Hillary Bernette." [The house has an outstanding mortgage of $50,000, for which Hillary will become responsible.]

"I leave my stocks [worth $28,000] to Stanley Mark."

"I leave the rest of my property to Denise Everread." [Although not spelled out in the will, this property consists of a savings account ($16,000), a car ($5,000), and a camera ($1,000).]

Ella decides to designate assets to be used to pay her debts, and not leave this matter to be decided by her executor. So she prepares a will from Chapter 11 and specifies that her savings account and stock be used, in that order, to pay debts and expenses. When Ella dies, she owes $8,000, and the expenses of probating her estate total $5,000 for a total of $13,000. Let's assume her property hasn't changed in value (that's unrealistic, but keeps the example from becoming too unwieldy). Following Ella's instructions, her executor would close the savings account and use $13,000 for debts. The balance of $3,000 would be distributed to Denise.

EXAMPLE 2:

Now suppose Ella's debts total $18,000 when she dies. Her executor, following the same instructions, would use all of the savings account ($13,000) and $5,000 worth of stock to pay the debts. The stock market account would be worth $23,000 when Stanley receives it.

State and Federal Estate Taxes

Your estate may be liable for estate taxes. The federal government imposes the stiffest taxes. In addition, some states impose estate or inheritance taxes.

You can use your will to direct your executor how to pay any estate taxes assessed against your estate. But before focusing on how you want your estate taxes to be paid, consider whether you need to be concerned about these types of taxes at all. Most people do not.

> **CAUTION**
>
> **Avoiding probate doesn't avoid taxes.** Some people confuse probate avoidance devices, such as living trusts and joint tenancy, with schemes to save on estate taxes. Unfortunately, avoiding probate does not reduce estate taxes at all.

Federal Estate Taxes

Few people need to concern themselves with federal estate tax. Presently, only if your estate is worth more than $2 million (net) could your estate be subject to that tax. Moreover, the federal estate tax exemption will rise to $3.5 million in 2009, and then be repealed entirely for one year, 2010. But under current federal law, the estate tax exemption will be reduced to $1 million for 2011 and thereafter. Clearly, it's odd to have an unlimited exemption for one year (2010) and an exemption reduced to $1 million for future years. Congress will likely revisit the estate tax law before 2010, and deal with this anomaly. Learn more about the changes to the federal estate tax laws at www.nolo.com.

If you're a member of a couple and planning to leave most or all of your property to your spouse or partner, you may want to estimate whether the survivor's estate is likely to exceed $2 million. If so, consider planning that could reduce or eliminate any estate taxes on the estate of the second spouse to die, if that spouse dies before 2010.

The rules and uncertainties of federal estate tax planning are discussed in Chapter 14.

State Estate and Inheritance Taxes

The following states impose an inheritance tax on property left by the deceased: Iowa, Indiana, Kentucky, Maryland, Nebraska, New Jersey, Ohio, Oklahoma, Pennsylvania, and Tennessee. These states impose tax on:

- all property of residents of the state, no matter where the property is located, and
- all real estate located in the state, no matter where the deceased resided.

The tax rates vary depending on the state and the relationship of each beneficiary to the deceased. A surviving spouse may owe no tax, or be taxed at the lowest rate. Non-family members are taxed at the highest rate. Technically, inheritance taxes are levied on the recipients of a deceased person's property rather than the property itself, but the reality is that the money comes out of the deceased person's estate.

All states that impose inheritance taxes provide some exemptions. Certain inheritors (usually spouses and immediate family members) are exempt from all or a portion of any inheritance tax.

Even if your estate is not exempt from state inheritance taxes, they do not normally take a deep enough bite to cause serious concern unless your estate is very large. Still, your executor must use your assets to pay any state taxes and will pay them according to the laws of your state, unless you specify a different payment method in your will.

SEE AN EXPERT

Get help with large estates. As you might imagine, financial planning experts have devised many creative ways to plan for paying or avoiding estate taxes. If your estate is large enough to warrant concern about federal or state estate taxes, it is large enough for you to afford a consultation with an accountant, estate planning specialist, or lawyer specializing in estates and trusts. You could simply ignore estate tax planning by taking the following gamble: you won't die before 2010, the estate tax repeal will prove to be truly permanent, and your estate, therefore, will not be taxed. This is quite a risk, however, when tax planning now could save your inheritors large amounts of money.

Pick-Up Tax

Many states have adopted a new type of estate tax that is different from the traditional inheritance tax. This new estate tax is designed to replace revenue states lost because of changes in federal estate tax law. Here's the story.

Before 2002, most states did not collect estate or inheritance taxes. However, almost all states collected what was called a "pick-up" tax from an estate large enough to have to pay federal estate taxes. This "pick-up" tax didn't increase the overall tax amount paid by an estate. Rather, the state was entitled, under federal law, to receive a certain percentage of the federal tax due.

Congress changed this system in 2002. Under current federal law, states receive no "pick-up" taxes from the federal government. To make up for this loss of revenue, many states have enacted a new estate tax, which is no longer connected to the federal system. Essentially this new tax is a "pick-up replacement" tax. Other states are likely to adopt similar laws soon. The details of these new laws can vary between different states. The common denominator is that some estates may have to pay a "pick-up replacement" tax even if they are not large enough to pay federal estate tax.

SEE AN EXPERT

Learning your state's pick-up replacement tax law. In most cases, a state pick-up replacement tax amount will be minor. But if you are prosperous and concerned about this new state tax, see a lawyer who can bring you up to date on this rapidly changing area of the law.

Providing for Payment of Taxes

The book follows the same approach for payment of taxes as it does for debts. If you select a fill-in-the-blanks will from Chapter 10, you cannot choose how taxes are to be paid; it will be up to your executor. If you want to specify how any taxes are to be paid, you must use a will clause from Chapter 11. You have three options:

Authorize your executor to decide how any taxes are to be paid. This means your executor has discretion to decide how any taxes are paid, following any guidelines set out by state law. The advantage here is that your executor is alive when the tax bill comes, and can take all existing circumstances into account when deciding where the money should come from. A possible disadvantage is that your executor may decide to use funds (or sell property to raise funds) that you'd definitely wanted to go to the named beneficiary. One possible compromise is to specify in your will that certain gifts cannot be used to pay any taxes due, but that otherwise it's up to your executor to make the decision.

Designate specific assets. If you designate a bank, brokerage, or money market account to be used to pay taxes, and it contains enough to pay these obligations, the other gifts you leave will not be affected. But if the resources you specified for payment are insufficient, your executor will face the problem of which property to use make up the difference. So, again, it's a good idea to list several resources, to be used in the order listed.

Direct that taxes be paid from all property you own. You can decide that any estate taxes your estate owes be paid proportionately from all property you own, whether that property is transferred by will or not. This option can be very sensible if you transfer assets of significant value by methods other than your will. There are a range of possible other methods, including joint tenancy, living trust, pay-on-death bank accounts, and life insurance. If you transfer valuable assets by such methods, why should only your will property be liable for taxes? After all, for the purpose of computing estate tax liability, your estate consists of all property you legally own at your death, whether it passes under the terms of your will or not.

Directing that taxes be paid proportionately means that all beneficiaries' gifts, no matter how transferred, will be reduced by the same percentage to raise necessary cash. For example, someone who inherits half your property is responsible for half the estate taxes assessed, no matter what method is used to transfer that property.

EXAMPLE:

Julie Johanssen, a widow, owns a house (worth $1 million), stocks ($400,000), jewelry ($150,000), and investments as a limited partner in a number of rental properties ($800,000). Julie puts the house in a living trust for her eldest son Warren and the stocks in a living trust for another son, Alain. She uses her will to leave the jewelry to a daughter, Penelope, and the investments to her two surviving brothers, Sean and Ivan. She specifies that all beneficiaries of property in her taxable estate share in paying any estate and inheritance taxes.

When Julie dies in 2008, the net worth of her estate, which consists of all the property mentioned, is $2,350,000. Because this taxable estate is over the $2 million estate tax threshold for 2008, it owes federal estate tax.

Each of Julie's beneficiaries will be legally responsible for paying a portion of this liability. Each portion will be measured by the proportion that beneficiary's inheritance has to the estate as a whole. ●

Choosing the Right Will Form

Now that you've assembled all the personal information you need to prepare your will, it's time to focus on actually preparing it. Unfortunately, no single generic will form suits all needs. Recognizing this, *Nolo's Simple Will Book* offers you two distinct methods for drafting your will.

A fill-in-the-blanks will. Seven forms are set out and explained in Chapter 10. Your job will be easiest if you can fit your desires within one of these wills.

A customized will. Chapter 11 contains an extensive selection of clauses for you to pick and choose from. This assemble-it-yourself will format allows you more options and flexibility in choosing what to include in your will.

All the will forms and will clauses in this book are available both on the tear-out forms and the CD-ROM included with the book. Using either method, first prepare a rough draft of your will. Then, after reviewing it and making any corrections or revisions you want, type or print out a clean version to sign in front of witnesses.

Basic Form Wills

If your desires are straightforward, one of the seven basic wills discussed in Chapter 10 will probably meet your needs. These wills are designed for the following situations:

Form 1. Will for a Married Person Leaving All or Bulk of Property to Spouse. This form allows you to leave up to three specific gifts, and leave all your other will property to your spouse. The will specifies that your children are the alternate beneficiaries, who share all property received equally.

Form 2. Will for a Single Person With No Minor Children. This form is also appropriate for a single person with adult children who are left gifts outright. However, if you want to leave gifts to young adult children in a child's trust, or plan to leave gifts to someone else's minor children, use Form 3.

Form 3. Will for a Single Person With Minor Children. This form is also appropriate if you want to leave gifts in trust to any young adults or to someone else's minor children.

Form 4. Will for a Married Person With No Minor Children. This form is also appropriate for a married person with no children or with adult children who are left gifts outright. However, if you want to leave gifts to young adult children in a child's trust, or plan to leave gifts to someone else's minor children, use Form 5.

Form 5. Will for a Married Person With Minor Children. This form is also appropriate if you're married and want to leave gifts in trust to any young adult children or to someone else's minor children.

Form 6. Will for an Unmarried Person With a Partner and No Minor Children. This form is also appropriate if you have adult children who are left gifts outright. However, if you want to leave gifts to young adults by a child's trust, or plan to leave gifts to someone else's children, use Form 7.

Form 7. Will for an Unmarried Person With a Partner and Minor Children. This form is also appropriate if you want to leave gifts in trust to any young adults or to someone else's children.

REMINDER

Prepare your own will. Each spouse must prepare his or her own will.

What You Can Accomplish With a Basic Will

You can use any of the Chapter 10 fill-in-the-blanks wills to:

- Leave your property to the people and organizations you choose, including your spouse, children, grandchildren, other relatives, friends, charitable institutions, or anyone else.

- Name one or more alternate beneficiaries for each specific gift, in case your first choice does not survive you.

- Name one or more residuary beneficiaries and alternate residuary beneficiaries to receive any will property not specifically left to other named beneficiaries.

- Establish a 45-day survivorship period for beneficiaries, including your spouse or mate (except alternate residuary beneficiaries).

- Appoint your executor and alternate executor.

- Appoint a personal guardian and alternate personal guardian to care for your minor children if you die before they reach 18 and a guardian is needed.

- Make gifts to your minor children, grandchildren, or other minors under the Uniform Transfers to Minors Act.

- Set up a family pot trust for your minor children.

- Set up a child's trust for any of your children who are minors or young adults.

- Appoint an adult to serve as property guardian, and one to serve as alternate property guardian, for your minor children, in case one is needed.

> ! **CAUTION**
>
> **Be careful.** As explained in Chapter 10, you can make minor changes in the printed text of a fill-in-the-blanks will, but the will form shouldn't be revised in any major way. If after you review the wills in Chapter 10, you find that one or more of your basic desires cannot be accommodated, either prepare your will from Chapter 11 or see a lawyer.

Making a Customized Will

Using Chapter 11, you can create your own will, clause by clause. You can select from a number of topics, beyond what must be included in any well-prepared will, and for some matters, choose among alternative clauses. You can address all the concerns covered in Chapter 10 wills, and also:

- Name two levels of alternate residuary beneficiaries.

- Impose a survivorship period of your choosing on your beneficiaries.

- Name a beneficiary for your interest in joint tenancy property if all joint tenants die simultaneously.

- Forgive debts and state why you forgave them.

- Appoint coexecutors.

- Appoint an ancillary executor to handle probate of real estate in another state.

- Require your executor to post a bond.

- Explain why you believe it's in your children's best interest for the person you named as their personal guardian to be legally appointed. You can also explain why you believe the other parent, if alive, would be harmful to the children as primary caretaker. Doing this is a very good idea if you think your choice for guardian may be contested after your death.

- Name different trustees for different children's trusts.

- Appoint different personal guardians or different property guardians for different minor children.

- Vary the normal statutory age at which a minor is entitled to receive a gift under the Uniform Transfers to Minors Act, if your state permits this.

- Specify assets to be used to pay liens or encumbrances, such as mortgages, so beneficiaries can receive the property (often real estate) free of all obligations.

- Provide for what happens if your estate doesn't have enough cash or liquid assets to cover all cash gifts you've left.

- Expressly disinherit a child or anyone else (except your spouse, in common law states).

- Specify how your debts and estate taxes are to be paid.

- Include a no-contest clause in your will.

- Include a specific clause providing that if you and your spouse or mate die simultaneously, you will be deemed to have survived him or her for purposes of your will.

- Provide for your pets.

Chapter 11 doesn't attempt to present every conceivable will clause. To do so would result in a book of encyclopedic length. Chances are, though, that your intentions and goals can be met using the clauses in Chapter 11. If you're the exception to this rule and you need to modify or add to the material presented, you'll have to do your own research or see a lawyer. (See Chapter 15.)

After You've Prepared Your Will

Once you've prepared the final version of your will, you must sign it in front of two, or preferably three, witnesses. Your witnesses must then in turn sign your will. Chapter 12 explains in detail how to accomplish this.

A will that has been prepared following the instructions in this book and has been properly signed and witnessed is valid. This means it will be implemented after your death.

Self-Proving Wills: Making Probate Easier

To get your will admitted to probate, your executor will have to convince the judge that the will is genuine—that is, that it's really your will. This is generally accomplished by having one or two of your witnesses testify to that effect, either in person or through a written sworn statement.

In the great majority of states, the need for this type of proof can usually be avoided if, when or soon after your will is prepared, you and your witnesses appear before a notary public and all sign an affidavit stating that your will was properly signed and witnessed. This procedure is aptly called "self-proving" your will. If you want to take this additional step, Chapter 12 provides detailed instructions.

Making a Fill-in-the Blanks Will

This chapter explains how to complete a basic fill-in-the-blanks will. This chapter's no-frills, no-fuss wills are both legal and practical. They are written in plain English, with a minimum of legal jargon. When you're finished, you should be able to read and understand every provision of your will, and be confident that it clearly expresses your wishes.

Seven different basic will forms are provided. If you aren't sure which one is best for you, see Chapter 9.

Getting Started

All the will forms in this chapter are available both as tear-out forms and on the CD-ROM included with this book. You can prepare your final will with a computer or typewriter.

CD-ROM

Note to Mac users. This CD-ROM and its files should work on Macintosh computers. Please note, however, that Nolo cannot provide technical support for non-Windows users.

Using a Computer and a Word Processor

The seven basic will forms discussed in this chapter are included as rich text format (RTF) files on the CD-ROM. For instructions on how to install and copy the form files from the CD-ROM onto your computer, please refer to Appendix A.

Finding the Will Form You Want

Windows users

- Each will form in this chapter is installed to the \Nolo's Will Forms\Fill-in-the-Blanks Will subfolder in the \Program Files folder of your computer.

- Open a file by selecting its "shortcut" as follows: (1) click the Windows "Start" button; (2) open the "Programs" folder; (3) open the "Nolo's Will Forms" subfolder; (4) open the "Fill-in-the-Blanks Will" subfolder; and (5) click on the shortcut to the form you want to work with.

Mac users

- Each will form in this chapter is located in the "Fill-in-the-Blanks Will" subfolder in the "Nolo's Will Forms" folder.

- Open a file as follows: (1) use the Finder to go to the "Fill-in-the-Blanks Will" folder; (2) open it; and (3) double-click on the specific file you want to open.

The file names are the same as the ones used in Appendix A. For example, Form 2, the Will for a Single Person With No Minor Children, is FORM2.RTF. All forms and their file names are listed in Appendix A.

Drafting Your Will

When you open a will file, you'll see that it contains blank lines, which show you where you need to type in information. In most cases, the blanks are followed by bracketed instructions about what information is required. Fill in the appropriate information, following the instructions and samples in this chapter. *Be sure to delete the blank underlines and the bracketed instructional text from your final document.* Because the formatting of the files has been simplified, the clauses may look slightly different from the samples in the book. If you want your final document to look just like the forms in the book, you'll need to format it with your word processor.

If you do not know how to use your word processor to edit a document, you will need to look through the manual for your word processing program—Nolo's technical support department will not be able to help you with the use of your word processing program.

After filling in the form, use your word processor's "Save As" command to save and rename the file. Because all the files are "read-only," you will not be able to use the "Save" command. This is for your protection. *If you save the file without renaming it, the underlines that indicate where you need to enter your information will be lost and you will not be able to create a new document with this file without recopying the original file from the CD-ROM.*

If you do not know how to use your word processor to save a document, you will need to look through the manual for your word processing program—again, Nolo's technical support department will not be able to help you with the use of your word processing program.

Using a Typewriter

If your will is going to be typed, follow these steps:

Step 1. Tear out or photocopy the will form you want.

Step 2. Use the form as a worksheet, following the instructions in "Filling in the Will Form," below, to prepare a draft of your will. You may want to use a pencil, so you can easily make changes or revisions.

If you need more space than is provided to complete a particular blank, here's what to do: Put the extra information on a blank sheet of paper and label it "Attachment 1." Then put "continued on Attachment 1" in the blank on the will form. If you need another attachment, repeat the process.

Step 3. Prepare your final will from your draft by following the directions in "Preparing Your Final Will," below. Be sure to incorporate the information you put on any attachments.

Filling in the Will Form

This section goes through all the clauses included in the basic will forms. These clauses are presented to get you familiar with your will form. After reading here about one clause, you may want to turn to the same clause in the will form you've selected and complete that clause. Or you may decide to read through all the clauses here, making notes as you go, and then complete your form. Do whatever works best for you.

Will Identification
(this clause is not numbered)

Will of _____
your name

I, _____,
your name

a resident of _____, _____,
city   _county_

_____, declare that this is my will.
state

Your will should identify you by the name you currently use when you sign legal documents and other important papers. You do not have to list any previous names you've used, unless it's necessary to help identify property you own. For example, if you've changed your last name because of marriage, divorce, or both, you need only use your current last name. By contrast, suppose you own property in two different names. Then it might help clarify what property you owned to list both names. For example, if you changed your name to Jerry Adams but still own some real estate in the name of Jerry Adananossos, identify yourself as "Jerry Adams aka [also known as] Jerry Adananossos," and sign your will that way.

Providing your city, county, and state can help eliminate any doubt about the state in which you reside. (If you move to another state, your will remains valid. See Chapter 13 for a discussion of when you need to revise your will if you move.)

Clause 1. Revocation of All Prior Wills

1. **Revocation of Prior Wills.** I revoke all wills and codicils that I have previously made.

This is a standard clause that revokes all previous wills, including any handwritten ones. It helps prevent confusion or litigation regarding the validity of prior wills. To be safe, a revocation clause is used whether or not you have in fact made a previous will. All wills in this chapter contain a revocation clause; you don't have to add anything.

Clause 2. Personal Information

2. **Personal Information.** I am married to

_____,
name

and all references in this will to my

_____ are to _____.
wife/husband   him/her

How this clause works depends on your marital status. If you use a form for an unmarried person, Clause 2 simply states that fact, and you don't need to add any information. If you are married, this clause asks for information regarding your spouse.

TIP

If you're a member of an unmarried couple, you may want to select Will Form 6 or 7. In these forms, the personal information clause provides a space for you to name your partner and to state that all references to your partner are to that person.

Clause 3. Children

3. **Children.** I have _____ _____
number   child/children

whose name(s) and date(s) of birth _____:
is/are

_____
Name   Date of Birth

_____
Name   Date of Birth

[The will forms contain space to enter the names of more children.]

Here, obviously, you list all your children and their birth dates. The forms also contain space for you to list any children of a deceased child; if that part of the clause doesn't apply to you, simply delete it. However, if it does apply to you, do be sure to complete it, to make sure you haven't overlooked a grandchild who might, if overlooked, have rights to a portion of your estate. (See Chapter 5.)

When you use a will from this chapter, your will should both name and leave something to all of your children and all children of a deceased child. This includes children of previous marriages, children born outside of marriage, and legally adopted children. It is sufficient to name a child as an alternate beneficiary or alternate residuary beneficiary. (If you fail to name a child as a beneficiary, that child is disinherited under the terms of the will. See Chapter 5.)

Clause 4. Specific Gifts

4. **Specific Gifts.** I leave the following specific gifts:

I leave _____
description of gifts

to _____ or, if _____
beneficiary/beneficiaries   he/she/they

_____ not survive me, to _____.
do/does   alternate beneficiary/beneficiaries

[The will forms contain space to leave several specific gifts.]

Here, enter each specific gift you want to leave by describing the property and entering the name of one or more beneficiaries, and the alternate beneficiary or beneficiaries. If you filled out the beneficiary worksheet discussed in Chapter 5, just transfer the information you listed there to your will form. If you didn't, you may want to review the instructions in Chapter 5 covering how to describe property in your will.

To remind you, it is perfectly okay to leave a number of property items in one blank—such as, "I leave my gold watch, skis, and coin collection to Wilfred Brown." If you run out of room on the form, prepare an attachment, following the instructions at the beginning of this chapter.

If you name a minor as a beneficiary (or alternate) here, later in the will form you can arrange for an adult to manage any property that beneficiary inherits while still young. There is one clause for using the Uniform Transfers to Minors Act to appoint a custodian to manage property left to minors (available in every state but South Carolina and Vermont). There's another clause for creating a family pot trust, and a third to establish an individual child's trust.

If you are leaving any specific gifts to be shared by two or more beneficiaries, how you fill in the will form depends on who you want to name as alternates. If you want the surviving cobeneficiaries to inherit the share of any beneficiary who doesn't survive you, use just one paragraph for the gift. If, however, you want to name different alternates for each cobeneficiary, use a separate paragraph for each cobeneficiary. This is explained in Chapter 5.

If you want to include comments on your gifts in your will, you can do so here. If you're typing your will, create an attachment for your comments and insert them in the typed, final document. If you're using a computer, simply add the comments after identifying the gift.

> ### Special Instructions for Will Form 1
>
> This form has space for only three specific gifts, because the purpose of this will is to leave most or all property to your spouse. The will form specifies that your spouse is the residuary beneficiary, and your children are the alternate residuary beneficiaries. In other words, this will is "hardwired" to make it as easy as possible to prepare. If you are married and want to leave more specific gifts to other people, use Will Form 4 or 5.

Clause 5. Residuary Estate

5. Residuary Estate. I leave my residuary estate, that is, the rest of my property not otherwise specifically and validly disposed of by this will or in any other manner, including lapsed or failed gifts, to

_____
residuary beneficiary/beneficiaries

or, if _____ _____ not survive me, to
he/she/they   *does/do*

_____ .
alternate residuary beneficiary/beneficiaries

As you know by now, your residuary estate is exactly what it sounds like: any will property that remains after all specific gifts have been distributed. As I've said, some people leave all their property in their residuary estate, leaving no specific gifts.

In this clause, enter the name of your residuary beneficiary or beneficiaries, and any alternates. If you named them in the beneficiary worksheet discussed in Chapter 5, simply transfer that information to this clause. (If you have questions about choosing your residuary beneficiary, review Chapter 5.)

If you name more than one residuary beneficiary, the will forms state that if one of them doesn't survive you, his or her share goes to the other surviving residuary beneficiaries in equal shares. If you want to name different alternates for different residuary beneficiaries, you'll need to use Chapter 11 to make your will.

Clause 6. Beneficiary Provisions

This clause contains five rules regarding beneficiaries. Section A imposes a 45-day survivorship period on all beneficiaries of your will, except alternate residuary beneficiaries. Each beneficiary must survive you by that period to inherit.

Section B establishes rules for shared gifts. In Will Forms 2 through 7, the three rules discussed below apply. Will Form 1 contains somewhat different rules because it is, as I've discussed, a hardwired form. Form 1 provides that the residue must be left to your spouse, or if she or he doesn't survive you, to your children in equal shares.

In Will Forms 2 through 7, the first sentence of Section B covers what happens if your will names multiple beneficiaries but doesn't state what percentage or fraction of the gift each should receive: if you don't specify, each beneficiary receives an equal share.

The second sentence covers shared gifts left in a single paragraph of Clause 4, Specific Gifts. As discussed earlier, you can leave shared specific gifts either by a single paragraph, or create a separate paragraph for each beneficiary of that shared gift. If you want the surviving beneficiaries of a shared gift to inherit a deceased beneficiary's share, you simply name all the beneficiaries in a single specific gift paragraph. This second sentence specifies that the surviving beneficiaries share equally in a deceased beneficiary's portion. In other words, if you leave a shared gift in a single paragraph, any alternate you name would inherit only if all the primary beneficiaries for the gift didn't survive you.

The third sentence covers what happens if a residuary beneficiary for a shared gift does not survive you, and you haven't made specific provision for that possibility in your will. In that case, the surviving residuary beneficiaries share equally in the deceased residuary beneficiary's share. The alternate residuary beneficiary inherits only if all residuary beneficiaries do not survive you.

Section C of Clause 6 provides that all gifts you leave in your will pass with any liens or obligations on that property. If you want to direct your executor to pay these obligations, so that the beneficiary will inherit the property free and clear, you need to make a will from Chapter 11. (See Chapter 8.)

Clause 7. Your Executor

7. Executor

A. Nomination of Executor. I nominate

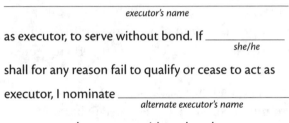

as executor, to serve without bond. If _____ she/he shall for any reason fail to qualify or cease to act as executor, I nominate _____ alternate executor's name as executor, also to serve without bond.

[In the will forms, this clause also contains Section 7(B), an extensive list of the executor's powers.]

Here you name your executor and alternate executor, the people you've chosen to be responsible for supervising the distribution of your property. (If you have questions about this, see Chapter 6.)

> **! CAUTION**
>
> **Special rule for Texas residents.** If you live in Texas, it is desirable that your executor or "personal representative" can act under the Texas Independent Administration of Estates Act (Tex. Prob. Code Ann. §145). This law gives your executor very wide powers, largely free of court supervision. However, at least one Texas court has held that invoking this Act and also listing specific executor's powers in your will creates a possible ambiguity that could leave your executor with

a legal mess. Therefore, rather than mentioning the Act itself in your will, Texas residents should delete all of Section B, Executor's Powers, from Clause 7, and replace it with the paragraph below.

> **B. Personal Representative's Powers.** Except as otherwise required by Texas law, I direct that my personal representative shall take no other action in the county court in relation to the settlement of my estate than the probating and recording of this will, and the return of an inventory, appraisement, and list of claims of my estate.

REMINDER

Payment of debts and taxes. The wills in this chapter provide that your debts and any taxes owed will be paid as your executor decides is best, unless state law requires otherwise. If you don't want your executor to decide how your debts and taxes are paid, you must prepare a will from Chapter 11.

Clause 8. Personal Guardian for Your Minor Children

Note: Will Forms 2, 4, and 6 are for people who do not have minor children and are not leaving gifts to minors or young adults in a child's trust. They do not contain Clauses 8 through 12, which address these matters.

8. Personal Guardian. If at my death any of my children are minors and a personal guardian is needed, I nominate _____

personal guardian's name

to be appointed personal guardian of my minor children.

If _____ cannot serve as personal guardian, I

he/she

nominate _____

alternate personal guardian's name

to be appointed personal guardian.

I direct that no bond be required of any personal guardian.

If you have minor children, use Clause 8 to name the adult you want to serve as their personal guardian. You should also name an alternate personal guardian. (Selecting a personal guardian is discussed in Chapter 7.)

TIP

Naming different personal guardians for different children, or explaining your reasons. If you want to name different personal guardians for different children, or if you want to explain why you named the personal guardian you did, you'll need to prepare your will from Chapter 11.

Clause 9. Property Guardian for Your Minor Children

9. Property Guardian. If at my death any of my children are minors, and a property guardian is needed, I appoint _____

property guardian's name

as the property guardian of my minor children. If

_____ cannot serve as property guardian, I appoint

he/she

_____ as property guardian.

successor property guardian

I direct that no bond be required of any personal guardian.

If you have minor children, you should name a property guardian for them in your will. The property guardian will manage any of the children's property that doesn't come with a built-in adult supervisor. (See Chapter 7.)

Clause 10. Property Management for Minor Children

If you want to include property management for minor children in your basic will, you must use *only one* of the three alternative clauses below. See Chapter 7 to decide which option is best for you. When you make your will, delete the two alternative clauses you don't use. If you want to include more than one alternative because you want to make different plans for different children, do not use this will form—use a Chapter 11 will instead.

Alternative 1. Gifts Under the Uniform Transfers to Minors Act

10. Gifts Under the Uniform Transfers to Minors Act.

All property left by this will to _____
minor's name

shall be given to _____
custodian's name

as custodian for _____ under the
minor's name

Uniform Transfers to Minors Act of _____.
your state

If _____ cannot serve as custodian,
custodian's name

_____ shall serve as custodian.
alternate custodian's name

The Uniform Transfers to Minors Act (UTMA) offers a simple, effective way to manage property left to a minor. (See Chapter 7.) If you decided to use the UTMA for gifts to one or more beneficiaries or alternate beneficiaries, you've surely decided by now on the custodian and alternate custodian you want to appoint.

> **(!) CAUTION**
>
> **Two states don't allow this.** You cannot use the UTMA if you live in South Carolina or Vermont.

If you live in a state that allows you to change the age at which the custodianship ends and the minor receives the property outright, and you want to do so, you'll need to prepare your will from Chapter 11. The states that allow this are Alaska, Arkansas, California, Maine, Nevada, New Jersey, North Carolina, Oregon, Pennsylvania, Tennessee, and Virginia. (See Chapter 7 for a discussion of these states' rules on varying an age.)

Complete a separate UTMA clause for each minor for whom you want to name a custodian. Just fill in:

- the name of the minor, the custodian, and alternate custodian (remember, you can appoint only one custodian and one alternate custodian per child), and
- the name of your state.

The will forms state that all property you leave through your will to the named minor will be managed by the UTMA custodian. There's no need for you to itemize the property here. The custodian will have authority over anything the minor receives under the terms of your will.

Alternative 2. Family Pot Trust

11. Family Pot Trust. All property I leave by this will to the children listed in Section A below shall be held for them in a single trust, the family pot trust.

A. Trust Beneficiaries

_____

_____

_____

_____

If all of the beneficiaries of the family pot trust are age 18 or older at my death, no family pot trust shall be established, and the property left to them shall be distributed to them outright.

If a beneficiary survives me but dies before the family pot trust terminates, that beneficiary's interest in the trust shall pass to the surviving beneficiaries of the family pot trust.

B. Trustee of the Family Pot Trust. The trustee

shall be _____ or, if _____
trustee's name she/he

cannot serve as trustee, the trustee shall be

_____.
successor trustee's name

No bond shall be required of any trustee.

[In the will forms, this clause also sets out the trustee's duties and authority and defines how the trust ends.]

If you've decided that you want to leave property to your children in a family pot trust, use this clause. (Pot trusts are discussed in Chapter 7.)

! **CAUTION**

If you create a family pot trust, don't appoint a custodian under the UTMA for any of your minor children. A family pot trust will take care of all property left to all of your minor children.

To create a family pot trust in your will, list each minor child's name in Section A of this clause. Then name the trustee and alternate trustee for the trust. You do not specify in this clause the property that may go into the trust. Any property left by your will to any of your children named in this clause will automatically go into the family pot trust. You can't create a pot trust for your minor children and also leave one or more of them a specific gift of property outside the pot trust.

Alternative 3. Individual Trusts for Property Left to Children

12. Child's Trusts

All property I leave in this will to a child listed in Section A below shall be held for that child in a separate trust.

A. Trust Beneficiaries and Age Limits. Each trust shall end when the beneficiary becomes 35, except as otherwise specified in this section:

Trust for	Shall end at age
_____	_____
_____	_____
_____	_____

B. Trustee. The trustee of each child's trust shall be _____, or, if _____ cannot serve
        trustee's name   *she/he*

as trustee, the trustee shall be _____ .
                                    successor trustee's name

No bond shall be required of any trustee.

[In the will forms, this clause also sets out the trustee's duties and authority, and defines how each trust ends.]

If you've decided to create a child's trust, use this clause. (See Chapter 7.) A separate child's trust is created for each child.

You can create a child's trust in your will for:

• any of your minor children

• any adult child under age 35, or

• any other beneficiary under age 35.

In this clause, you list each beneficiary's name, and the age he or she must reach to receive the trust property outright. Then name the trustee and successor trustee for every child's trust. In a Chapter 10 will, you must appoint the same trustee and the same successor trustee for all child's trusts. If you want to name different trustees or different successor trustees for different trusts, you'll need to prepare a will from Chapter 11.

You do not, in this clause, specify the property that you want to go into a child's trust. All property left through your will to the child will go into that child's trust, if at your death the child has not reached the age you specified.

Signature Clause

Leave the signature clause blank until you sign the final version of your will in the presence of your witnesses. (Instructions are in Chapter 12.) In addition, if you decide to make your will self-proving, to make it easier for a court to accept its validity after your death, follow the instructions in Chapter 12.

Sample Filled-in Basic Will

Before filling in your will form, take a look at the sample draft below. (A sample finished, final will is in Chapter 1.) Hopefully, examining this will reassure you (once again) that it really isn't hard to do your own will.

This is the will of Mark, a married man in his 40s who has two young children. Mark wants to leave much of his property to his wife, but also plans to leave several valuable gifts to friends, relatives, and charities. Mark concludes that the best will for him to use is Will Form 5, for a married person with minor children. He doesn't use Will Form 1, for a married person leaving all or bulk of property to spouse, because he wants to make more specific gifts than that form allows.

Mark lives in a community property state, and all of his assets are the community property of Mark and his wife. His wife agrees (in writing) to allowing Mark to make separate gifts of their property.

Here is Mark's will after he's drafted it, ready to be typed into the final version. (Obviously, if you're using a word processor, your draft won't contain handwritten material.)

Will for a Married Person With Minor Children

Will of _____ Mark P. Creery _____
your name

I, _____ Mark P. Creery _____, a resident of

_____ Hayward _____, _____ Alameda County _____, _____ California _____,
    city   *county*   *state*

declare that this is my will.

1. **Revocation of Prior Wills.** I revoke all wills and codicils that I have previously made.

2. **Personal Information.** I am married to _____ Linda F. Creery _____,
                                                 spouse's name

and all references in this will to my _____ wife _____ are to _____ her _____.
                                    husband/wife   *him/her*

3. **Children.** I have _____ two _____ children _____ whose name(s) and date(s) of birth _____ are ___:
              number   *child/children*   *is/are*

_____ Anthony A. Creery _____   10/1/89 _____
                    name   *date of birth*

_____ Jennifer S. Creery _____   11/7/91 _____
                    name   *date of birth*

_____   _____
                    name   *date of birth*

_____   _____
                    name   *date of birth*

_____   _____
                    name   *date of birth*

(repeat as needed)

There _____ _____ living _____ of my deceased child _____:
     is/are   *number*   *child/children*   *name*

_____   _____
              name of grandchild   *date of birth*

_____   _____
              name of grandchild   *date of birth*

_____   _____
              name of grandchild   *date of birth*

(repeat as needed)

If I do not leave property in this will to a child or grandchild listed above, my failure to do so is intentional.

4. **Specific Gifts.** I leave the following specific gifts:

I leave _____ $5,000 _____
                                description of gift(s)

to _____ Mary Creery Noonan _____ or, if _____ she _____
                   beneficiary/beneficiaries   *she/he/they*

_____ does ___ not survive me, to _____ my children in equal shares _____.
  does/do   *alternate beneficiary/beneficiaries*

I leave __my power tools_____
description of gift(s)

to _____John Creery_____ or, if _____he_____
beneficiary/beneficiaries she/he/they

__does__ not survive me, to _____my wife_____.
does/do alternate beneficiary/beneficiaries

I leave __my 1950 Ford convertible_____
description of gift(s)

to _____my best friend, Ray Ellington_____ or, if _____he_____
beneficiary/beneficiaries she/he/they

__does__ not survive me, to _____my wife_____.
does/do alternate beneficiary/beneficiaries

I leave __50 shares of UniCompuTechno Corp_____
description of gift(s)

to _____Albert Creery_____ or, if _____he_____
beneficiary/beneficiaries she/he/they

__does__ not survive me, to _____my wife_____.
does/do alternate beneficiary/beneficiaries

I leave _____
description of gift(s)

to _____ or, if _____
beneficiary/beneficiaries she/he/they

_____ not survive me, to _____.
does/do alternate beneficiary/beneficiaries

5. Residuary Estate. I leave my residuary estate, that is, the rest of my property not otherwise specifically and validly disposed of by this will or in any other manner, including lapsed or failed gifts, to _____
__my wife_____
residuary beneficiary/beneficiaries

or, if _____she_____ __does__ not survive me, to _____my children in equal shares_____.
she/he/they does/do alternate residuary beneficiary/beneficiaries

6. Beneficiary Provisions. The following terms and conditions shall apply to the beneficiary clauses of this will.

A. 45-Day Survivorship Period. As used in this will, the phrase "survive me" means to be alive or in existence as an organization on the 45th day after my death. Any beneficiary, except any alternate residuary beneficiary, must survive me to inherit under this will. If there are no surviving beneficiaries for a specific gift, that gift shall become part of my residuary estate.

B. Shared Gifts. If I leave property to be shared by two or more beneficiaries, it shall be shared equally between them unless this will provides otherwise.

If any beneficiary of a shared specific gift left in a single paragraph of the Specific Gifts clause, above, does not survive me, that deceased beneficiary's portion of the gift shall be given to the surviving beneficiaries in equal shares.

If any residuary beneficiary of a shared residuary gift does not survive me, that deceased beneficiary's portion of the residue shall be given to the surviving residuary beneficiaries in equal shares.

C. Encumbrances. All property that I leave by this will shall pass subject to any encumbrances or liens on the property.

7. Executor. The following terms and conditions shall apply to the executor of this will.

A. Nomination of Executor. I nominate _____Linda F. Creery_____
— executor's name —

as executor, to serve without bond. If _____she_____ shall for any reason fail to qualify or cease to act as executor,
— she/he —

I nominate _____John Creery_____
— alternate executor's name —

as executor, also to serve without bond.

B. Executor's Powers. I direct that my executor take all actions legally permissible to have the probate of my will conducted as simply and as free of court supervision as possible, including filing a petition in the appropriate court for the independent administration of my estate.

I grant to my personal representative the following powers, to be exercised as he or she deems to be in the best interests of my estate:

1. To pay, as my executor decides is best (unless state law requires a specific method for payment), all my debts and taxes that may, by reason of my death, be assessed against my estate or any portion of it.

2. To retain property without liability for loss or depreciation resulting from such retention.

3. To dispose of property by public or private sale, or exchange, or otherwise, and receive or administer the proceeds as a part of my estate.

4. To vote stock, to exercise any option or privilege to convert bonds, notes, stocks, or other securities belonging to my estate into other bonds, notes, stocks, or other securities, and to exercise all other rights and privileges of a person owning similar property in his or her own right.

5. To lease any real property that may at any time form part of my estate.

6. To abandon, adjust, arbitrate, compromise, sue on, defend, or otherwise deal with and settle claims in favor of or against my estate.

7. To continue, maintain, operate, or participate in any business which is a part of my estate, and to effect incorporation, dissolution, or other change in the form of organization of the business.

8. To do all other acts, which in his or her judgment may be necessary or appropriate for the proper and advantageous management, investment, and distribution of my estate.

The foregoing powers, authority, and discretion are in addition to the powers, authority, and discretion vested in him or her by operation of law and may be exercised as often as is deemed necessary or advisable without application to or approval by any court in any jurisdiction.

8. Personal Guardian. If at my death any of my children are minors, and a personal guardian is needed, I nominate
_____my wife's sister, Joan Roye_____
— personal guardian's name —

to be appointed personal guardian of my minor children. If ____she_____ cannot serve as personal guardian,
— she/he —

I nominate _____Mary Roye_____
— alternate personal guardian's name —

to be appointed personal guardian.

I direct that no bond be required of any personal guardian.

9. Property Guardian. If at my death any of my children are minors, and a property guardian is needed, I appoint

Joan Roye
property guardian's name

as the property guardian of my minor children. If _____she_____ cannot serve as property guardian, I appoint
she/he

Mary Roye as property guardian.
alternate property guardian's name

I direct that no bond be required of any property guardian.

[Include only ONE Clause 10, below. Choose Uniform Transfers to Minors Act, the Family Pot Trust, OR the Child's Trust.]

10. Gifts Under the Uniform Transfers to Minors Act. All property left by this will to _____
minor's name

_____ shall be given to _____
custodian's name

as custodian for _____ under the Uniform Transfers to
minor's name

Minors Act of _____. If _____
your state _____ custodian's name

cannot serve as custodian, _____ shall serve as custodian.
alternate custodian's name

(repeat as needed)

10. Family Pot Trust. All property I leave by this will to the children listed in Section A below shall be held for them in a single trust, the family pot trust.

    A. Trust Beneficiaries

    Anthony A. Creery
child's name

    Jennifer S. Creery
child's name

    _____
child's name

    _____
child's name

If all of the beneficiaries of the family pot trust are age 18 or older at my death, no family pot trust shall be established, and the property left to them shall be distributed to them outright.

If a beneficiary survives me but dies before the family pot trust terminates, that beneficiary's interest in the trust shall pass to the surviving beneficiaries of the family pot trust.

    B. Trustee of the Family Pot Trust. The trustee shall be _Joan Roye_
trustee's name

_____ or, if _____she_____ cannot serve as trustee, the trustee shall be
she/he

Mary Roye .
successor trustee's name

No bond shall be required of any trustee.

C. Duties of the Family Pot Trust Trustee

1. The trustee may distribute trust assets (income or principal) as the trustee deems necessary for a beneficiary's health, support, maintenance, and education. Education includes, but is not limited to, college, graduate, postgraduate, and vocational studies, plus reasonably related living expenses.

2. In deciding whether or not to make distributions, the trustee shall consider the value of the trust assets, the relative current and future needs of each beneficiary, and each beneficiary's other income, resources, and sources of support. In doing so, the trustee has the discretion to make distributions that benefit some beneficiaries more than others or that completely exclude others.

3. Any trust income that is not distributed by the trustee shall be accumulated and added to the principal.

D. Termination of the Family Pot Trust. When the youngest surviving beneficiary of this family pot trust reaches 18, the trustee shall distribute the remaining trust assets to the surviving beneficiaries in equal shares.

If none of the trust beneficiaries survives to the age of 18, the trustee shall distribute the remaining trust assets to my heirs at the death of the last surviving beneficiary.

E. Powers of the Trustee. In addition to all other powers granted a trustee in any portion of this will, the trustee of the family pot trust shall have the power to make distributions to the beneficiaries directly or to other people or organizations on behalf of the beneficiaries.

10. Child's Trusts. All property I leave by this will to a child listed in Section A below shall be held for that child in a separate trust.

A. Trust Beneficiaries and Age Limits. Each trust shall end when the beneficiary becomes 35, except as otherwise specified in this section.

Trust for	**Shall end at age**
_____	_____
_____	_____
_____	_____
_____	_____
_____	_____
_____	_____
_____	_____
_____	_____

B.   Trustees. The trustee of each child's trust shall be _____

trustee's name

_____ or, if _____ cannot serve as trustee, the trustee shall be

she/he

_____.

successor trustee's name

No bond shall be required of any trustee.

C. Duties of the Trustee

1. The trustee may distribute trust assets (income or principal) as the trustee deems necessary for the beneficiary's health, support, maintenance, and education. Education includes, but is not limited to, college, graduate, postgraduate, and vocational studies, plus reasonably related living expenses.

2. In deciding whether or not to make a distribution, the trustee may take into account the beneficiary's other income, resources, and sources of support.

3. Any trust income that is not distributed by the trustee shall be accumulated and added to the principal of that child's trust.

D. Termination of Trust. A child's trust shall terminate when any of the following events occurs:

1. The beneficiary becomes the age specified in Section A of this trust clause;

2. The beneficiary dies before becoming the age specified in Section A of this trust clause;

3. The trust is exhausted through distributions allowed under these provisions.

If a trust terminates for reason one, the remaining principal and accumulated net income of the trust shall pass to the beneficiary. If a trust terminates for reason two, the remaining principal and accumulated net income of the trust shall pass to the trust beneficiary's heirs.

E. Powers of the Trustee. In addition to all other powers granted the trustee in this will, the trustee shall have the power to make distributions to a child's trust beneficiary directly or to other people or organizations on behalf of that child.

[Delete Clause 11 if in Clause 10 you selected Gifts Under the Uniform Transfers to Minors Act.]

11. General Trust Administrative Provisions. Any trust established under this will shall be managed subject to the following provisions.

A. Intent. It is my intent that any trust established under this will be administered independently of court supervision to the maximum extent possible under the laws of the state having jurisdiction over the trust.

B. No Assignment. The interests of any beneficiary of any trust established under this will shall not be transferable by voluntary or involuntary assignment or by operation of law and shall be free from the claims of creditors and from attachment, execution, bankruptcy, or other legal process to the fullest extent permitted by law.

C. Trustee's Powers. In addition to other powers granted the trustee in this will, the trustee shall have all the powers generally conferred on trustees by the laws of the state having jurisdiction over this trust and the powers to:

1. Invest and reinvest trust funds in every kind of property and every kind of investment, provided that the trustee acts with the care, skill, prudence, and diligence under the prevailing circumstances that a prudent person acting in a similar capacity and familiar with such matters would use.

2. Receive additional property from any source and acquire or hold properties jointly or in undivided interests or in partnership or joint venture with other people or entities.

3. Enter, continue, or participate in the operation of any business, and incorporate, liquidate, reorganize, or otherwise change the form or terminate the operation of the business and contribute capital or loan money to the business.

4. Exercise all the rights, powers, and privileges of an owner of any securities held in the trust.

5. Borrow funds, guarantee or indemnify in the name of the trust, and secure any obligation, mortgage, pledge, or other security interest, and renew, extend, or modify any such obligations.

6. Lease trust property for terms within or beyond the term of the trust.

7. Prosecute, defend, contest, or otherwise litigate legal actions or other proceedings for the protection or benefit of the trust; pay, compromise, release, adjust, or submit to arbitration any debt, claim, or controversy; and insure the trust against any risk and the trustee against liability with respect to other people.

8. Pay himself or herself reasonable compensation out of trust assets for ordinary and extraordinary services, and for all services in connection with the complete or partial termination of this trust.

9. Employ and discharge professionals to aid or assist in managing the trust and compensate them from the trust assets.

D. Severability. If any provision of any trust is held invalid, that shall not affect other trust provisions that can be given effect without the invalid provision.

E. "Trustee" Defined. The term "trustee" shall include all successor trustees.

Signature

I subscribe my name to this will the _____ day of _____, _____, at

month   year

_____, _____, _____,

city   county   state

and do hereby declare that I sign and execute this instrument as my last will and that I sign it willingly, that I execute it as my free and voluntary act for the purposes therein expressed, and that I am of the age of majority or otherwise legally empowered to make a will, and under no constraint or undue influence.

_____

your signature

Witnesses

On this _____ day of _____, _____, _____

month   year   your name

declared to us, the undersigned, that this instrument was ____his____ will and requested us to act as witnesses

his/her

to it. ____He____ thereupon signed this will in our presence, all of us being present at the same time. We now, at

He/She

____his____ request, in ____his____ presence and in the presence of each other, subscribe our names as

his/her   his/her

witnesses and declare we understand this to be ____his____ will, and that to the best of our knowledge the

his/her

testator is of the age of majority, or is otherwise legally empowered to make a will, and under no constraint or undue influence.

We declare under penalty of perjury that the foregoing is true and correct, this _____ day of _____, _____, at _____.

        month   *year*   *city and state*

_____

witness's signature

_____ residing at _____,

witness's typed name   *address*

_____, _____, _____.

         city   *county*   *state*

_____

witness's signature

_____ residing at _____,

witness's typed name   *address*

_____, _____, _____.

         city   *county*   *state*

_____

witness's signature

_____ residing at _____,

witness's typed name   *address*

_____, _____, _____.

         city   *county*   *state*

Preparing Your Final Will

After you've filled in the blanks on the will form of your choice, review your draft (print one out if you're using a word processor) until you're confident your will does what you want it to. Then you're ready to prepare the final version.

> ⚠ **CAUTION**
>
> **Don't change the language in a will form.** The purpose of a basic will form is to provide clarity and simplicity. To warn you again, if you change anything, you risk creating a confusing and possibly even an ineffective document. This risk is especially high for computer-prepared wills. As I can attest, when word processing, it's distressingly easy to cut and paste incorrectly, or to mush words or sentences around so that meaning is lost.

Delete All Instructions

Your final will must have all extraneous material removed. Don't include any of the instructions below the blank lines or the lines themselves.

Delete All Clauses You Didn't Use

If a portion of the form doesn't apply to you, simply draw a line through it so you, or your typist, will know to leave it out of the final draft. For example, each will form contains a clause in which you list your children. (Even if you have no minor children, and leave no gifts to minors, adult children should be listed in your will.) The clause contains space for listing five children. If you have two children, delete the last three spaces for listing children. And, of course, if you have no children, delete the entire clause. If you eliminate an entire clause, be sure to renumber the rest of the clauses.

Type or Print Out the Entire Will

Your final will—the one you will sign—must be completely typewritten using a typewriter or a computer. Do not, for your final will, simply type in information on the blank lines of a form from this book. Such a will would probably be invalid. Use whatever works best for you—an old portable typewriter or a brand new laser printer. What matters is that the machine prints clearly.

Your final will should be on regular 8½" x 11" white bond typing paper. It's preferable not to use erasable typing paper. Paper with a high rag content looks nicer, but cheap paper is just as legal. I recommend double spacing, because that's the way wills are normally done, although single spacing is permissible. Spacing should be uniform throughout the will. Normal side and top margins (one inch) are recommended, and no abnormal gaps should be present. Pages should be numbered at the bottom.

Proofread the Will Carefully

Once you have a final version, review it again to be sure it does what you want and that there are no typing errors. If you find any mistakes, do not fix them by hand—your corrections must be typed. If you used a computer to make your will, print out a corrected version. If you used a typewriter and you found only minor mistakes, you can use correction tape and make your corrections with the typewriter. But if you find substantial errors, you must retype the entire page.

Keep in mind that your primary mission when you type or print out your will is to avoid any remote suspicion that you or anyone else changed your will after you signed it in front of witnesses.

Accordingly, if a mistake is made on a sensitive item—say, a beneficiary's name—retype or reprint the whole page rather than using white-out or something similar. You don't want to create the possibility that a beneficiary, a would-be beneficiary, or the probate judge will question the validity of the change.

Again, there can be no handwritten corrections or cross-outs in your final document. If you X out or type over a mistake, you may invalidate at least a portion of your will.

> **CAUTION**
>
> **Don't add ANYTHING handwritten to your completed will.** What should you do if your name, or the name of someone else mentioned in your will, is properly spelled with special characters, such as an accent mark or umlaut? If your typewriter or word processing program allows you to create the characters you desire, do it. But do NOT ink in such a character on your will. Handwritten entries on a printed will can cause difficulties, or at the worst, invalidate part or even all of your will when it is probated. Don't risk it. The fact that a special character is missing may understandably be displeasing to you, but it will have no adverse impact on your will's legality or effectiveness.

Once your will is complete you may want to staple it to a heavy sheet of backing paper (typically, blue) that identifies it as your will. You can purchase a backing sheet from a stationery store. Otherwise, simply staple the pages together in the upper left-hand corner.

Your final act is signing your will in front of your witnesses, and also in front of a notary if you choose to have a "self-proving" will. Signing instructions are detailed in Chapter 12. ●

Making a Customized Will

You can use this chapter to prepare your own personally designed will. From the clauses provided here, pick the ones you want, find them on the CD-ROM, and include them in your will.

How to Prepare Your Will

This chapter presents a series of will clauses identified by capital letters, beginning with "A" and concluding with "CC," which is the clause for signing and witnessing your will. Each lettered clause is accompanied, where appropriate, by:

- a brief discussion of the reasons for its inclusion
- a cross-reference to the section of the book where the legal issue covered in the clause is discussed in more detail, and
- an indication of whether or not that clause must be included in your will. Some clauses are mandatory; others are optional, depending on your family situation and personal desires.

Optional. Any clause that doesn't apply to everyone making a will is labeled "**Optional**"—even though it may be vital for you. For example, Clause R covers naming personal guardians for minor children. This clause is labeled **Optional** because many readers don't have minor children. However, if you do have minor children, you definitely should use one of the alternatives in Clause R.

Alternatives. For several will clauses, I present two or more choices, labeled "**Alternatives**." *You cannot use more than one alternative.* There are accompanying explanations to help you decide which one to choose.

EXAMPLE:

Clause P is "Nomination of Executor—Mandatory." This means you must include an executor's clause in your will. There are two alternative versions of this clause. Alternative 1 is for appointing a single executor. Alternative 2 is for the appointment of coexecutors. After referring back to Chapter 6, where you already tentatively chose one or more executors, select the clause you want and write in the appropriate name or names.

Additions. In a few of the clauses, there are also some additional possibilities, labeled "**Additions**." An Addition is a will provision you can use or not as you wish. You do not have to choose between it and another clause. (By contrast, when there are "Alternatives," you can select only one.)

EXAMPLE:

Clause F is for leaving specific gifts. Addition 1 of this clause allows you to leave your share of joint tenancy property to a specific beneficiary (effective only if no joint tenant owner survives you). When you prepare Clause F for specific gifts, you can include Addition 1 or not.

To use this chapter to prepare your will, read it through at least once. Then, go through the clauses one by one with pencil in hand, following the steps below.

Step 1. Identify All Mandatory Will Clauses

This is easy, because in this chapter we've labeled them "**Mandatory**." In addition, all mandatory clauses are marked with a large check mark in the box in the margin, like this: ☑. If there are alternatives, select the one that best meets your needs.

Step 2. Choose What Else to Include

Identify the optional will clauses (marked "**Optional**") you want in your will. When you decide to use an optional clause, place a check mark in the empty box ☐ in the margin next to

Using the CD-ROM to Create a Customized Will

The will clauses discussed in this chapter are in rich text format (RTF) files that can be copied onto your computer from the CD-ROM at the back of this book. You can use these files to draft a customized will. You'll still follow Steps 1 through 8 in this section. For instructions on how to install and copy the form files from the CD-ROM onto your computer, please refer to Appendix A.

! **CAUTION**

Note to Mac users. This CD-ROM and its files should work on Macintosh computers. Please note, however, that Nolo cannot provide technical support for non-Windows users.

💡 **TIP**

Work through the forms on paper first. Before you use the files from the CD-ROM and your word processor to create your will, we suggest using this chapter to work through all the sample clauses on paper first. Place a check mark next to the clauses you want to include in your will and fill in the appropriate blanks.

Finding the Clauses You Want

Windows users

- Each will clause in this chapter is installed to the \Nolo's Will Forms\Custom Will subfolder in the \Program Files folder of your computer.

- Open a file by selecting its "shortcut" as follows: (1) click the Windows "Start" button; (2) open the "Programs" folder; (3) open the "Nolo's Will Forms" subfolder; (4) open the "Custom Will" subfolder; and (5) click on the shortcut to the clause you want to work with.

Mac users

- Each clause in this chapter is located in the "Custom Will" subfolder in the "Nolo's Will Forms" folder.

- Open a file as follows: (1) use the Finder to go to the "Custom Will" folder; (2) open it; and (3) double-click on the specific file you want to open.

Except where noted, file names are the same as the clause names. For example, the clause for forgiving any debts you are owed is in CLAUSEG.RTF. All forms and their file names are listed in Appendix A.

Drafting Your Customized Will

When you're ready to begin assembling your will, open the file Clause A, B, C, & AA: My Will (MYWILL .RTF), which contains the mandatory opening and closing clauses. After filling in the preliminary information, you can start opening, copying, and pasting from the custom clause files into the MYWILL file. When you open a clause file, you'll see that it contains blank lines, which show you where you need to type in information. In most cases, the blanks are followed by bracketed instructions about what information is required. After pasting a clause into your will document, fill in the appropriate information, following the instructions and the samples in this chapter. *Be sure to delete the blank underlines and the bracketed instructional text from your final document.*

Alternatives. For will clauses with two or more alternative versions, all alternatives are included in the same file. In the sample clauses in the book, they are preceded by a number symbol and a blank line (#__). Since you cannot use more than one alternative, be sure to delete the alternatives you don't want to include.

Additions. As discussed, in a few of the clauses, there are also some additional possibilities, labeled "Additions." Be sure to delete any additions you don't want to include in your will document.

Because the formatting of the files has been simplified, the clauses may look slightly different from the samples in the book. If you want your final document to look just like the sample clauses in the book, you'll need to format it with your word processor.

Using the CD-ROM to Create a Customized Will (continued)

If you do not know how to use your word processor to edit a document, you will need to look through the manual for your word processing program—Nolo's technical support department will not be able to help you with the use of your word processing program.

The clause forms on the CD-ROM are not numbered. Blanks are provided for numbering the clauses in your final document (see Step 4, below).

After filling in the form, use your word processor's "Save As" command to save and rename the file. Because all the files are "read-only," you will not be able to use the "Save" command. This is for your

protection. *If you save the file without renaming it, the underlines that indicate where you need to enter your information will be lost and you will not be able to create a new document with this file without recopying the original file from the CD-ROM.*

If you do not know how to use your word processor to save a document, you will need to look through the manual for your word processing program— Nolo's technical support department will not be able to help you with the use of your word processing program.

---

the selected clause. These check marks can help you avoid overlooking a clause when it comes time for you to prepare the final version of your will.

Step 3. Fill in the Blanks

Fill in all necessary information in the blanks in each will clause you've selected. You can do this right in the book, or can use the clauses on the CD-ROM to create a draft of your will and fill in the blanks on that. Which way you do this is up to you. Some people will want to get their thoughts down right in the book, others may prefer to create a draft so that they don't fill the book with personal information or because they like seeing everything laid out before they start.

If you do decide to make a draft of your will at this point, see the long sidebar, above, for instructions.

Step 4. Number Each Clause

Number all of the clauses you've chosen to include in your will—sequentially, starting with number 1. Put the numbers in the blank in the margin next to the clause. (The identification provisions at the top of the form, where you fill in your name, do not have a number.) These same numbers will be included on your final will, to identify each clause.

EXAMPLE:

Clause C, Revocation of Prior Wills, appears at the beginning of your will after the unnumbered identification provisions. It is mandatory and therefore is always numbered 1. If you use the next clause, Personal Information (Clause D), give it the number 2. However, if you have no children and are not married, and so have no need for this clause, the next clause you would probably use would be the Specific Gifts clause (Clause F), so you'd number it 2.

> **CAUTION**
>
> **Don't change the wording.** If you make substantive changes in the language of a will clause printed in this chapter, you're running a risk that:
>
> - you won't accomplish what you wish to, and
> - you will create ambiguities that could interfere with your will's effectiveness.
>
> For these reasons, I urge you not to change the wording of any of these clauses. If you make a change, carefully evaluate whether it's desirable to have your will reviewed by an attorney or research the legal issue involved yourself. (See Chapter 15, Lawyers and Doing Your Own Legal Research.)

Step 5. Prepare the Final Draft of Your Will

Next, you will work on the final draft of your will. If you haven't already done so, create a draft of your will using the file MYWILL which contains the essential clauses of your will. Resave that document with a new name, perhaps on your desktop or to your My Documents folder. Then find each clause you need on the CD-ROM and paste it into a new document. (See the long sidebar above, for specific instructions on how to do this.) Then,

- Type in all of your answers on the blank lines. Reread the notes that accompany each clause in the book to double check that your filling it in correctly.

- Copy and paste any clauses that you need to repeat and delete all of the alternative clauses that you don't need.

- Delete all extraneous material from your draft, like the instructions in brackets and italics.

For example, the identification clause at the beginning of our will looks like this:

Will of ___ *[your name]* ___

You should type in your name and delete the line and the instructions, so that it looks like this:

Will of Mary Jones

Step 6. Print Out and Proofread Your Will

After you have completed all of the clauses in your will and deleted all of the extraneous material, print out your will and read it carefully. Does it accomplish what you want it to accomplish? Is everything spelled correctly? Are all of the lines and instructions removed?

If you find a mistake, use the computer to fix it and print out a fresh copy. Each time you print out a new draft, review your document until you find no mistakes.

> **CAUTION**
>
> **Don't add ANYTHING handwritten to your completed will.** What should you do if your name, or the name of someone else mentioned in your will, is properly spelled with special characters, such as an accent mark or umlaut? If your typewriter or word processing program allows you to create the characters you desire, do it. But do NOT ink in such a character on your will. Handwritten entries on a printed will can cause difficulties, or at the worst, invalidate part or even all of your will when it is probated. Don't risk it. The fact that a special character is missing may understandably be displeasing to you, but it will have no adverse impact on your will's legality or effectiveness.

Step 7. Sign and Date Your Will and Have It Witnessed

Once the final version of your will is ready, you must sign and date it, and have it witnessed. Instructions are in Chapter 12.

Will Clauses

Now it's time to complete the clauses you want in your will.

☑ Clause A. Will Heading— Mandatory

This unnumbered heading is typed at the top of your will.

Use the name you commonly use for signing legal papers and other important documents.

If for any reason you've used different names and still own property in both names, identify yourself using both these names. For example, if you changed your name to Albert Burnstone but still own some property in the name of Albert Bones, identify yourself using both names, "Albert Burnstone aka Albert Bones," and sign your will that way.

Will of _____
your name

☑ Clause B. Personal Identification— Mandatory

This unnumbered provision identifies you. Use the same form of your name set out in clause A, and your permanent address. If there's any question about where you reside, review Chapter 2.

I, _____,
your name

a resident of _____,
city

_____, _____
county   *state*

declare that this is my will.

☑ Clause C. Revocation of Prior Wills— Mandatory

This clause revokes all previous wills and codicils (formal amendments to a will) that you've made. This is the first numbered clause of your will.

If you have made prior wills, and you know the date of the most recent one, it's helpful to both enter that date here and destroy that will and all copies, but this isn't required. If you don't know the date of your prior will, or haven't made a prior will, delete everything after the word "made."

1. **Revocation of Prior Wills.** I revoke all wills and codicils that I have previously made (including the will dated _____, 20___).

☐ Clause D. Personal Information— Mandatory If You Are Married or Have Children

If you are not married and do not have any children, skip this clause. Otherwise, place a check in the box in the margin to indicate that this clause is to be included in your will and place number 2 on the blank line to indicate that it is the second clause in your will. Then fill in the blanks by listing your spouse, if you're married. List all your children, and any grandchild of yours who's the son or daughter of a child who has died. You must provide in your will for each living child (and any children of a deceased child) or that child is disinherited under the terms of the will. (See Chapter 5.) To remind you, naming a child as an alternate beneficiary, or alternate residuary beneficiary, means you have "provided" for that child.

#_. **Personal Information.** I am married to

_____,
spouse's name

and all references in this will to my _____
husband/wife

are to _____.
him/her

I have _____ _____ now living,
number *child/children*

whose name(s) and date(s) of birth _____:
is/are

_____ _____
name *date of birth*

_____ _____
name *date of birth*

_____ _____
name *date of birth*

_____ _____
name *date of birth*

_____ _____
name *date of birth*

[repeat as needed]

There _____ _____ living _____
is /are *number* *child/children*

of my deceased child, _____,
name

whose name(s) and date(s) of birth are:

_____ _____
name of grandchild *date of birth*

_____ _____
name of grandchild *date of birth*

_____ _____
name of grandchild *date of birth*

[repeat as needed]

If I do not leave property to a child or grandchild listed above, my failure to do so is intentional.

☐ Clause E. Disinheritance— Optional

If you want to explicitly disinherit a child, a child of a deceased child, or anyone else, use this clause. Check the box in the margin and number this clause with the next number. Otherwise, leave both box and line blank and simply skip this clause.

#_. **Disinheritance.** I direct that _____ be disinherited and receive nothing from my estate.

[repeat as needed]

☐ Clause F. Specific Gifts—Optional (though very common)

Here you complete the clauses necessary to leave specific gifts, from cash to heirlooms to real estate. If you wish to make specific gifts, check the box and keep reading. If you wish to leave all your property to one beneficiary, or a group of them, without singling out any items, leave the box blank and proceed to Clause G.

Hopefully, you made your decisions regarding specific gifts in Chapter 5. If you haven't made up your mind yet, this is the time to do it. If you completed the Beneficiary Worksheet in Chapter 5, you need only transfer that information to the appropriate lines below. If you didn't use the worksheet, review the guidelines for describing property in Chapter 4 before you list items here.

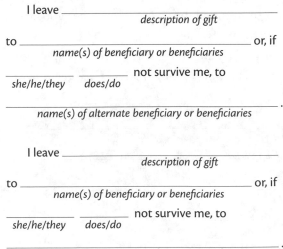

TIP

Leaving shared gifts to multiple beneficiaries. If you want to leave shared gifts to two or more beneficiaries, be sure you've reviewed the discussion in Chapter 5.

#_. **Specific Gifts.** I leave the following specific gifts:

I leave _____
description of gift

to _____ or, if
name(s) of beneficiary or beneficiaries

_____ _____ not survive me, to
she/he/they *does/do*

_____.
name(s) of alternate beneficiary or beneficiaries

I leave _____
description of gift

to _____ or, if
name(s) of beneficiary or beneficiaries

_____ _____ not survive me, to
she/he/they *does/do*

_____.
name(s) of alternate beneficiary or beneficiaries

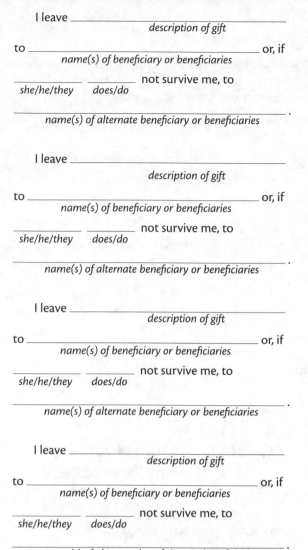

I leave _____
description of gift

to _____ or, if
name(s) of beneficiary or beneficiaries

_____ _____ not survive me, to
she/he/they *does/do*

_____ .
name(s) of alternate beneficiary or beneficiaries

I leave _____
description of gift

to _____ or, if
name(s) of beneficiary or beneficiaries

_____ _____ not survive me, to
she/he/they *does/do*

_____ .
name(s) of alternate beneficiary or beneficiaries

I leave _____
description of gift

to _____ or, if
name(s) of beneficiary or beneficiaries

_____ _____ not survive me, to
she/he/they *does/do*

_____ .
name(s) of alternate beneficiary or beneficiaries

I leave _____
description of gift

to _____ or, if
name(s) of beneficiary or beneficiaries

_____ _____ not survive me, to
she/he/they *does/do*

_____ .
name(s) of alternate beneficiary or beneficiaries

☐ Addition 1: Naming a Beneficiary for Joint Tenancy Property

At your death, your interest in joint tenancy property goes to the surviving joint tenants. However, if you and all the other joint tenants die simultaneously, your share of the property is transferred by your will. Unless you have named a specific beneficiary for it in your will, your share goes to your residuary beneficiary. You can leave all such property to a specific beneficiary by using Addition 1, below. (See Chapter 5.)

#__. Joint Tenancy Property

I leave any interest in joint tenancy property subject to this will to:

_____
beneficiary/beneficiaries

or, if _____ do not survive me, to
she/he/they

_____ .
alternate beneficiary/beneficiaries

☐ Addition 2: Making Comments About Your Gifts

If you want to include comments on the reasons for making your gifts, as discussed in Chapter 5, you can do it here. If you are going to type your will, you'll probably have to prepare an attachment to have space to set forth your reasons. Then be sure that language from the attachment is included in the final, typed version. If you prepare your will using the forms on the CD-ROM, simply type in your comments after the clause that leaves the property.

☐ Clause G. Debts Forgiven—Optional

You can use your will to forgive debts. (If you have questions about this, see Chapter 5.) You may also, if you wish, include an explanation of why you forgave the debt. Don't put in the amount of the debt, because that will probably change over time.

> **CAUTION**
>
> **Forgiving marital debts.** If you're married and wish to use your will to forgive all of a debt, be sure you have power to do so. This may not be the case if the money is owed to both you and your spouse. (See Chapter 3.)

#__. Debts Forgiven

I forgive my interest in the following _____,
debt/debts

including all interest accrued as of the date of my death:

Person or Organization Owing Debt   Date of Loan

_____   _____

_____   _____

_____   _____

☐ **Addition 1: Explaining Why You Forgave Debts**

If you want to state in your will why you forgave a debt, you can express yourself here. Your comments become the second part of the Debts Forgiven clause. They are not given a separate number.

I forgive the debts owed me by _____

_____ because
debtor

_____

_____

_____.

[repeat as needed]

☐ **Clause H. Real Estate Encumbrances— Optional**

When you leave real estate through your will, the recipient becomes responsible for all encumbrances on it, such as mortgages, deeds of trust, and liens, unless you specify differently in your will. If you want to relieve the beneficiary of the obligation to pay a mortgage or other encumbrance, you must put a clause in your will directing your executor to use certain other assets to pay off the encumbrance. (The real estate itself should be left by a specific gifts clause, not as part of the residuary estate.) Of course, you must be sure there's enough property elsewhere in your estate to pay the encumbrances. (See Chapter 8.)

The clause below applies to one specific gift of real estate. If you want to leave more than one

gift of real estate free of encumbrances, repeat this clause for each such gift.

#__. Real Estate Encumbrances

I direct that the gift of real estate,

_____,
address or description of property

left to _____,
name(s) of beneficiary/beneficiaries

be made free of all encumbrances on that property at my death, including, but not limited to, any mortgages, deeds of trust, real property taxes and assessments, and estate and inheritance taxes, and that such encumbrances shall be paid by my executor from the assets below, in the order listed:

_____

_____

_____
description of assets

[repeat as needed]

☐ **Clause I. Personal Property Encumbrances— Optional**

If any gift of personal property (anything but real estate) is encumbered by a lien or other debt, that obligation goes with the property, unless you specify otherwise. If you want to leave an encumbered item, such as a car with a loan on it, free of that obligation, you must expressly state so in your will and direct your executor to pay the debt from other identified assets. (The property itself must be left by a specific gift clause, not as part of the residuary estate.) Of course, you must be sure there's enough property elsewhere in your estate to pay the debt. (See Chapter 8.)

#__. Personal Property Encumbrances

I direct that the following gift, _____,
description of gift

left to _____,
beneficiary/beneficiaries

be made free of all loans, liens, debts, or other obligations on that property, and that all such obligations shall be paid by my executor from the assets below, in the order listed:

_____

_____

_____

assets

[repeat as needed]

☑ Clause J. Shared Gifts— Mandatory

This clause establishes three rules for shared gifts. Section A covers what happens if your will names multiple beneficiaries but doesn't state what percentage or fraction of the gift each should receive: if you don't specify, each beneficiary receives an equal share.

Section B covers shared gifts left in a single paragraph of the Specific Gifts clause. As discussed earlier, you can leave shared specific gifts either by a single paragraph, or create a separate paragraph for each beneficiary of that shared gift. (See Chapter 5.) If you want the surviving beneficiaries of a shared gift to inherit a deceased beneficiary's share, you simply name all beneficiaries for the gift in a single specific gift paragraph. Section B of Clause J specifies that the surviving beneficiaries share equally in a deceased beneficiary's portion. In other words, if you leave a shared gift in a single paragraph, any alternate you name would inherit only if all the primary beneficiaries for the gift didn't survive you.

Section C covers what happens if a residuary beneficiary for a shared gift does not survive you, and you haven't made specific provision for that possibility in your will. In that case, the surviving residuary beneficiaries share equally in the deceased beneficiary's share. The alternate residuary beneficiary would inherit only if all residuary beneficiaries did not survive you.

#___. Shared Gifts

A. If I leave property to be shared by two or more beneficiaries, it shall be shared equally between them unless this will provides otherwise.

B. If any beneficiary of a shared specific gift left in a single paragraph of the Specific Gifts clause, above, does not survive me, that deceased beneficiary's portion of the gift shall be given to the surviving beneficiaries in equal shares.

C. If any residuary beneficiary of a shared residuary gift does not survive me, that deceased beneficiary's portion of the residue shall be given to the surviving residuary beneficiaries in equal shares, unless this will provides otherwise.

☑ Clause K. Residuary Estate— Mandatory

As previously discussed, the "residue" of your estate is exactly what it sounds like—all that remains after all specific gifts of personal property and real estate have been distributed, and any encumbrances you directed to be paid off have been satisfied.

Following are four alternative residuary clauses. Using any of them, you should always name at least one residuary beneficiary and an alternate residuary beneficiary. (See Chapter 5 for discussion of selecting a residuary beneficiary clause.)

Alternative 1. Standard Residuary Estate Clause

This is a standard, common residuary beneficiary clause, the one used in the fill-in-the-blanks wills of Chapter 10. Using this clause, you simply name your residuary beneficiary or beneficiaries. If you name more than one residuary beneficiary, the clause states that property is left to them in equal shares unless you provided differently. The clause also provides that if you name more than one residuary beneficiary, the survivors share equally the portion of any residuary beneficiary who dies before you do. The alternate residuary beneficiary inherits only if all residuary beneficiaries fail to survive you.

#__. **Residuary Estate**

I leave my residuary estate, that is, the rest of my property not otherwise specifically and validly disposed of by this will or in any other manner, including lapsed or failed gifts, to

_____ ,
residuary beneficiary/beneficiaries
(specify percentages, if desired)

or, if _____ _____ not survive me, to
she/he/they   *does/do*

_____ .
alternate residuary beneficiary/beneficiaries

If any residuary beneficiary does not survive me, the surviving residuary beneficiaries shall receive the deceased residuary beneficiary's share of the residuary estate in equal shares, unless this will provides otherwise. If there is more than one alternate residuary beneficiary, they shall receive the residuary estate in equal shares.

Alternative 2. More Than One Residuary Beneficiary, With Different Alternates

This clause may be desirable if you name more than one residuary beneficiary. It allows you to name different alternates for each residuary beneficiary. For example, you could name your three children as residuary beneficiaries, and name each child's children (your grandchildren) as alternate residuary beneficiaries for each child's share.

#__. **Residuary Estate**

I leave my residuary estate, that is, the rest of my property not otherwise specifically and validly disposed of by this will or in any other manner, including lapsed or failed gifts, to the following beneficiaries in the following shares:

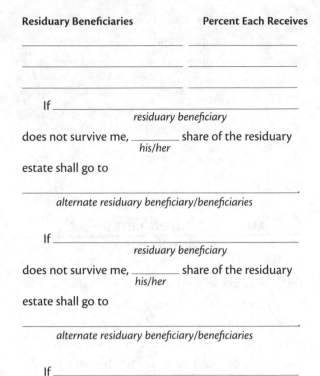

Residuary Beneficiaries	Percent Each Receives
_____	_____
_____	_____
_____	_____

If _____
residuary beneficiary

does not survive me, _____ share of the residuary
his/her

estate shall go to

_____
alternate residuary beneficiary/beneficiaries

If _____
residuary beneficiary

does not survive me, _____ share of the residuary
his/her

estate shall go to

_____
alternate residuary beneficiary/beneficiaries

If _____
residuary beneficiary

does not survive me, _____ share of the residuary
his/her

estate shall go to

_____
alternate residuary beneficiary/beneficiaries

[repeat as needed]

Alternative 3. One Residuary Beneficiary With Two Levels of Alternate Residuary Beneficiaries

This clause allows you to name two levels of alternate residuary beneficiaries for a single residuary beneficiary. In other words, you can name alternates for your alternates, if you want to carry your contingency planning this far. If you want to name more than one first level beneficiary, you should use Alternative 4.

#__. **Residuary Estate**

I leave my residuary estate, that is, the rest of my property not otherwise specifically and validly disposed of by this will or in any other manner, including lapsed or failed gifts, to

_____ ,
residuary beneficiary

or, if _____ does not survive me, to
she/he

_____
alternate residuary beneficiary/beneficiaries

or, if _____ does not survive me, to
she/he

_____
second alternate residuary beneficiary/beneficiaries

Alternative 4. More Than One Residuary Beneficiary With Two Levels of Alternate Residuary Beneficiaries

This clause allows you to name two levels of alternate residuary beneficiaries to a number of residuary beneficiaries.

#__. Residuary Estate

I leave my residuary estate, that is, the rest of my property not otherwise specifically and validly disposed of by this will or in any other manner, including lapsed or failed gifts, to the following beneficiaries in the following shares:

Residuary Beneficiaries	Percent Each Receives
_____	_____
_____	_____
_____	_____

If _____
residuary beneficiary
does not survive me, _____ share of the residuary
his/her
estate shall go to

_____
alternate residuary beneficiary/beneficiaries

If _____
alternate residuary beneficiary/beneficiaries
does not survive me, _____ share of the
his/her/their
residuary estate shall go to

_____
alternate residuary beneficiary/beneficiaries

If _____
residuary beneficiary
does not survive me, _____ share of the residuary
his/her

estate shall go to

_____
alternate residuary beneficiary/beneficiaries

If _____
alternate residuary beneficiary/beneficiaries
does not survive me, _____ share of the
his/her/their
residuary estate shall go to

_____
alternate residuary beneficiary/beneficiaries

If _____
residuary beneficiary
does not survive me, _____ share of the residuary
his/her
estate shall go to

_____
alternate residuary beneficiary/beneficiaries

If _____
alternate residuary beneficiary/beneficiaries
does not survive me, _____ share of the
his/her/their
residuary estate shall go to

_____
alternate residuary beneficiary/beneficiaries

[repeat as needed]

☐ Clause I. Survivorship Period— Optional

To remind you, a "survivorship period" clause requires all beneficiaries (except alternate residuary beneficiaries) to survive you by a specified time in order to inherit under your will. (See Chapter 5.) If a beneficiary doesn't survive you by this period, the property goes to the alternate beneficiary (or for a shared gift, to the surviving beneficiaries, if that's what you chose). If you do not include a survivorship period in your will, beneficiaries will inherit the gifts you leave them even if they outlive you by only a few minutes.

Below are two alternative survivorship clauses for you to choose between. The first is a standard 45-day survivorship period, the one used in the basic wills of this book. It works fine for most people.

The second alternative allows you to choose any period you want. For instance, if some beneficiaries are in ill health, you may want to require a longer survivorship period, to lessen the possibility your gift would simply wind up as part of someone else's estate. Since probate usually takes at least six months, a survivorship period of up to 180 days can be reasonable, depending on the circumstances. A longer period risks needlessly tying up your property.

Alternative 1. 45-Day Survivorship Period

#__. Survivorship Period

As used in this will, the phrase "survive me" means to be alive or in existence as an organization on the 45th day after my death. Any beneficiary, except any alternate residuary beneficiary, must survive me to inherit under this will. If there are no surviving beneficiaries for a specific gift, that gift shall become part of my residuary estate.

Alternative 2. Other Survivorship Period

#__. Survivorship Period

As used in this will, the phrase "survive me" means to be alive or in existence as an organization on the _____th day after my death. Any beneficiary, except any alternate residuary beneficiary, must survive me to inherit under this will. If there are no surviving beneficiaries for a specific gift, that gift shall become part of my residuary estate.

☐ Clause M. Abatement—Optional

Here are two versions of a clause that lets you specify what happens if, at your death, you don't own enough property to cover all your cash gifts after your debts and taxes are paid. (This matter is discussed in Chapter 5.)

Alternative 1. Abatement First From Residue

#__. Abatement

If my estate is not sufficient to pay in full all gifts of set dollar amounts made in this will, my executor shall first sell personal property, and then real property, in my residuary estate, in the amount necessary to pay these gifts.

Alternative 2. Abatement Pro Rata From Cash Gifts

#__. Abatement

If my estate is not sufficient to pay in full all gifts of set dollar amounts made in this will, my executor shall make an appropriate pro rata reduction of each cash gift.

☐ Clause N. Payment of Estate Taxes—Optional

Your estate is obligated to pay any taxes you or your estate owe, including all estate taxes. (Chapter 14 discusses these taxes.) These may be minimal, or even nonexistent, and thus not worth bothering about in your will. However, if your estate may be subject to federal estate taxes, you may want to specify that certain assets be used to pay those taxes using Alternative 1.

Many readers will not transfer any significant amount of property by methods other than their will. However, if you do, and you want all your inheritors to be responsible for any estate taxes in the proportion of the value of property they receive compared to the total estate, use Alternative 2.

If you don't use either of these alternatives, the Executor's Powers clause you'll find later in the will gives your executor the authority to decide how any estate taxes are to be paid.

Alternative 1. Payment From Specific Assets

#__. Payment of Estate Taxes

I direct my executor to pay all estate taxes assessed against my estate, or taxes payable by beneficiaries for property received from my estate, from the following assets, in the order listed:

_____

_____

_____

description of assets

Alternative 2. Payment From All Property in Estate

#__. Payment of Estate Taxes

I direct that all estate taxes assessed against my estate, or payable by beneficiaries for property received from my estate, be paid out of all the property in my taxable estate, no matter how transferred, on a pro rata basis by or on behalf of the recipients of the property.

☐ Clause O. Payment of Debts—Optional

If you anticipate you'll have significant debts, you may want to earmark assets to be used to pay them. Again, if you don't, your executor will decide how they are to be paid under the standard Executor's Powers clause of your will. This can be fine if you expect only routine debts, such as charge accounts with modest balances, or household bills.

#__. Payment of Debts

I direct my executor to pay all debts and expenses of my estate from the assets listed below, in the order listed, except that liens and encumbrances placed on property as security for repayment of a debt or loan pass with that property, unless I specifically provide otherwise in this will.

_____

_____

_____

description of assets

☑ Clause P. Nomination of Executor—Mandatory

By now, you should have decided who you want to name as your executor and alternate executor. Below are two alternative executor clauses. The first is for naming one executor. The second is for naming two or more. Remember that with this clause, each executor can act for your estate. (See Chapter 6.)

You can add Addition 1 to either alternative, naming an ancillary executor for a state other than the one you live in, in case an in-state executor is needed in that state to handle probate of real estate located there. (See Chapter 6.)

Both alternatives state that your executor will not be required to post a bond. However, Addition 2 allows you to require that your executor must post a bond. If you have no one you really trust to serve as your executor, you may want the person you name to have to post a bond. Before deciding on this, be sure to review the discussion of executor's bonds in Chapter 6.

Alternative 1. Sole Executor

#__. Executor

I nominate _____
                    executor's name

as executor. If _____
                    executor's name

shall for any reason fail to qualify or cease to act as executor, I nominate _____,
                              alternate executor's name

as executor.

No bond shall be required by any executor.

Alternative 2.　More Than One Executor

#__. Executors

I nominate _____
executors' names

to serve as executors without bond. Each executor may act for my estate. If any of them fail to qualify or cease to serve as executor, the surviving executor(s) shall serve as executor(s), also without bond. If none of them are available to serve, I nominate

_____
alternate executor's name

as executor, to serve without bond.

☐ Addition 1: Appointing an Ancillary Executor

If an executor is needed in

_____, I nominate
state where real estate is located

_____ to serve as
ancillary executor's name

executor there, without bond.

☐ Addition 2: Requiring Executor to Post Bond

If you want to require that your executor post a bond, add this provision to your Executor's clause, and delete the statement that no bond is required.

Any person serving as executor under this will must post a bond, in an amount determined by the court supervising the administration of this will.

☑ Clause Q. Executor's Powers— Mandatory

This clause gives your executor a good deal of flexibility, which is desirable.

> ⚠ **CAUTION**
>
> **Special clause for Texas residents.** Texas residents should not use the Executor's Powers clause below. Instead, use the special Texas Personal Representative's Powers Clause that follows. Using it should make your Texas executor's court job significantly easier, because it authorizes him or her to act under the Texas

Independent Administration of Estates Act. This Act enables the executor to minimize paperwork. (The Act can be used in many states. However, only in Texas have courts shown a willingness to interpret the Act to require both specific language authorizing it in the will, and no other listing of executor's powers.)

Alternative 1.　Standard Executor's Powers Clause

#__. Executor's Powers

I direct that my executor take all actions legally permissible to have the probate of my estate done as simply as possible, including filing a petition in the appropriate court for the independent administration of my estate.

I grant to my executor the following powers, to be exercised as my executor deems to be in the best interests of my estate:

a. Except as otherwise provided in this will, my executor shall pay, as my executor decides is best (unless state law requires a specific method for payment), all my debts and all taxes that may, by reason of my death, be assessed against my estate or any portion of it.

b. To retain property without liability for loss or depreciation resulting from such retention.

c. To dispose of property by public or private sale, or exchange, or otherwise, and receive or administer the proceeds as a part of my estate.

d. To vote stock, to exercise any option or privilege to convert bonds, notes, stocks, or other securities belonging to my estate into other bonds, notes, stocks, or other securities, and to exercise all other rights and privileges of a person owning similar property in his or her own right.

e. To lease any real property that may at any time form part of my estate.

f. To abandon, adjust, arbitrate, compromise, sue on, defend, or otherwise deal with and settle claims in favor of or against my estate.

g. To continue, maintain, operate, or participate in any business which is a part of my estate, and to effect incorporation, dissolution, or other change in the form of organization of the business.

h. To do all other acts, which in his or her judgment may be necessary or appropriate for the proper and advantageous management, investment, and distribution of my estate.

The foregoing powers, authority, and discretion are in addition to the powers, authority, and discretion vested in him or her by operation of law and may be exercised as often as is deemed necessary or advisable without application to, or approval by, any court in any jurisdiction.

Alternative 2. Special Executor's Clause for Texas

#__. Personal Representative's Powers

Except as otherwise required by Texas law, I direct that my personal representative shall take no other action in the county court in relation to the settlement of my estate than the probating and recording of this will, and the return of an inventory, appraisement, and list of claims of my estate.

☐ Clause R. Personal Guardian of Minor Children— Mandatory If You Have Minor Children

If you have minor children, by now you should have decided on the people you want to serve as their personal guardian and alternate personal guardian. Now it's time to put your choices in your will. (If you have any questions, review Chapter 7.)

Alternative 1. Other Parent as First Guardian

Use this version if you want the child's other parent to serve as first personal guardian if you die. You don't name that parent to be personal guardian. You are naming someone to raise the children only if both you and the other parent cannot. Also use Alternative 1 if you know that the other parent won't, for some reason, be, or desire to be, the personal guardian. If you wish, you can also set out your reasons for your choices.

#__. Personal Guardian

If at my death any of my children are minors, and a personal guardian is needed, I nominate

_____ to

personal guardian's name

be appointed as personal guardian of my minor children. If _____ cannot serve as guardian,

she/he

I nominate _____

alternate personal guardian's name

to be appointed as personal guardian.

I direct that no bond be required of any personal guardian.

☐ Addition: Statement of Reasons for Your Choice

I believe it is in the best interests of my

_____ for _____

child/children   *personal guardian's name*

to be _____ personal guardian because

his/her/their

_____

_____

_____

_____

_____

_____

Alternative 2.   Guardian in Place of Other Parent

If you don't want the other parent to get custody, use Alternative 2. Be sure you've read the discussion in Chapter 7 and have taken stock of the reality that the other natural parent usually gets custody, if he or she desires it, unless it's proven to be harmful to the child. In this situation, you should include a brief explanation of your reasons.

#___. Personal Guardian

If at my death any of my children are minors, I nominate _____ to be

personal guardian's name

appointed as personal guardian of my minor

children. If _____ cannot serve as guardian,

she/he

I nominate _____

alternate personal guardian's name

to be appointed as personal guardian.

I direct that no bond be required of any personal guardian.

I believe it is in the best interests of my children for

_____ to be their personal

name

guardian, rather than _____ because

biological or legal parent's name

_____

_____

_____

Alternative 3.   Different Personal Guardians for Different Children

Use this version if you want to name different personal guardians for different children.

#___. Personal Guardian

If at my death any of my children are minors, and a personal guardian is needed:

I nominate _____

personal guardian's name

to be appointed as personal guardian of my child(ren)

_____ .

name of child/children

If _____

personal guardian's name

cannot serve as guardian, I nominate

_____ to

alternate personal guardian's name

be appointed as personal guardian for these children.

I nominate _____

personal guardian's name

to be appointed as personal guardian of my child(ren)

_____ .

name of child/children

If _____

personal guardian's name

cannot serve as guardian, I nominate

_____ to

alternate personal guardian's name

be appointed as personal guardian for these children.

I direct that no bond be required of any personal guardian.

I believe these people are the best personal guardians for the respective children because

_____

_____

_____

☐ Clause S. Gifts Under the Uniform Transfers to Minors Act—Optional

> **CAUTION**
>
> **Don't use this clause in South Carolina or Vermont.** You cannot make gifts in your will using the Act if you live in South Carolina or Vermont.

After reading Chapter 7, you should have decided whether or not you want to leave gifts to minors under your state's Uniform Transfers to Minors Act (UTMA). Here you list each such child's name, the adult "custodian" and "alternate custodian" for each child, and complete the clause by filling in the name of your state.

To remind you, you've already left your gifts to minors in the clauses above. Here you're simply plugging the UTMA into your will for those minors you want to use the Act for.

You must complete a separate clause for each minor whose gifts you want to be supervised by a custodian under the Act. You can appoint only one custodian and one alternate custodian per minor. You cannot appoint joint custodians.

Most states that have adopted the UTMA set either 18 or 21 as the age at which the custodian must turn over the property to the minor. (See list in Chapter 7.) However, a few states allow you to vary the statutory age within set limits. If you live in one of the states listed below, and you've decided to vary the age at which a minor is to receive a gift, complete the additional portion of clauses applicable for your state.

TIP

Remember that there are three distinct ways you can include property management for minor children in your will—the UTMA, a pot trust, and a child's trust. You can only choose one method per child, but you can include different methods for different children. See Chapter 7 to decide which is right for your situation.

#__. Gifts to Minors Under the Uniform Transfers to Minors Act

All property left in this will to _____

_____
minor's name
shall be given to _____
custodian's name
as custodian for _____
minor's name
under the Uniform Transfers to Minors Act of

_____ .
your state
If _____
custodian's name
cannot serve as custodian, _____

States That Let You Change the Age at Which a Minor Receives Property		
State	**Statutory Age for Receiving Gift**	**You Can Change to Age:**
Alaska	18	19 to 25
Arkansas	21	20 to 18
California	18	19 to 25
Maine	18	19 to 21
Nevada	18	19 to 25
New Jersey	21	20 to 18
North Carolina	21	20 to 18
Oregon	21	22 to 25
Pennsylvania	21	22 to 25
Tennessee	21	22 to 25
Virginia	18	19 to 21

_____
alternate custodian's name
shall serve as custodian.

All property left in this will to _____

_____
minor's name
shall be given to _____
custodian's name
as custodian for _____
minor's name
under the Uniform Transfers to Minors Act of

_____ .
your state
If _____
custodian's name
cannot serve as custodian, _____

_____
alternate custodian's name
shall serve as custodian.

All property left in this will to _____

_____
minor's name

shall be given to _____
                            custodian's name

as custodian for _____
                            minor's name

under the Uniform Transfers to Minors Act of

_____ .
your state

If _____
                     custodian's name

cannot serve as custodian, _____

_____
alternate custodian's name

shall serve as custodian.

All property left in this will to _____

_____
minor's name

shall be given to _____
                            custodian's name

as custodian for _____
                            minor's name

under the Uniform Transfers to Minors Act of

_____ .
your state

If _____
                     custodian's name

cannot serve as custodian, _____

_____
alternate custodian's name

shall serve as custodian.

[repeat as needed]

☐ Addition: Varying the Age at Which Minor Receives Gift

If you want to vary the age at which a minor receives an UTMA gift outright, in states where that is permitted, complete and add the following sentence to your UTMA clause:

The custodianship for _____
                                     minor's name

_____

shall end when _____ becomes age
                         he/she

_____ .
specify age allowed by your state

☐ Clause T. Family Pot Trust— Optional

By now you've likely decided whether or not you want to create a family pot trust for property you leave to your minor children. (If you have questions about this, review Chapter 7.) To remind you, you can create only one family pot trust. The trustee can spend different amounts for different children as he or she decides their needs warrant.

To complete the family pot trust clause, list all of your minor children. Then name the trustee and successor trustee.

#__. **Family Pot Trust.** All property I leave by this will to the children listed in Section A below shall be held for them in a single trust, the family pot trust.

    A. Trust Beneficiaries.

_____
child's name

_____
child's name

_____
child's name

_____
child's name

If all of the beneficiaries of the family pot trust are age 18 or older at my death, no family pot trust shall be established, and the property left to them shall be distributed to them outright.

If a beneficiary survives me but dies before the family pot trust terminates, that beneficiary's interest in the trust shall pass to the surviving beneficiaries of the family pot trust.

    B. Trustee of the Family Pot Trust. The trustee shall be _____
                                     trustee's name

or, if _____ cannot serve as trustee, the trustee
         she/he

shall be _____ .
                     successor trustee's name

No bond shall be required of any trustee.

    C. Duties of the Family Pot Trust Trustee.

    1. The trustee may distribute trust assets (income or principal) as the trustee deems necessary for a

beneficiary's health, support, maintenance, and education. Education includes, but is not limited to, college, graduate, postgraduate, and vocational studies, plus reasonably related living expenses.

2. In deciding whether or not to make distributions, the trustee shall consider the value of the trust assets, the relative current and future needs of each beneficiary and each beneficiary's other income, resources, and sources of support. In doing so, the trustee has the discretion to make distributions that benefit some beneficiaries more than others or that completely exclude others.

3. Any trust income that is not distributed by the trustee shall be accumulated and added to the principal.

D.   Termination of the Family Pot Trust. When the youngest surviving beneficiary of this family pot trust reaches 18, the trustee shall distribute the remaining trust assets to the surviving beneficiaries in equal shares.

If none of the trust beneficiaries survives to the age of 18, the trustee shall distribute the remaining trust assets to my heirs at the death of the last surviving beneficiary.

E.   Powers of the Trustee. In addition to all other powers granted a trustee in any portion of this will, the trustee of the family pot trust shall have the power to make distributions to the beneficiaries directly or to other people or organizations on behalf of the beneficiaries.

☐ Clause U. Child's Trusts—Optional

By now you should have decided which children (if any) you want to leave gifts to, using a child's trust. (See Chapter 7.) If you want to create one or more child's trusts, list each trust beneficiary's name and the age each must reach to receive his or her trust property outright. (Remember that if you don't specify an age, all property left to each child will be turned over to him or her at age 35.) Then name

the trustee and successor trustee for each child's trust.

If you want to name different trustees for different child's trusts, you can do that in this clause. If you want to name the same trustee and successor trustee for more than one child, simply list those children's names together in Section B of the clause, and name that trustee and successor trustee once.

#__. Child's Trusts

All property I leave by this will to a child listed in Section A below shall be held for that child in a separate trust.

A. Trust Beneficiaries and Age Limits. Each trust shall end when the beneficiary becomes 35, except as otherwise specified.

Trust for	Shall end at age
_____	_____
_____	_____
_____	_____
_____	_____

B. Trustees

The trustee for _____
name of child or children

_____

shall be _____ ,
trustee's name

or, if _____ cannot serve as trustee, the trustee
he/she

shall be _____ .
successor trustee's name

The trustee for _____
name of child or children

_____

shall be _____ ,
trustee's name

or, if _____ cannot serve as trustee, the trustee
he/she

shall be _____ .
successor trustee's name

The trustee for _____
name of child or children

_____

shall be _____,
<small>trustee's name</small>

or, if _____ cannot serve as trustee, the trustee
<small>he/she</small>

shall be _____.
<small>successor trustee's name</small>

[repeat as needed]

No bond shall be required of any trustee.

C. Duties of the Trustee.

1. The trustee may distribute trust assets (income or principal) as the trustee deems necessary for the beneficiary's health, support, maintenance, and education. Education includes, but is not limited to, college, graduate, postgraduate, and vocational studies, plus reasonably related living expenses.

2. In deciding whether or not to make a distribution, the trustee may take into account the beneficiary's other income, resources, and sources of support.

3. Any trust income that is not distributed by the trustee shall be accumulated and added to the principal of that child's trust.

D. Termination of Trust. A child's trust shall terminate when any of the following events occurs:

1. The beneficiary becomes the age specified in Section A of this trust clause;

2. The beneficiary dies before becoming the age specified in Section A of this trust clause;

3. The trust is exhausted through distributions allowed under these provisions.

If a trust terminates for reason one, the remaining principal and accumulated net income of the trust shall pass to the beneficiary. If a trust terminates for reason two, the remaining principal and accumulated net income of the trust shall pass to the trust beneficiary's heirs.

E. Powers of the Trustee. In addition to all other powers granted the trustee in this will, the trustee shall have the power to make distributions to a child's trust beneficiary directly or to other people or organizations on behalf of that child.

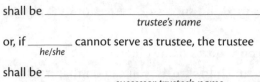

Clause V. Trust Administrative Provisions—Mandatory If You Create a Family Pot Trust or Child's Trust

If you create a child's trust or a family pot trust in your will, include this clause. It gives the trustee of the trust essential powers. You don't have to add anything to this clause; just include it as is.

#__. General Trust Administrative Provisions

Any trust established under this will shall be managed subject to the following provisions.

A. Intent. It is my intent that any trust established under this will be administered independently of court supervision to the maximum extent possible under the laws of the state having jurisdiction over the trust.

B. No Assignment. The interests of any beneficiary of any trust established under this will shall not be transferable by voluntary or involuntary assignment or by operation of law and shall be free from the claims of creditors and from attachment, execution, bankruptcy, or other legal process to the fullest extent permitted by law.

C. Trustee's Powers. In addition to all other powers granted the trustee in this will, the trustee shall have all the powers generally conferred on trustees by the laws of the state having jurisdiction over this trust and the powers to:

1. Invest and reinvest trust funds in every kind of property and every kind of investment, provided that the trustee acts with the care, skill, prudence, and diligence under the prevailing circumstances that a prudent person acting in a similar capacity and familiar with such matters would use.

2. Receive additional property from any source and acquire or hold properties jointly or in undivided interests or in partnership or joint venture with other people or entities.

3. Enter, continue, or participate in the operation of any business, and incorporate, liquidate, reorganize, or otherwise change the form or terminate the operation of the business and contribute capital or loan money to the business.

4. Exercise all the rights, powers, and privileges of an owner of any securities held in the trust.

5. Borrow funds, guarantee or indemnify in the name of the trust and secure any obligation, mortgage, pledge, or other security interest, and renew, extend, or modify any such obligations.

6. Lease trust property for terms within or beyond the term of the trust.

7. Prosecute, defend, contest, or otherwise litigate legal actions or other proceedings for the protection or benefit of the trust; pay, compromise, release, adjust, or submit to arbitration any debt, claim, or controversy; and insure the trust against any risk and the trustee against liability with respect to other people.

8. Pay himself or herself reasonable compensation out of trust assets for ordinary and extraordinary services, and for all services in connection with the complete or partial termination of this trust.

9. Employ and discharge professionals to aid or assist in managing the trust and compensate them from the trust assets.

D. Severability. The invalidity of any provision of this trust instrument shall not affect the validity of the remaining provisions.

E. "Trustee" Defined. The term "trustee" includes all successor trustees.

☐ Clause W. Property Guardian for Your Minor Children— Mandatory If You Have Minor Children

If you have minor children, you should always name a property guardian and alternate property guardian in your will. (See Chapter 7.) If you want to explain the reasons for your choices in your will, you can add a brief statement.

Alternative 1. One Property Guardian for All Children

#___. Property Guardian

If at my death any of my children are minors, and a property guardian is needed, I appoint

_____
property guardian's name
as property guardian of my minor children. If

_____ cannot serve as property guardian, I
she/he
appoint _____
alternate property guardian's name
as property guardian.

I direct that no bond be required of any property guardian.

Alternative 2. Different Property Guardians for Different Children

#___. Property Guardian

If at my death any of my children are minors, and a property guardian is needed, I appoint

_____
property guardian's name
to be appointed as property guardian of my child(ren)

_____.
name of child/children

If _____
property guardian's name
cannot serve as guardian, I nominate

_____ to
alternate property guardian's name
be appointed as property guardian for these children.

If at my death any of my children are minors, and a property guardian is needed, I appoint

_____
property guardian's name

to be appointed as property guardian of my child(ren)

_____ .
name of child/children

If _____
property guardian's name

cannot serve as guardian, I nominate

_____ to
alternate property guardian's name

be appointed as property guardian for these children.

[repeat as needed]

I direct that no bond be required of any property guardian.

☐ Addition: Explaining the Reasons for Your Choice—Optional

I believe these are the best property guardians for these children because:

_____

_____

☐ Clause X. No-Contest Clause— Optional

A no-contest clause is designed to discourage lawsuits. It disinherits any will beneficiary who unsuccessfully challenges your will in court. (See Chapter 5.)

#__. No-Contest Clause

If any beneficiary under this will in any legal manner contests or attacks this will or any of its provisions, any property, share, or interest in my estate left to the contesting beneficiary under this will is revoked and shall be disposed of as if that contesting beneficiary had predeceased me without children.

☐ Clause Y. Simultaneous Death— Optional

As I've discussed, quite a number of people wonder and worry about what happens if they die at the same time as their spouse (or mate or lover) who is a major beneficiary under their will. Who gets what? As discussed in Chapter 5, the survivorship clauses in this book's wills provide an orderly method for determining who inherits a spouse's property when it's impossible to tell which spouse died first. If you included a survivorship period (Clause I, above), all property you left to your spouse or partner will pass to the alternate beneficiaries you named in the event of simultaneous death.

However, you may want to specifically address simultaneous death of spouses or mates, even if doing so is legally redundant. Only if there's no survivorship period in a will can a simultaneous death clause come into operation. But if you wish to include it in your will (it can't hurt), complete the clause below.

#__. Simultaneous Death

If my _____ , _____
wife/husband/mate   *name*

_____

and I should die simultaneously, or under such circumstances as to render it difficult or impossible to determine by clear and convincing evidence who predeceased the other, I shall be conclusively presumed to have survived my _____ for purposes
                                wife/husband/mate

of this will.

☐ Clause Z. Pets—Optional

If you want to leave a pet—and perhaps a sum of money—to a friend who has agreed to care for the animal, use this clause. (For a discussion of arranging for pet care after your death, see Chapter 5.)

#___. Pets

I leave my pet(s) _____
_____ *pet's name(s)*
_____

to _____ .
       name or names

☐ Addition: Money for Your Pet's New Owner—Optional

To help _____
                    name or names
*care for my pet, I also leave the sum of $*_____

to _____ .
       him/her/them

☑ Clause AA. Signature and Witnessing— Mandatory

This is the final clause of your will. It is not numbered. Detailed instructions for how to sign your will, have it witnessed, and use a "self-proving affidavit," if you choose to, are in the next chapter.

Signature

I subscribe my name to this will the _____

day of _____ , _____ , at
                month   *year*
_____ ,
                       city
_____ , _____ .
          county   *state*

and do hereby declare that I sign and execute this instrument as my last will, and that I sign it willingly,

that I execute it as my free and voluntary act for the purposes therein expressed, and that I am of the age of majority or otherwise legally empowered to make a will, and under no constraint or undue influence.

_____
                your signature

Witnesses

On this _____ day of _____ ,
               day   *month*
_____ , _____
    year   *your name*
declared to us, the undersigned, that this instrument was

_____ will and requested us to act as witnesses to
  his/her

it. _____ thereupon signed this will in our presence,
    He/She

all of us being present at the same time. We now, at

_____ request, in _____
  his/her   *his/her*

presence and in the presence of each other, subscribe our names as witnesses and declare we understand this

to be _____ will, and that to the best of our
        his/her

knowledge the testator is of the age of majority, or is otherwise legally empowered to make a will, and under no constraint or undue influence.

We declare under penalty of perjury that the foregoing is true and correct, this _____ day

of _____ , _____ , at
              month   *year*
_____ ,
                       city
_____ , _____ .
          county   *state*

_____
                witness's signature
_____ , residing at
          witness's typed name
_____
                     address
_____ ,
                       city
_____ , _____ .
          county   *state*

_____
witness's signature

_____ , residing at
witness's typed name

_____
address

_____ ,
city

_____ , _____ .
county   _state_

_____
witness's signature

_____ , residing at
witness's typed name

_____
address

_____ ,
city

_____ , _____ .
county   _state_

Making Your Will Legal

Let's focus now on the formal requirements necessary to make your will legal, and where to store it once it's done. Fortunately, the formalities are easy. All you need to do is:

- make sure your will is neatly typed or printed, and
- sign it in front of two, or preferably three, witnesses and then have them sign it. Three witnesses are legally required only in Vermont, but are preferable in any state.

If your will doesn't comply with these requirements—say it was printed but not witnessed—it cannot be validated by the probate court, and your property will pass as if no will existed. It's not hard to prepare a will correctly. But it's absolutely essential that you do so.

Signing and Witnessing Your Will

Now let's look at the proper procedures for signing and witnessing your will.

Signing Your Will

In legalese, signing your will is called "executing" it. You must date the will and sign it, in ink, at its end, in the presence of witnesses. The date is the day, month, and year you sign the will. Your signature should be exactly the same name you used earlier in your will. For example, if you start your will with the name of Elissa T. James, sign it the same way, not in another form, such as "E. T. James" or "Elissa Thelma James."

Be sure you sign your will in the state of your residence. Otherwise, there might be problems regarding use of the correct self-proving affidavit, if you use one. A self-proving affidavit is a document that can make it easier, after your death, to prove to the probate court that your will is genuine.

SEE AN EXPERT

If you can't sign your name, consult a lawyer. In many states, if you're too ill to sign your own name, you can direct that a witness or an attorney sign it for you. In this unusual situation, you should have a lawyer's assistance, especially if substantial amounts of property are involved. Someone might later claim that if you were too ill to sign your name, you weren't mentally competent. In any subsequent court challenge to the will, the lawyer's testimony or other evidence of your competence, including a videotape of you stating that you know you're signing your will, could be very important.

Signing or Initialing Every Page

You aren't legally required to sign or initial every page of your will. However, if you're the cautious type, feel free to do so in the lower right-hand corner. The purpose of initialing every page of a will is to protect against the remote chance that some evildoer will remove a page from your will and substitute a fraudulent page after you die.

Witnessing Your Will

Under the law of every state, your signature on a formal typed or computer-printed will must be witnessed to be valid. This means that your witnesses must watch you sign the will and then sign their names below your signature.

How Many Witnesses to Use

All states require the use of a minimum of two witnesses. If it's feasible, use three. That way, there will be one more person to testify that your signature is valid, should that become necessary during probate.

Who to Select as Your Witnesses

Here are the guidelines you should follow in selecting your witnesses:

Each witness must be a legally competent adult. That means they must be age 18 or older.

Your witnesses must not be beneficiaries (even alternates) of your will. This is important—a witness who is left property in your will may be disqualified from inheriting, or the entire will may even be invalidated.

Relatives and family members who do not receive gifts in your will may be witnesses. Because your children should be left property or be expressly disinherited, you cannot use any of them as witnesses.

If possible, choose witnesses you believe will be easy to locate when you die. This usually means selecting people who know you and who live in your area, don't seem likely to move around a lot, and are younger than you are. Of course, stating this is a lot easier than having confidence it will happen. Obviously, you cannot know now where your witnesses will be when you die, or even if they will be alive. Fortunately, the need to locate witnesses can be largely eliminated by using a "self-proving" affidavit with your will.

Using witnesses who live far away doesn't invalidate your will, but it can make it more difficult for your executor to produce the witnesses in court should this be required as part of probating your estate. If you can keep track of your witnesses without much bother, do so. A record of your witnesses' current addresses would be quite helpful for your executor.

What Your Witnesses Do When You Sign Your Will

When you're ready to sign your will, assemble your witnesses. The witnesses do *not* need to read your will. However, they must all realize that you intend the document to be your will. Sometimes lawyers encourage a ritual dialogue that sounds like something from a Gilbert and Sullivan operetta, but does satisfy the technicalities of the law:

You say: "This is my will."

Your witnesses say (in unison or individually): "He says it's his will."

However you communicate that the document is your will, you then sign and date it. Immediately after that the witnesses sign it, also in ink, with their normal signatures. The witnesses' addresses aren't legally required, but it can be a good idea to list them, for identification and possibly to help locate the witnesses after your death.

An example of a completed will signature clause is in the sample will in Chapter 1.

What Witnesses Do After Your Death

The whole point of having witnesses sign your will is to ensure that someone will be around to prove, in the probate court proceeding after your death, that the document is genuine and that you really signed it.

Your witnesses probably won't have to go to court, however, for several reasons. First, many states have substantially eliminated the requirement that a witness actually appear in court and testify in the probate proceeding, unless a will is contested. Instead, the witnesses just have to sign a written affidavit (sworn statement) and submit it to the probate court.

Second, in most states, you can attach a simple, notarized document called a self-proving affidavit to your will. The probate court should accept it in lieu of testimony from your witnesses. (See below.)

A few states, however, still require witnesses to testify in court. Also, in rare circumstances, such as a lawsuit challenging the validity of a will, the court testimony of your witnesses could be crucial.

"Self-Proving" Wills: Using a Notary Public

In no state does a will legally have to be notarized (except in Louisiana, where this book doesn't apply and shouldn't be used).

However, in most states you can most likely simplify the probate process if you and your witnesses sign a simple statement, called an affidavit, in front of a notary public. The affidavit declares that the document presented is your will and that it was properly executed (signed and witnessed). This affidavit, sometimes called a self-proving affidavit, is then attached to your will. This whole process is called creating a "self-proving" will.

Making a will self-proving has absolutely nothing to do with your will's legality. The reason for a self-proving will is to eliminate any need for witnesses to appear at a routine probate proceeding after your death. (If the proceeding is contested, which is very rare, witnesses may have to appear anyway.) Obviously, a self-proving will is crucial if none of your witnesses can be located. So using a self-proving affidavit frees you from trying to keep track of where your witnesses live or, more commonly, worrying about not keeping track of them. In this mobile society, not having to bother with where your witnesses live can be quite a relief.

TIP

Use the notary's affidavit. The notary public may have your state's standard form for making your will self-proving. If so, use that form. If not, use the correct form from this book.

If you want to make your will self-proving, take the following steps:

1. Either arrange to have a notary present when you and your witnesses are going to sign the will, or find one later. Either way, you and all your witnesses must personally appear before the notary and be prepared to identify yourselves. Finding a notary shouldn't be a problem—you can find a local notary online or through the Yellow Pages. Or check with your bank, which may provide notarizations as a service to customers. Real estate offices and title companies also have notaries.

2. Tell the notary that you want to make your will self-proving and ask whether he or she has a form for doing that. If so, use that form and follow the notary's instructions.

3. If the notary doesn't have a form, use one of the four affidavits provided in Appendix B. (The table below tells you which one is correct for your state.) The forms are available on the CD-ROM and as tear-outs. If you use a tear-out, you'll need to retype it, deleting all extraneous material on the book's form—that is, the form's title ("Self-Proving Affidavit") and the page footer (for example, "Affidavit Form 1" and the Nolo icon).

4. Put your name and your witnesses' names in the spaces indicated in the affidavit, and give it to the notary. After you and your witnesses swear to the truth of the statement in the affidavit (basically the same statements you made when the will itself was signed and witnessed), the notary will date and sign the affidavit and put a notarial seal on it.

5. Staple the affidavit to your will. If you ever make a new will or codicil, you should also redo your affidavit.

CD-ROM

Using the CD-ROM. The files for the three self-proving affidavits are included on the Forms CD-ROM. See the table above to see which form you should use.

REMINDER

Reminder. The affidavit and will are two separate documents. You and your witnesses must sign both of them.

Which Self-Proving Affidavit Form to Use					
If you live in:	Use Tear-Out Form:	CD-ROM Form:	If you live in:	Use Tear-Out Form:	CD-ROM Form:
Alabama	1	SP_AFF1	Missouri	2	SP_AFF2
Alaska	1	SP_AFF1	Montana	1	SP_AFF1
Arizona	1	SP_AFF1	Nebraska	1	SP_AFF1
Arkansas	1	SP_AFF1	Nevada	1	SP_AFF1
California	None. The witnesses' declaration in the will is enough; you don't need a separate affidavit.		New Hampshire	See a lawyer for the precise wording of the affidavit.	
Colorado	1	SP_AFF1	New Jersey	2	SP_AFF2
Connecticut	1	SP_AFF1	New Mexico	1	SP_AFF1
Delaware	2	SP_AFF2	New York	1	SP_AFF1
District of Columbia	Does not accept self-proving affidavits.		New Jersey	2	SP_AFF2
Florida	2	SP_AFF2	North Dakota	1	SP_AFF1
Georgia	2	SP_AFF2	Ohio	Does not accept self-proving affidavits.	
Hawaii	1	SP_AFF1	Oklahoma	2	SP_AFF2
Idaho	1	SP_AFF1	Oregon	1	SP_AFF1
Illinois	1	SP_AFF1	Pennsylvania	Pennsylvania	SP_PENN
Indiana	1	SP_AFF1	Rhode Island	2	SP_AFF2
Iowa	2	SP_AFF2	South Dakota	1	SP_AFF1
Kansas	2	SP_AFF2	Tennessee	1	SP_AFF1
Kentucky	2	SP_AFF2	Texas	Texas	SP_TEXAS
Maine	1	SP_AFF1	Utah	2	SP_AFF2
Maryland	Does not accept self-proving affidavits.		Virginia	1	SP_AFF1
Massachusetts	2	SP_AFF2	Washington	1	SP_AFF1
Michigan	1	SP_AFF1	West Virginia	1	SP_AFF1
Minnesota	1	SP_AFF1	Wisconsin	1	SP_AFF1
Mississippi	1	SP_AFF1	Wyoming	2	SP_AFF2

After Your Will Is Completed

After your will has been typed or printed, double-checked, then signed and witnessed (in front of a notary if you want it to be self-proving), you're done. Congratulations! You've completed an important job.

For some, a party celebrating the completion of the will can be fun. Why not gather those you love, break out some good brandy (or soda, if you prefer), reveal as much (or as little) of your will as you want to, and enjoy?

Your next concern is normally where to keep your will and, perhaps, who should get copies of it. Here are some ideas.

Storing Your Will

After you've prepared a valid will, what do you do with it? Your main goal should be that, upon your death, the right people—at a minimum, your executor and preferably at least one other person whom you trust—know that your will exists and how to get it.

Keep your will in a safe, accessible location. There's no one best place. It can be stored in a safe deposit box if you're sure your executor will have access to it after your death. (Check with your bank.) In a number of states, safe deposit boxes of a person who died (even those owned in joint tenancy) are "sealed" under state law until taxing authorities make an inventory or release a tax lien, and aren't instantly accessible by your executor. If a safe deposit box might cause problems, you can store the will in a safe place in your home or office, such as a fireproof box.

 CAUTION

Don't lose your will. Do your best to make sure that your will does not get lost or misplaced. If you discover it has been lost or misplaced, make a new will. You or your executor cannot use a photocopy of your will to serve as a valid original. Only the document you and your witnesses signed is your legal will.

 RESOURCE

Getting organized. Despite good intentions, it's sometimes hard to find a will at death, and even harder to find other important documents such as bank books and insurance policies. You can save grieving loved ones the hassles of searching for your will and other important papers by maintaining one clear record of all your important documents. To help you accomplish this, Nolo offers *Get It Together: Organize Your Records So Your Family Won't Have To*, by Melanie Cullen with Shae Irving. This workbook with CD-ROM provides a complete system you can use to organize important legal, financial, and personal information.

Making Copies

Some people wonder if it's sensible to prepare more than one separately typed, signed, and executed original of their will in case one is lost or somehow inaccessible. I strongly advise against it.

If you later decided to change your will by adding a codicil (see Chapter 13), you would have to change every original. Likewise, if you wanted to revoke your will (see Chapter 13), you'd have to locate and revoke each original. Tracking down all original versions of your will could be quite a burden. Worse, you might forget one or more of the duplicate original wills, and wind up changing or revoking some but not others, thus creating a confusing mess and potentially a legal disaster.

That said, it can be a good idea to make several *unsigned* copies of your will. You may want to give one to your executor or to loved ones, so they know your plans. To share your will, make multiple copies after you've finalized the document but before you sign it and have it witnessed. You may want to keep an unsigned copy yourself. If you need more copies later, you can simply photocopy the unsigned will.

On the other hand, you may not want to reveal its contents to anyone. Giving loved ones a copy of your unsigned will may be a good idea if all is peace and harmony, but there are sometimes lots of practical reasons not to. In any case, whether or how much to reveal your will is a purely personal decision, not a legal one. ●

Changing or Revoking Your Will

Once you've prepared your will using *Nolo's Simple Will Book*, it's extremely important that you not alter it by inserting handwritten or typed additions or changes. You cannot simply cross out something in your will or write in a change. Doing so may invalidate your entire will.

By law, to change your will, you must either:

- make a new signed and witnessed will, or
- add a signed and witnessed addition, called a codicil, to the existing one.

To revoke a will, you should make a written declaration that you intend to revoke the old will. The wills in this book contain a statement revoking all prior wills.

Revising Your Will or Revoking It

It may sound simpler and easier to make a codicil and just add it to your original will than make a whole new will. But some of the work required is the same in either case. A codicil must be signed in front of witnesses, just as your original will was, and a new will must be, too. Whether to use a codicil or new will for changes depends first on whether you've made your will with a computer or a typewriter, and, for typed wills, on the extent of the changes.

The Work Required

If you prepared your will on a computer, it should be just as easy to prepare a new will as to prepare a codicil. The obvious advantage of using a computer is that you don't have to retype the document to make a change. You can simply make all the changes you want, leave the rest of the document as is, and print out your new will.

If you prepared a typewritten will, changes are often easier to make by codicil, so you don't have to retype your entire will. Whether it's advisable to use a codicil or create a new will depends on how much you want to change.

How Extensive Your Changes Are

Although there's no blanket rule covering when you should make a new typed will, or when a codicil suffices, here's a general guideline: Simple changes, such as a change of one beneficiary, the addition of one gift, or a change in an executor, can be accomplished by codicil. More extensive changes generally require revoking your existing will and creating a new one.

For example, suppose one of your beneficiaries dies. If you now want the alternate beneficiary to receive the gift, you could amend your will by codicil, naming the former alternate as the primary beneficiary and naming a new alternate. Here are some more examples of changes that can usually be taken care of in codicils:

- **You want to change your nomination for someone you named to care for your children or a child's property.** This includes a child's personal guardian or alternate personal guardian; a custodian or alternate custodian for any gifts under the Uniform Transfers to Minors Act; trustees or successor trustees for any child's trust created in your will; and a child's property guardian or alternate property guardian.

- **You want to name a different executor.** As you know, the executor of your estate is charged with making sure your wishes are faithfully complied with. You may discover that the person or institution you originally named would really not be the best person for this task. For example, if you originally named your spouse, who has subsequently become seriously ill, you may want to substitute one of your children.

But if you want a major revision of the will, don't use a codicil. A will that has been substantially rewritten by a codicil (or more than one) is likely to be confusing and awkward to read at best. At worst, there may be ambiguity or even conflict between the codicil and the original will. Definitely consider making a new will if:

- **You change your mind about who you want to inherit a significant portion of your property.**

- **You're married and move from a community property state to a common law property state, or vice versa.** For a list of which states fall into which category, see Chapter 3. Community property and common law property states view the ownership of property by married couples differently. This means that what both you and your spouse own may change if you move from one type of state to the other. Of course, if you plan to leave all or the bulk of your property to your spouse, this change is immaterial to you. Likewise, if you move from one common law state to another in the same category, it's not necessary to change your will. But do check the rules if you move from one community property state to another.

- **You marry or divorce.** If you don't make a new will, your new spouse will be entitled to claim a share of your property, which may not be what you wish. And a divorce may not automatically revoke an existing will as regards an ex-spouse.

- **One of your children dies, leaving children of his or her own.** These children (your grandchildren) may be entitled to claim a share of your estate (in some states) unless they receive property under the will or you've specifically disinherited them. (See Chapter 5.)

- **The property you left in your will expands or shrinks substantially.** Review your will to make sure it realistically reflects your current situation. This is especially true if you acquire or sell real estate or expensive personal property.

Making Simple Changes in Your Will by Codicil

In a codicil, you can revoke a clause in the will and then substitute a new clause. Or you can simply add a new provision, such as a new gift of an item of property.

EXAMPLE 1:

Since Alex wrote his will ten years ago, his brother Jim has lost interest in music. Alex now wants to leave the player piano he'd left to Jim to Jim's son, Fred. Here is the codicil Alex types and signs:

"First: I revoke the provision of Clause 4, Specific Gifts, of my will that left my player piano to my brother, Jim Sincowitz.
"Second: I add the following provision to Clause 4 of my will: I leave my player piano to my nephew, Fred Sincowitz."

EXAMPLE 2:

Consuela buys a new gold necklace that she wants to leave to her favorite niece, Maria. She executes the following codicil:

"I add the following provision to Clause 4, Specific Gifts, of my will:
"I leave my gold necklace to my niece, Maria Wallace, or, if she fails to survive me by 45 days, to Tom Wallace."

EXAMPLE 3:

Tsui has a falling-out with his executor, Raymond. So Tsui replaces him with the former alternate executor, and names a new person for that role. Tsui's codicil reads:

"First: I revoke the provisions of Section 7, Executor, of my will nominating Raymond Wong as my executor and Lau Ching Leong as my alternate executor.

"Second: I add the following provision to Section 7, Executor, of my will:

"A. Nomination of Executor. I nominate Lau Ching Leong as executor, to serve without bond. If he shall for any reason fail to qualify or cease to act as executor, I nominate Mary Kam as executor, also to serve without bond."

A codicil, being a sort of legal "P.S." to the will, must be executed with all of the formalities of a will. (See Chapter 12.) It must be typewritten, not handwritten, and it must be dated and signed by you in front of at least two witnesses. You don't have to use the same witnesses who signed your will, but you can. As with your original witnesses, your codicil witnesses must not be named as any type of beneficiaries in your will.

If you used a self-proving affidavit for your will, you must prepare a new affidavit for your codicil, following the instructions in Chapter 12. Be sure the completed, notarized self-proving affidavit is attached to the completed codicil.

The codicil doesn't have to be made part of the signature page of the original will. It must, however, refer to that will. This can be simply accomplished by labeling the codicil "First Codicil of the Will of [your name], dated [giving date will was originally prepared]."

A fill-in-the-blanks codicil form you can use or adapt is in Appendix B. It is also available on the CD-ROM included with this book.

To prepare a codicil, fill in the blanks and add whatever other information you need. Cross out all instructions and delete any unused language. Then have the codicil form typed or printed out for you and your witnesses' signatures.

! **CAUTION**

Number codicils correctly. The codicil form states that it is the first codicil of your will. If you are making a second or subsequent codicil, replace "first" with the correct number.

Be sure anyone with an unsigned copy of your will also receives an unsigned copy of the codicil. This may be a nuisance, but it can prevent confusion, or even conflict, later.

Revoking Your Will

Anyone who writes a will should understand how it can be revoked. There are only two reliable ways: in writing or by operation of law.

Written Revocation

If you want to revoke a prior will, you should do so by making an express written statement in your new will. All wills prepared with this book include a clause that revokes all prior wills.

If you later revoke the new will, the old one won't be revived unless the revocation states that this is what you want, or you "republish" the first will by signing it in front of witnesses again.

EXAMPLE:

Marguerite makes a will and then later makes a second will expressly revoking the first one. If Marguerite tears up the second will, the first one doesn't become valid again.

Tearing Up Your Will

In many states, a will (or codicil) can be revoked by being "burnt, torn, concealed, defaced, obliterated, or destroyed," if you intended to revoke it. You can also direct someone else to destroy the will to accomplish revocation. The problem with destroying a will, or having someone else do so, is that it revokes the will only if you intend it to. After your death this can become a matter of controversy, especially if you've distributed copies of your original will. So, if you want the satisfaction of destroying a revoked will, go right ahead, but be sure you've also revoked it in writing. This is the only good way to make your intention clear.

Revocation of a Will by Law

Your will, or parts of it, can be revoked if your spouse or children are entitled to claim more of your estate than you left them. In common law states, a spouse has a statutory right to claim a certain percentage of the other spouse's estate, unless that right has been waived in writing. (See Chapter 3.) Children not mentioned in a will may also have statutory rights to a part of a parent's estate. (See Chapter 5.)

If, after your death, your spouse or children do make a successful claim for more of your property, the provisions in your will that concerned your spouse or the children are revoked. Other provisions aren't affected—although the effects of giving more property than you intended to

a spouse or child will obviously send ripples all through your estate plan.

With a will drafted from this book, you shouldn't have to concern yourself with this. If you followed instructions, you've suitably provided for your spouse and mentioned all your children in your will, and have either left something to each of your children or expressly disinherited them.

> ! **CAUTION**
>
> **Make a new will after a divorce.** In several states, a final judgment of divorce (or annulment) has no effect on any gift made by your will to your former spouse; in other states it revokes such a gift. And in a few others, divorce revokes the entire will. Therefore, after a divorce make a new will.

Estate Planning

M aking a will is the first estate planning step that everyone should take. For many people, it's the only one they need. Whether or not that's true for you depends on your unique life circumstances: your age, finances, family situation, and your desire to plan for the future.

Basically, estate planning is concerned with avoiding probate and reducing estate taxes. It can also involve other personal concerns, such as:

- providing for a child with a disability
- establishing a scholarship fund for grandchildren
- handling potential inheritance conflicts when one has children from a prior marriage
- making charitable gifts, or
- planning for what will happen if you ever become incapacitated and unable to handle your own medical or financial affairs.

The more an estate is worth, the more important estate planning becomes. If you have relatively little property (say less than $100,000), a will handles your major estate planning concerns, because your estate won't be subject to federal estate tax or substantial probate fees.

If you expect to leave an estate worth more than $100,000, you might consider the pros and cons of probate court (required for most wills), and probate avoidance. Are the savings to your inheritors worth the time, effort, and possible costs of probate avoidance? Is a will sufficient for your needs now, with probate avoidance to be considered (much) later?

People with large estates, over $2 million, will probably want to both make a will and consider whether they should plan to reduce possible estate taxes.

This chapter summarizes common techniques used for probate avoidance and estate tax reduction and discusses how trusts can be used to handle personal problems. It also discusses planning for

incapacity and making final arrangements. This overview of basic estate planning methods should help you decide whether you want to investigate the matter further.

RESOURCE

More information about estate planning. A good source of in-depth estate planning information (I say modestly) is *Plan Your Estate*, by Denis Clifford and Cora Jordan (Nolo). That book treats estate planning questions thoroughly, and I believe that anyone with even a moderate-sized estate will benefit from reading it.

Here at the start, I want to assure you that extensive estate planning is certainly not mandatory. (I mean "mandatory" if you want to be considered a prudent adult.) Experience has taught me that many, many people need no more than a will. To remind you, a will achieves the essential goals of distributing your property as you want and providing for care of your minor children, if you have any.

Probate

Property left by a will must go through probate, the legal process that includes filing a deceased person's will with a court, locating and gathering the assets, paying off debts and taxes, and (eventually) distributing what's left as the will directs. Many states exempt small estates from normal probate procedures (discussed below).

Drawbacks of Probate

Probate has drawbacks. The probate process often takes six months to a year, and sometimes even longer. Further, probate normally requires lawyers, which automatically means attorneys' fees. Indeed, the executor and the attorney are both paid from the estate property. Either by law or custom, in a number of states the fees of the attorney who guides your estate through the probate court are a percentage of the probate estate's value. Moreover, in a few states the fees are computed from the estate's total gross market value, not the net estate.

California is one of those states. So, if Harry dies with a gross estate—that is, the total value of everything he owns, without subtracting any debts owed on the property—of $500,000, the attorney's fee under the state statute would be $13,000. The fee is based on the $500,000 figure, even if Harry's house has a $200,000 mortgage on it, so his real (net) estate totals $300,000. If Harry's will left everything to his children, and one of them acts as executor and probated the estate without an attorney, the process could be accomplished through the mail for approximately $650.

RESOURCE

Specialized help for executors of Californian estates. *How to Probate an Estate in California,* by Julia Nissley (Nolo) gives executors of estates in California step-by-step instructions for probating an estate without a lawyer. Executors in other states may also find this book helpful to gain a general understanding of the probate process.

Reducing Probate Fees

It is both legal and safe to avoid probate. Clearly, where probate fees are based on the size of the probate estate, you can reduce the fees by reducing the probate estate's worth. One approach to reducing probate fees is to transfer big-ticket items—for example, your house and stock portfolio—outside of probate, and transfer only the less valuable items by your will.

Probate fees can also be reduced if the attorney who handles the work agrees to take less than the conventional fee. State statutory or court fee schedules aren't mandatory—no matter what a lawyer may indicate.

The executor of the will is legally responsible for selecting the probate attorney. The will writer cannot legally hire the probate attorney, because the attorney must be responsible to a living person, not a deceased one. So, practically, it's up to the executor to negotiate a reasonable fee agreement with a probate attorney.

Why Wills Are Necessary

Before discussing the principal probate avoidance devices, let's deal with an obvious question: "If a will puts property into the probate system and this results in delays and attorney fees, why have a will at all if there are good alternatives?" I believe you should always have a will, no matter what other estate planning devices you use. Here are several good reasons:

- A will is an easy way to make a quick estate plan that can be refined later on, as you get older and (presumably) acquire more property. Probate avoidance techniques pay dividends in the form of saving on probate fees, but only at your death. In the meantime, unfortunately, some of them involve at least some paperwork (such as living trusts), and others actually require you to give up control over some or all of your property (for example, making gifts or transferring property into joint tenancy). Accordingly, many younger people decide to rely primarily on a will to dispose of their property should they die unexpectedly and wait to make a probate-avoiding estate plan until they're older—often in their 50s, or even 60s.

- Wills are usually the most effective and practical device for transferring some types of property, such as personal checking accounts or vehicles.

- In a will you can achieve the vital goal of naming a personal guardian for your minor children.

- A will enables you to appoint a property guardian for any property your minor children acquire that doesn't come with a built-in adult supervisor.

- Even if you leave your existing property by some other device than a will, you may end up acquiring valuable property shortly before death, ranging from a sudden inheritance to winning a lottery. You must take specific actions to transfer newly acquired property by devices other than a will. In contrast, with a will, newly acquired property will go to your residuary beneficiary without any further action on your part. Hence, a will is a necessary backup for other estate planning devices.

- Many states allow estates worth less than a certain amount (ranging from $500 to $200,000, depending on the state) to be left by will either free of probate or subject only to a simpler probate process. The details vary significantly from state to state. A few states also simplify or eliminate probate for property left by one spouse to the other.

RESOURCE

More information on small estates. Each state's "small estate" law is outlined in *Plan Your Estate*, by Denis Clifford and Cora Jordan, *8 Ways to Avoid Probate*, by Mary Randolph, and *The Executor's Guide: Settling a Loved One's Estate or Trust*, by Mary Randolph, all published by Nolo.

Probate Avoidance Methods

Here's a brief review of the principal probate avoidance methods.

Living Trusts

A revocable living trust is justifiably the most popular probate avoidance device. Under a living trust ("inter vivos" in Latin, for "among the living"), title to property is transferred by its living owner (called a "grantor") to a trust created by a document (in legalese, a "trust instrument"). A "trustee," normally the same person who created the trust, manages the trust property. A trusted person is named as "successor trustee" to take over trust management when the grantor/trustee dies. The trust "beneficiaries" are named by the person who sets up the trust. When the grantor/trustee dies, the successor trustee transfers trust property to these beneficiaries, free of probate.

A revocable living trust allows you, as the grantor, to retain full control over your property before you die. You do this by naming yourself as the initial trustee, retaining full rights to use of and income from all trust property until you die. You also keep the right to sell or give away trust property. And you can revoke the trust at any time, for any (or no) reason.

EXAMPLE:

James wants to leave his valuable painting collection to his son Bill, but wants total control over it until he dies. He doesn't want the value of his collection, $800,000, included in his probate estate. So he establishes a revocable living trust and transfers ownership of the paintings to the trust. James names himself as trustee while he lives, and his younger brother Ed to be successor trustee, to act after James's death. James names his son as the trust beneficiary.

When James dies, the successor trustee, Ed, will transfer the paintings to Bill outside of probate. However, should James want to sell a painting, or all the paintings, before he dies, he can do so at any time. Similarly, if James subsequently decides he wants to leave the paintings to a museum, he can readily change the trust's beneficiary to provide for that.

The only real drawback of a living trust as an estate planning device is that certain formalities are required. A formal trust document must be prepared. If property has a document of legal title (such as a house deed or stock account form), it must be actually transferred to the trustee's name.

For example, if you put your house in a living trust, you must properly execute and record a deed transferring ownership to the trustee. However, as long as you remain the trustee, no trust income tax returns are required, and separate trust records don't have to be maintained.

RESOURCE

How to create your own trust. Living trusts are explained in depth in *Make Your Own Living Trust,* by Denis Clifford (Nolo), which contains basic living trust forms and thorough instructions for how to prepare one. You can also prepare a living trust with *Quicken WillMaker Plus* (software for Windows from Nolo).

Using a "Pour-Over" Will

A "pour-over" will is one which directs that the property subject to it go to (be "poured over" into) another legal entity, often a living trust. In other words, a person's living trust is the beneficiary of the will. After the will property is poured into the living trust, it is distributed as the trust directs.

In my opinion, there's rarely a sensible reason to use a pour-over will. The purpose of using a living trust is to avoid probate. Using a pour-over will ensures that some property that will eventually wind up in the trust must go through probate first. This can be desirable, though, in a few situations. For instance, if you create a family pot trust or child's trust as part of a living trust, you may want to pour over any will property to the trust, to have that property become part of that trust.

It's my impression that some lawyers push pour-over wills because they not only sound sophisticated, but also ensure that some probate attorney fees can be collected.

Finally, don't confuse pour-over wills with "back-up" wills. Every estate plan should include a will, at least as a backup, to cover any property that isn't transferred by other devices.

Pay-on-Death Bank Accounts

Pay-on-death bank accounts (sometimes called "Totten trusts") are a very simple way to avoid probate. You open a bank account—for example, savings, certificate of deposit, or money market—in your name and add a designation naming a pay-on-death (P.O.D.) beneficiary. You keep complete and exclusive control over the money in the account until your death, at which point any money left in the account belongs to the named beneficiary without any necessity for probate. If all the money has been withdrawn, the beneficiary gets nothing. If you want to establish this type of account, visit your bank and complete the appropriate forms. They're simple.

TIP

Personal checking accounts. While you can set up a pay-on-death designation for your checking account, those accounts often contain relatively small amounts of money, used to pay monthly bills. So a pay-on-death arrangement for a checking account may not be worth the minor hassle required to create it, in contrast to a bank account where you maintain substantial funds.

CAUTION

Check pay-on-death account rules. A few states, generally ones with state estate taxes, impose barriers and hassles on collecting a pay-on-death account after the depositor dies. For example, Ohio requires that a state tax lien form be filled out before any cash is released to the beneficiary. Ask at your bank if there are any special rules before deciding to create a pay-on-death account.

Joint Tenancy and Tenancy by the Entirety

Joint tenancy is a form of shared property ownership that avoids probate. When one coowner dies, the surviving owner(s) automatically inherit his or her interest, through a "right of survivorship." In many states, there is a special form of joint tenancy for married couples, called tenancy by the entirety. (For a married couple to hold property in tenancy by the entirety, a certificate of title for the property—normally, a real estate deed—must specify that it is held in tenancy by the entirety. When one spouse dies, the entire interest in the property belongs automatically to the surviving spouse.)

States That Allow Tenancy by the Entirety

* Alaska	Missouri
Arkansas	New Jersey
Connecticut	* New York
Delaware	* North Carolina
District of Columbia	** Ohio
Florida	Oklahoma
Hawaii	* Oregon
* Illinois	Pennsylvania
* Indiana	Rhode Island
* Kentucky	Tennessee
Maryland	Utah
Massachusetts	Vermont
Michigan	Virginia
Mississippi	Wyoming

*Allows tenancy by the entirety only for real estate.

**Only if created before 4/4/85.

Joint tenancy can be a useful probate-avoidance device for people who buy property together, if each is sure they want their share of the property to go to the other owner(s) when they die. If you want to leave your share to anyone else, joint tenancy is not for you.

Transferring your solely owned property into joint tenancy, with the intention that the property will be transferred outside of probate when you die, is generally a bad idea. You have no control over the new joint tenant's share of the property. The new joint tenant can sell his interest in the property or pledge it as security for a loan. Also, this interest can be foreclosed on by creditors of the new joint tenant. Further, federal gift taxes are assessed if you transfer property worth more than $12,000 to a new joint tenant in one year. Finally, complicated federal tax basis rules (which determine taxable profit when property is eventually sold) make transfers of property that has appreciated in value into joint tenancy undesirable.

By contrast, a revocable living trust is a far better probate-avoidance method for solely owned property. The beneficiaries of a living trust have no rights to your property while you live, and you can change the beneficiary or end the trust at any time. In addition, the federal basis rules have no negative impact on appreciated property transferred to inheritors by a living trust.

Both real estate and personal property (everything else) can be held in joint tenancy, as long as there is a written document to that effect. Joint tenancy bank accounts, for example, require a written form signed by the joint tenants. Likewise, automobiles, securities, and business interests can be held in joint tenancy by appropriate registration on the ownership documents.

Naming a Beneficiary for Stocks and Bonds

In all states except New York, North Carolina, and Texas, you can add a pay-on-death designation to individual securities (stocks and bonds) or broker accounts under the Uniform Transfer-on-Death Securities Registration Act. Your broker should have a form to allow you to use transfer-on-death registration for a securities account. For individual stock or bond certificates, contact the company's transfer agent.

Transfer-on-Death Deeds for Real Estate

In some states, you can prepare and record a deed now that takes effect to transfer that real estate only when you die. The states that allow transfer-on-death real estate deeds are Arizona, Arkansas, Colorado, Kansas, Missouri, New Mexico, Nevada, Ohio, and Wisconsin.

Real estate transferred this way does not go through probate. The deed must be prepared, signed, notarized, and recorded just like a regular deed. The deed should expressly state that it does not take effect until your death. Unlike a regular deed, you can revoke a transfer-on-death deed at any time during your life—for example, if you want to sell the property or name a new beneficiary to receive it after your death.

> **CAUTION**
>
> **Don't try this unless you know your state law authorizes it.** You cannot use a deed to transfer real estate at your death unless your state law (or the state law where the real estate is located) specifically allows it.

Transfer-on-Death Vehicle Registration

Only a few states currently allow this sensible form of vehicle registration: California, Connecticut, Kansas, Missouri, and Ohio. In these states, if the registration shows a transfer-on-death beneficiary, the vehicle does not need to go through probate. Contact your local department of motor vehicles office to learn more.

Making Gifts While You're Alive

As you know by now, the word "gifts," as used so far in this book, means property left by a will. However, it has another common meaning, which is any property transferred freely, without commercial intent, from a living person. It's this meaning of the word "gifts" that is discussed here.

Property given away before death is, obviously, not part of the probate estate of the giver. For property to be considered a valid legal gift, you must actually surrender ownership and control of the property while you are living. (Tax consequences of gifts are discussed below.)

Life Insurance

Life insurance benefits paid on your death rarely go through probate. When you name a beneficiary in your life insurance policy, the proceeds of the policy pass under the terms of the policy rather than under the terms of your will; they don't go through probate. However, if for some reason you designate your estate (as opposed to a person or institution) as the beneficiary of the policy, the proceeds would be part of your probate estate. This is rarely done.

401(k)s, IRAs, and Other Retirement Plans

Many retirement plans, including 401(k) plans and IRAs, allow you to name a beneficiary, or any number of them, to receive any funds remaining in the plan when you die. The beneficiary receives any such funds directly, outside of probate.

Debts and Taxes

Transferring some, or all, of your property outside of probate can raise questions about how any debts and estate taxes are to be paid. If your estate is likely to be liable for taxes, or if you have serious debts, you should consider what assets you want used to pay those debts and taxes. With a will from Chapter 11, you can designate certain assets to be used, or specify that all your property, whether transferred by will or otherwise, is proportionally liable for any debts and taxes your estate owes.

Estate Taxes

When you die, your estate may be subject to federal estate tax. However, federal law provides substantial exemptions from that tax, so that most estates don't owe anything. All estates worth under $2 million (net) are exempt for deaths that occur in 2007 and 2008. This exemption rises to $3.5 million by 2009. (See the chart below for exact exemption amounts.)

Your estate may also owe inheritance tax, if the state where you live imposes it and the value of your estate is over any applicable state exemptions.

The combined net worth of all your property determines the value of your taxable estate. This includes property transferred by your will and also property passed outside of probate, including property held in joint tenancy, a living trust, retirement accounts such as IRAs or 401(k) plans, a pay-on-death bank or stock account, and the full dollar value of all insurance paid from a life insurance policy you owned. Only if you actually give property away before death do the taxing authorities consider it outside your taxable estate. However, large gifts made during your lifetime are subject to federal gift taxes, which are basically the same as estate taxes. So giving property away

doesn't reduce your tax liability, with one major exception: currently you may give away $12,000 per person per year free of gift tax.

One goal of sophisticated estate planning is to reduce estate taxes. For those with estates worth less than the estate tax exemption (discussed below), there are only a few possible means to reduce taxes, which are discussed here. If your estate is larger, you'll be wise to invest a few of those dollars in a consultation with a tax attorney, accountant, or both.

Should You Worry About Estate Tax?

Before concerning yourself with reducing death taxes, be sure you need to bother with the matter at all.

As mentioned in Chapter 1, the federal estate tax may be permanently repealed. Congress may well make permanent the estate tax law changes introduced in 2001. Under the 2001 law, the amount of the personal estate tax exemption will rise from $2 million to $3.5 million in 2009. The tax is repealed entirely for 2010.

However, under current law, the estate tax is scheduled to return, with an exemption of $1 million, in 2011. The chart below sets out the estate tax exemptions by year.

Year	Estate tax exemption	Gift tax exemption	Highest estate and gift tax rate
2007	$2 million	$1 million	45%
2008	$2 million	$1 million	45%
2009	$3.5 million	$1 million	45%
2010	Estate tax repealed	$1 million	Top individual income tax rate (gift tax only)
2011	$1 million	$1 million	55%

Planning Difficulties Under the Estate Tax Law

The uncertain future of the estate tax for 2010 and thereafter means that tax planning for wealthy couples may not be easy over the next few years. Indeed, currently, expert estate planners are not certain about how to engage in long-term estate tax planning. The consensus is—for now—do nothing new or different. Though the amounts of the personal estate tax exemption will continue to rise until 2009, the estate tax game otherwise remains the same as it has been up to now. As we get closer to 2010, however, the game will likely change entirely and many revised plans will be prepared.

If your estate is under $1 million, you can safely continue with your existing plan, or use current planning devices such as the AB trust, discussed below. If you are wealthier, you can continue with your existing plan, or current planning devices, but you'll need to keep up on estate tax law changes. And, you'll need to see an estate planning expert as we get closer to 2010.

CAUTION

Check the current estate tax laws. If you have a large estate, you should keep up with any estate tax law changes. It's not clear, as of the printing of this book, what all the details of the estate tax repeal will be. After any new law is passed and adopted, you can find details on Nolo's website: www.nolo.com.

Because, except for the year 2010, the amount of the personal exemption depends on the year of death, no one dollar figure can define the amount of an estate that can be transferred tax free under this exemption. So I use the term "estate tax threshold" to mean the amount of the personal exemption in any and all years. Thus "estate tax threshold" refers to the exemption and the range of exempt amounts, ranging from $2 million to $3.5 million.

All property left to a surviving spouse who is a U.S. citizen is exempt from federal tax.

So, in general, if you expect your net estate to be under the estate tax threshold, and you haven't already made large gifts (more than $12,000 per person per year), you don't need to worry about how to reduce federal taxes.

If, on the other hand, your estate alone—or the combined value of your own and your spouse's estate, if you're leaving most of your property to each other—is likely to be larger than the estate tax threshold, then you may want to explore ways to reduce your taxes. Or you could just assume, or hope, that you—and your spouse if you have one—will live to at least 2010, and ignore estate tax planning (except to check that the "permanent" repeal stays permanent over the years).

Certain types of property do not have to be valued at their "best use" market value for federal estate tax purposes. These include family farmland and wooded land. Also, an estate can have up to 14 years to pay off estate taxes on a closely held business if the value of your interest in it exceeds 35% of the value of your estate. If you have any of these kinds of property and a net worth near or over $1 million, it could be wise to see an estate planner.

Estate Taxes and Foreign Citizens

If your spouse is not a U.S. citizen, you still have your personal estate tax exemption. It applies to property left to anyone, including your spouse.

If you leave property worth more than the amount of the personal exemption for the year of your death to your noncitizen spouse, property over that amount will be taxed when you die, unless you establish a type of trust authorized by federal law, called a "QDOT trust." It allows you to defer payment of estate taxes until your spouse's death. See a lawyer about drafting such a trust.

If you are a foreign citizen who has legal residence in the U.S., you can leave property worth up to the amount of the estate tax threshold without liability for federal estate tax. However, property in foreign countries—or property left to foreign, non-U.S. resident beneficiaries—is subject to the law of the foreign country or countries involved.

State Inheritance and Estate Taxes

There are two types of state taxes that may be imposed on the property you leave: inheritance tax and state estate tax.

Inheritance tax. Just a handful of states impose a traditional "inheritance tax" on property left by a deceased person. These states are Connecticut (being phased out by 2008), Indiana, Iowa, Kentucky, Maryland, Nebraska, New Jersey, Ohio, Oklahoma, Pennsylvania, and Tennessee.

State estate tax. Many states have adopted a new type of estate tax that is different from the traditional inheritance tax. This new estate tax is a "pick-up tax" replacement. See "State Estate Taxes" in Chapter 8.

SEE AN EXPERT

Learning your state's inheritance and estate tax rules. Inheritance tax rules for the states that impose them are summarized in *Plan Your Estate*, by Denis Clifford and Cora Jordan (Nolo). State estate tax rules are a bit trickier to pin down. The good news is that, even if it applies to you, a state estate tax amount will be minor. But if you are affluent and concerned about new state tax laws, see a lawyer who can bring you up to date.

Reducing Federal Estate Taxes

Let's now turn to some of the methods that have been most commonly used to reduce federal estate taxes.

Gifts

One way to reduce the size of your estate and save on federal estate taxes is to give away some of your property while you're still alive. Currently, you may give $12,000 per year, per recipient, free of gift taxes. Your spouse may do the same. For example, if a couple has three children, they could each give $12,000 to each child each year, thus transferring $24,000 free of federal gift tax per child; they could remove a total of $72,000 per year from their estate. In ten years, $720,000 could be transferred in this way, tax free. This would probably result in saving an even larger sum, because of the interest and dividends this money earns, which would have ended up in the parents' estate. With a gift, the interest and dividends are instead earned by the people to whom you give the money, who may well be in a lower income tax bracket. (Unearned income over $750 per year that is received by a child under 18 is taxed at the highest of the parents' income tax rate.)

Other gifts are also tax exempt:

- amounts paid directly for someone's educational or medical costs
- gifts to tax-exempt charities

• gifts to your spouse who is a U.S. citizen. (You can give a noncitizen spouse up to $125,000 per year free of tax.)

One kind of property that can be suitable as a gift is a life insurance policy. The proceeds from life insurance are included in your taxable estate if you owned the policy at your death. If the policy has a large death benefit—say, hundreds of thousands of dollars—inclusion of that sum in the taxable estate can result in substantial federal estate taxes. The taxes attributable to the insurance proceeds can be eliminated if you (the insured) give the policy to someone else. Under IRS regulations, this gift must be made at least three years before your death.

Irrevocable Trusts

A number of types of irrevocable trusts can be used to save on estate taxes. An irrevocable trust is one that cannot be revoked or altered once it is established. By contrast, you can revoke your own living trust (discussed above), as long as you are alive. Below are two examples of using irrevocable trusts for tax savings.

"AB" Irrevocable Trusts

I'll start here by repeating a tax rule: All property, no matter what the amount, you leave to your (U.S. citizen) spouse is exempt from federal estate tax. This is called the "marital deduction."

Even so, traditionally, it often wasn't tax wise for one spouse to leave a large estate to the other. Why? Because if the survivor had property of his own, and that property, combined with what the other spouse left him, was worth more than the estate tax threshold, a large and unnecessary estate tax had to be paid when the second spouse died (unless the second spouse had given away or spent it down to under the estate tax threshold). Estate planners refer to this as the "second tax" problem.

In this situation, what's called an AB trust has been used to lower a couple's overall estate taxes. With this type of trust, each spouse leaves the use and income of his or her property to the other spouse only for that spouse's life (called a "life estate"). The spouse who receives the life estate has only the power to use the trust property, and receive its income, during her life; she cannot consume the principal of the trust or dispose of it as part of her own estate.

When the second spouse dies, the trust property goes to the final trust beneficiary—often, the couple's children. The property in the trust is subject to tax only when the first spouse dies. At the death of the second spouse, the one with the life estate interest in the trust property, that property is *not* subject to estate tax.

EXAMPLE:

Calvin and Phyllis, husband and wife, each have an estate worth $2.3 million, for a combined worth of $4.6 million. Calvin dies in 2008, leaving all his property to Phyllis. Because of the marital deduction, no estate tax is assessed. Phyllis dies in 2009, when the personal exemption is $3.5 million. Her estate is the entire $4.6 million. $1.1 million is subject to tax.

Now suppose Calvin hadn't left his property outright to Phyllis, but had established an AB trust, with Phyllis having a "life estate" in the trust property and their children serving as the final beneficiaries. The trust property is subject to estate tax when Calvin dies, but no tax is due because it falls below the estate tax threshold of $2 million for 2006. Phyllis has the right to the income and use of the trust property, but cannot spend the trust principal. And because Phyllis was named as trustee, she can manage the trust property. She is never the legal owner of the trust property, so it isn't included in her taxable estate when she dies. When Phyllis dies, her $2.3 million can be transferred to the children free of estate tax, as it is well under the personal exemption for the year of her death. No estate tax is paid at either death.

AB trusts can be particularly desirable for elderly and prosperous couples. If the surviving spouse probably won't outlive the other by many years, the survivor probably won't need to spend the trust principal. By contrast, younger spouses are often understandably reluctant to risk imposing these restrictions on property one spouse leaves for the other's benefit. Further, if the estate tax is entirely repealed for 2010 and thereafter, there will be no need for an AB trust after that repeal.

RESOURCE

Making your own AB trust. If you and your spouse have a combined estate worth under $4 million, you can prepare an AB trust yourself, without a lawyer, by using *Make Your Own Living Trust,* by Denis Clifford (Nolo) or *Quicken WillMaker Plus* (software from Nolo).

Generation-Skipping Irrevocable Trusts

Wealthy people can establish a "generation-skipping" trust for the benefit of grandchildren, instead of leaving the money directly to their children and hoping they pass it along when they die. With this kind of trust, only the income from the trust property goes to your children during their lives.

Under a special Internal Revenue Code provision, your estate pays an estate tax on all money in a generation-skipping trust when you die, but no additional tax is owed when the children die and the grandchildren get the money. The generation-skipping trust exemption is the same as the amount of the personal estate tax exemption. Obviously, establishing this sort of trust makes sense only if your children have enough money to get along with only the interest, not the principal, of the trust property.

SEE AN EXPERT

Get help with fancy trusts. An attorney's help is necessary to draft any irrevocable estate tax-saving trust, except the type of AB trust discussed above. IRS regulations applicable to irrevocable trusts are complicated, and a mistake can cost you all the tax savings you'd planned for. Also, irrevocable trusts are designed to last for quite a while, which means there must be a thorough consideration of contingencies over time. Finally, you need to evaluate what effect the estate tax repeal may have on your need for this type of sophisticated planning. Drafting such a trust is difficult. To learn about irrevocable estate tax-saving trusts before you see a lawyer—always a smart move—consult *Plan Your Estate*, by Denis Clifford and Cora Jordan (Nolo).

Placing Controls on Property

For any number of reasons, you may want to impose controls over property left to beneficiaries. The usual solution is to create a trust imposing the controls you want. Except for a family pot or simple child's trust, used in wills in this book, all require preparation by a lawyer. (Family pot trusts and child's trusts are discussed in Chapter 7.)

Restrictions on Your Spouse

If you are married and have children from a previous relationship, you may feel a fundamental conflict when it comes to making your will: What is a fair division of your property among all your loved ones? Especially if your current spouse and your kids don't get along, it can be a tough determination.

Some people enter into second or subsequent marriages unencumbered by grand concerns about estate planning. If each spouse has enough property of his or her own to live comfortably, there may be no real need for them to merge property. The simplest way to prevent thorny future battles may be to sign a prenuptial agreement making it clear that separate property stays separate; then each can make an independent estate plan for that property.

But you—or your current spouse—may really need income from, or the use of, the other's property to live comfortably. On the other hand, children from a former marriage may believe they are entitled to inherit the property once a parent dies. Even if the children are not insistent, they may have financial needs and resent their inheritance being tied up while the other spouse lives. This situation—which can be dicey at the best of times—becomes even more complicated if your spouse and children are estranged.

One possible way to balance the interests and needs of all concerned is to set up a special kind of trust, what I call a "marital property control trust." With this kind of trust, if your spouse survives you, he or she has some use of your property, or income from it, for as long as he or she lives—but does not have unlimited rights to use it. The goal is to preserve most or all of the trust principal intact for your children, who will inherit it after your spouse's death.

Your surviving spouse is the "life beneficiary" of the trust, and receives benefits from the trust while living. However, the rights to use trust property, receive trust income, or spend trust principal are limited, and the restrictions are expressly stated in the trust document.

A marital property control trust is in marked contrast to an AB trust intended to save on estate tax, where the surviving spouse is usually granted the maximum rights to use and spend trust property allowed under IRS rules. The purpose of restricting the surviving spouse's rights in a marital property control trust is to protect the trust principal, so that it remains until the surviving spouse dies. Then, the trust property goes outright to your children from a prior marriage, or other final beneficiaries you named.

EXAMPLE:

Sherry and Raymond, each of whom has children from a prior marriage, marry. They buy an expensive house together. Each contributes 50% of the purchase price and mortgage payments. If they die, each wants the other to be able to continue to live in the house for his or her life. But on the second spouse's death, each wants his or her share of the house to go to his or her own children.

Sherry and Raymond each create an AB trust for their share of the house. The surviving spouse will receive only the rights to lifetime use of the other's share of the house. If a surviving spouse wants to sell the house, the deceased spouse's children become cotrustees with that spouse, to ensure that their principal is protected. When the second spouse dies, each spouse's children receive a total of half the value of the house.

As discussed earlier, this type of trust must be geared to individual family needs, desires, and dynamics and must be drafted by a lawyer.

"Spendthrift" Trusts

If you want to leave property to an adult, but worry that the adult cannot sensibly handle that property, you can create a "spendthrift trust." It restricts the recipient's freedom to spend the trust property.

EXAMPLE:

Bill wants to leave a significant amount of money to 35-year-old Tim, but worries that Tim is improvident and easily influenced. So Bill leaves the money in a spendthrift trust that will end when Tim turns 50. Until then, the trustee controls distribution of the trust funds to Tim, who cannot legally pledge them or use them before actual receipt.

This is a different and more complex trust than the child's trust contained in this book's will forms. You will need to see a lawyer to draft a spendthrift trust.

Trusts for Loved Ones with Disabilities

A trust is often advisable if you want to leave money to a loved one with a physical or mental disability who receives government benefits. A gift left outright to your loved one would be considered income, and could easily jeopardize eligibility for benefits.

In this situation, it makes sense to leave the gift to a "special needs trust" managed by a competent adult for the benefit of your loved one. Doing this does not risk eligibility for benefits because your loved one never has access or control of the gift—that is left to the trustee.

EXAMPLE:

Elizabeth's daughter, who has Down syndrome, resides in a permanent care facility. Elizabeth leaves all her property in a special needs trust for her daughter, and names her best friend Mona as trustee.

RESOURCE

Be your own expert. *Special Needs Trusts: Protect Your Child's Financial Future,* by Stephen Elias (Nolo) lets you create a trust for a loved one with a disability. Using the book's clear instructions and forms, you can draft a trust that provides for your child without jeopardizing government benefits.

Flexible Trusts

For a variety of reasons, you may want to have a trustee determine how to spend or use the property you leave the beneficiaries after your death. You can accomplish this through a customized trust.

EXAMPLE:

Vivian leaves money for her six grandchildren. She wants the money used where it is most needed, which she realizes she can't determine in advance. So she leaves the money in a "sprinkling" trust, with the trustee having the power to distribute trust money as the trustee determines the beneficiaries need.

You should see a lawyer for a customized trust.

Planning for Incapacity

Your executor will handle your affairs after your death. But what if you need help before then? It's wise to prepare for the possibility that you might become incapacitated and unable to handle your own financial affairs or make medical decisions. There are basic legal documents you can prepare to appoint someone to manage your financial and business affairs, and to make health care decisions for you, should you become incapacitated.

There are two basic types of medical care documents. You need to prepare both. First, you need a "directive:" a written statement that you make directly to medical personnel that spells out the medical care you do or do not wish to receive if you become incapacitated. A directive functions as a contract with your treating doctors, who must either honor your wishes for medical care, or transfer you to other doctors or a facility that will honor them.

Second is what's often called a "durable power of attorney for health care." In this document you appoint someone you trust to be your "health care agent" or "attorney-in-fact" to see that your doctors and health care providers give you the kind of medical care you wish to receive. You can also give your health care agent broader authority to make decisions about your medical care—excluding, of course, matters you covered in your declaration. Some states combine both health care documents into a single form.

Planning for Incapacity: Vocabulary

Several terms used in this chapter sound similar but have distinct meanings. Here's a chart to help you keep them straight.

Term	Also Called	What It Means
Health Care Declaration	• Living Will • Directive to Physicians • Health Care Directive • Medical Directive	A legal document in which you state your wishes about life support and other kinds of medical treatments. The document takes effect if you can't communicate your own health care wishes.
Durable Power of Attorney for Health Care	• Medical Power of Attorney • Power of Attorney for Health Care • Designation of Surrogate • Patient Advocate Designation	A legal document in which you give another person permission to make medical decisions for you if you are unable to make those decisions yourself.
Advanced Health Care Directive		A legal document that includes both a health care declaration and a durable power of attorney for health care. It is currently used in more than one-third of the states.
Health Care Agent	• Attorney-in-Fact for Health Care • Patient Advocate • Health Care Proxy • Surrogate • Health Care Representative	The person you name in your durable power of attorney for health care to make medical decisions you if you cannot make them yourself.
Durable Power of Attorney for Finances		A legal document in which you give another person authority to manage your financial affairs if you become incapacitated.
Attorney-in-Fact for Finances	Agent for Finances	The person you name in your durable power of attorney for finances to make financial decisions for you if you cannot make them yourself.
Springing Power of Attorney		A durable power of attorney that takes effect only when and if you become incapacitated.

Take Time to Prepare Your Documents

Preparing your medical care documents is likely to be difficult and troublesome. First, you'll need to understand some basics about what kind of care you can select or prohibit. Next comes the often more disturbing process of facing up to what some choices may involve. For instance, do you want to allow, prohibit, or require that water or food be artificially administered to you through tubes if you are near death? If you prohibit this, you may die from dehydration or starvation. Is that a fate you want to risk choosing?

Further, you need to talk about your wishes with your health care agent. Making health care decisions for another person can be complex, even wrenching. The medical situation may be far from clear. Chances of recovery may be uncertain. The unfortunate truth is that not all possibilities can be anticipated, so precise instructions can't always be given in a durable power of attorney for health care. Your health care agent may be called upon to make hard choices. The more he or she understands about your wishes and desires regarding medical care, the better.

To arrange for someone to manage your money and property if you become incapacitated, you can use a durable power of attorney for finances. (In this way, you avoid the need for a court-appointed conservator.) You can tailor your durable power of attorney for finances to your specific financial situation, authorizing your attorney-in-fact to take care of financial matters ranging from paying bills to handling insurance or watching over your investments. You can also impose whatever restrictions you want on your attorney-in-fact. For instance, you can specify that he or she cannot sell your home.

A durable power of attorney for finances can go into effect as soon as you sign it, or only if you become unable to manage your own finances. (The latter is called a "springing" document.) And, as with a durable power of attorney for health care, you can change the attorney-in-fact or other terms of the document at any time, as long as you are of sound mind.

RESOURCE

Where to get the forms. Health care documents and durable powers of attorney for finances for your state are provided in *Quicken WillMaker Plus* (software for Windows from Nolo).

Health care documents are also offered by many state medical associations and hospitals. Or you can order them by calling the National Hospice and Palliative Care Organization at 800-658-8898 or download forms from their website at www.nhpco.org.

Making Final Arrangements

Estate planning can also include making plans for what happens after you die. Giving your loved ones clear instructions about what you want done with your body and what kind of services you'd like to have may greatly reduce stress and conflict in the days and weeks following your death.

Body or Organ Donation

If you want to donate organs, the best thing you can do is to make your wishes known. One good place to do this is in a health care directive. (See the discussion above.) Many states also have additional methods, such as a donor card or sticker to accompany your driver's license. It's fine to express your wishes in more than one place, as long as they don't conflict.

Whichever methods you choose, be sure your loved ones know what you want. Organs must be donated immediately after your death, and doctors will often turn to family members for guidance. If those close to you understand your wishes, they can direct medical personnel to carry them out as you intend.

If you want to donate your whole body for education or research, you must make these arrangements in advance. Contact a nearby medical school for information.

Cremation or Burial

You may also want to leave your loved ones instructions about what to do with your remains. For example, do you want your body to be cremated or buried? If you want to be cremated, will your ashes be scattered or kept? If you want to be buried, have you chosen a casket or a gravesite? Have you thought about what kind of grave marker you want or what your epitaph should be? Planning for these matters can provide valuable guidance for your loved ones and ensure you get the kind of send off you prefer.

For help with these arrangements, you can turn to a local mortuary or contact a nonprofit funeral or memorial society. A funeral or memorial society may be able to help you keep your plans simple and affordable. To locate an organization in your area, contact the Funeral Consumers Alliance (FCA) at www.funerals.org or 800-765-0107.

Services and Ceremonies

Along with instructions for burial or cremation, you can let your family and friends know what type of after-death ceremonies you'd prefer. You may have a favorite church, synagogue, or temple where you would like the service held, or a particular clergyperson to conduct it. Your wishes can be as simple or as detailed as you like, from a traditional religious funeral to an informal gathering that includes your unique preferences for readings, music, food, or flowers. Those close to you will likely accept your directions with gratitude.

Putting Your Wishes in Writing

Whatever your preferences for final arrangements, the most important thing you can do is write them down. Simple written instructions should be all you need, especially if your family members get along well. Talk with those who will be most likely to carry out your wishes and give them a copy of your instructions—or be sure they know where to find them when the time comes.

Even if your loved ones quarrel with each other— for example, if there's a disagreement between your partner or spouse and other relatives—funeral industry personnel are usually bound to follow any written instructions you left.

If you fear family squabbles, you can help by naming one trusted person to oversee your arrangements. You can provide more insurance by setting aside sufficient funds to cover the costs of the arrangements you've chosen.

Keep in mind that it may not be possible to make your wishes ironclad. (State laws on this subject vary widely, and many are unclear or full of loopholes.) But as long as your wishes are reasonable and financially feasible, they should be carried out as you intend.

RESOURCE

Help with final arrangements. Nolo offers two excellent resources to help you decide on final arrangements—from burial or cremation to memorial ceremonies—and leave instructions for loved ones. Nolo's *Quicken WillMaker Plus* software lets you use your computer to prepare a final arrangements letter that makes your wishes clear. Or, if you prefer to use a workbook, *Get It Together: Organize Your Records So Your Family Won't Have To,* by Melanie Cullen with Shae Irving, provides a complete system to help you organize all your important paperwork and personal information, including instructions for final arrangements. ●

Lawyers and Doing Your Own Legal Research

I believe most people can safely prepare their own will by using *Nolo's Simple Will Book* without any help from a lawyer. However, only you can decide whether you want or need legal assistance. For a variety of reasons, as discussed throughout this book, you may need a lawyer's services to prepare a will that suits your desires.

> Lawyer: "One skilled in circumvention of the law." Ambrose Bierce, *The Devil's Dictionary.*

Working With a Lawyer

For intelligent consumers, consulting a lawyer does not mean hiring one and saying, "I want a will, so please prepare one for me." At a minimum, you should take the time to understand your needs. Even better, prepare a rough draft of your will before consulting an expert. You may want your attorney to do little more than answer specific questions and ensure that the finished product achieves your goals. Whatever you decide, be clear about what you expect the lawyer to do. Don't let any lawyer cast you in the role of a passive client. (Interestingly, the Latin root of the word client translates as "to obey" or "to hear.") If your lawyer tries to do this, it's wise to hire someone else.

Hiring a Lawyer to Review Your Will

Hiring a lawyer solely to review a will you've prepared sounds like a good idea. It shouldn't cost much, and seems to offer a comforting security. Unfortunately, though, it may be difficult or even impossible to find a lawyer who will accept the job.

I'm not willing, however, to excoriate lawyers who won't review a do-it-yourself will. From their point of view, they are being asked to accept what might turn into a significant responsibility for inadequate compensation, given their usual fees. Any prudent lawyer sees every client as a potential occasion for a malpractice claim, or at least, serious later hassles—a phone call four years down the line that begins, "I talked to you about my will, and now…." Many experienced lawyers want to avoid this kind of risk. Also, many lawyers feel that if they're only reviewing someone else's work, they simply don't delve deeply enough into a situation to be sure of their opinions. Then there's the truth that beyond the few formal, legal requirements, there's no one right way to prepare a will. For some lawyers, though, this means that if you haven't prepared your will their way, you've done it wrong.

If you decide you really need an attorney to review your will, all I can suggest is that you keep trying to find a sympathetic lawyer—or be prepared to pay enough so the lawyer feels adequately paid for the work and assumption of responsibility.

Finding a Lawyer

If you want to hire a lawyer but don't know one, how do you find a good one? It's the "good one" part that presents the real challenge. Of course, there are plenty of lawyers out there—the trick is retaining a lawyer who is trustworthy, competent, and charges fairly. A few words of advice may be helpful.

First, decide what type of lawyer you need. This depends on what your problem is. If you need sophisticated estate planning, especially the creation of an irrevocable trust to save on estate taxes, see someone who specializes in the field. Irrevocable trusts are quite technical. Most general practice lawyers are simply not sufficiently educated in this field for you to rely on them. An expert may charge relatively high fees ($300 to $400 or more per hour), but a good expert is worth it. And if you need this sort of estate planning help, presumably you can afford it. On the other hand, if you want a lawyer to answer some questions about will drafting, a competent attorney in general practice should suffice.

Next, it's important that you feel a personal rapport with your lawyer. You want one who treats you as an equal. When talking with a lawyer on the phone, or at the first conference, ask some specific questions. If the lawyer answers them clearly and concisely—explaining but not talking down to you—fine. If he acts wise, but says little except to ask that the problem be placed in his hands (with the appropriate fee, of course), watch out. You're either talking with someone who doesn't know the answer and won't admit it (common), or someone who finds it impossible to let go of the "me expert, you peasant" way of looking at the world (even more common).

To find a lawyer you'll like, and who will do a good job, the best route is the traditional one—ask your friends. If a close friend of yours likes a certain lawyer, chances are you will, too. Otherwise, you've got work to do. Here are some suggestions on how you can find a lawyer you'll be pleased with:

- Check with people you know who own their own businesses. Almost anyone running a small business has a relationship with a lawyer. And chances are they've found one they like. If this lawyer doesn't handle wills, she'll know someone who does. And, best of all, because she has a continuing relationship with your friend, she has an incentive to recommend someone who's good, not just her brother-in-law who owes her money.

- Ask people you know in any political or social organization you're involved with. They may well know of a competent lawyer whose attitudes are similar to yours. Groups that advise and assist older people are particularly likely to have a list of local lawyers who specialize in wills and estate planning and are generally regarded as competent and caring.

- Consider getting advice by phone. For around $50, you can call a lawyer licensed in your state and talk as long as you want about a

---

The Nolo Lawyer Directory

At Nolo.com, you'll find our directory of qualified lawyers who can help you with a variety of issues and who will respect your desire to help yourself. Currently, the Nolo Lawyer Directory covers Arizona, California, Oregon, and Washington. If you live in one of those states, you can use the directory to locate lawyers in your area who specialize in the subject you need. You can then read an in-depth profile of each attorney to figure out which might be best for you.

---

personal (not business-related) legal matter. This "Ask an Attorney" service is offered by ARAG, a large provider of prepaid legal insurance, at www.aragdirect.com. There's a money-back guarantee if you're not satisfied.

- Evaluate joining a prepaid legal plan that offers advice, by phone or in person, at no extra charge. These plans aren't as easy to find as they once were. If you do find one, there's no guarantee that the lawyers available are of the best caliber. These plans are sometimes inaccurately called "prepaid legal insurance." The plans are not insurance per se; rather, they offer an initial level of service for a low fee, then charge more for further work. Many prepaid plan providers have websites explaining the terms of their plans, so you can do some comparison shopping online. You may also be able to find a list of companies licensed to offer prepaid legal plans from your state's consumer affairs agency; call the agency or check out your state's website.

- Some unions, employers, and consumer action organizations offer group legal plans to their members or employees, who can obtain comprehensive legal assistance free or for low rates. If you're a member of such a plan, check with it first for a lawyer referral to find out whether your problem is covered free of charge. However, if the plan gives you only a slight reduction in a lawyer's fee, as many do, keep in mind that you may be referred to a lawyer whose main virtue is the willingness to reduce his price in exchange for a high volume of referrals. There are better criteria for picking a good lawyer.

- Most county bar associations maintain referral services that will give you the names of some attorneys who practice in your area. Usually you can get a referral to an attorney who specializes in wills, and offers an initial consultation for a low fee. A problem is that most referral services do little screening of the attorneys listed, which means those who participate may not be the most experienced or competent. It may be possible to find a skilled attorney willing to work for a reasonable fee following this approach; be sure to ask the attorney about credentials and experience.

- Check the Yellow Pages under "Attorneys." Quite a few attorneys are not interested in handling court-contested matters but do provide consultations and will drafting at relatively low rates. This could be just what you need.

Paying Your Lawyer

As you undoubtedly know, lawyers are expensive. They charge fees ranging from $100 to $300 and up per hour. While fancy office trappings, dull dress, and solemn faces are no guarantee (or even any indication) that a lawyer is good, or is the best person for you to work with, this conventional style will almost always ensure that you'll be charged a fee towards the upper end of this range. But high fees and quality service don't necessarily go hand in hand. The attorneys I think most highly of tend to charge moderate fees (for lawyers, that is).

Be sure you've established your fee arrangement at the start of your relationship. Generally, fees in the range of $100–$200 per hour are reasonable, depending on the area of the country and what you want the lawyer to do. In addition to the amount charged per hour, you want a clear commitment from the lawyer concerning roughly how many hours your problem will probably take. If a lawyer merely tells you that wills are complex, and it will take many hours to handle your problems, go somewhere else.

Doing Your Own Research

If you don't want to, or can't afford to, hire a lawyer to resolve legal issues that affect your will, you can do your own legal research. Not only will you save some money, but you'll also gain a sense of mastery over an area of law, generating a confidence that will stand you in good stead should you have other legal problems.

Fortunately, researching wills and related issues is generally well suited to doing your own legal research. Many problems don't involve massive or abstruse legal issues. Perhaps you need only check the statutes of your state to find one particular provision. Or you can learn how to use legal form books, the very books lawyers often refer to in order to solve a problem.

If you decide to do your own research, how do you go about it? First, it surely helps to have a research aid. If you can't hire your own law librarian, the best book explaining how to do your own legal work is *Legal Research: How to Find and Understand the Law*, by Stephen R. Elias and Susan Levinkind (Nolo). It tells you all you need to know to do effective research.

Next, locate a law library or a public library with a good law collection. There's usually a law library in your principal county courthouse. These law libraries are supported by tax dollars or by the fees paid to file legal papers, and are open to the public. The librarians in county law libraries are generally most helpful and courteous to nonlawyers doing their own legal research. Ask them how you can locate your state's laws (which may be called "codes" or "statutes," depending on the state). Usually what you want is called the "annotated version," which contains both your state's statutes and excerpts from any relevant judicial decisions and cross-references to related articles and commentaries.

Once you've found your state's statutes, check the index for provisions dealing with wills or the specific subject that concerns you. Generally, you'll find what you want in the statutes dealing with your state's basic civil or probate laws. These are usually called a name such as "Civil Code" or "Probate Laws." These codes are numbered sequentially, and once you get the correct number in the index, it's easy to find the statute you need. If you have trouble, the law librarian will usually be happy to help.

Read the statutes in the hardcover volume and check the paper "pocket part" at the back of the book for any amendments made since the main volume was printed. Then you'll probably want to skim the summaries of recent court decisions contained in the "Annotations" section immediately following the text of the statute itself. If a summary looks like it might help answer your question, read the full court opinion that the summary was taken from. A law librarian can help you find the published opinion.

Legal Information Online

Another way to approach legal research is to use the Internet. If you want information about a recent court decision, a new statute or a current legal issue about wills, you'll probably be able to find it somewhere online.

For example, you can look up any section of your state statutes by visiting Nolo's legal research center at www.nolo.com/statute/state.cfm. Once there, follow these steps to look up the law you need:

1. Click "State Laws."
2. Choose your state.
3. Follow the instructions on your state's website to search for the statute you want to read.

It's usually not difficult to do. You can also browse Nolo's website for lots of other helpful legal information and links. The best place to start is the free legal encyclopedia, which contains dozens of articles on wills and estate planning.

You can also hunt down information using one of the many search engines available online. A search engine asks you to type one or more key words or phrases in a text entry box, and then produces a list of materials that contain them. For example, if you want to locate information about a recent U.S. Supreme Court case dealing with generation skipping trusts, you would type in the words "generation skipping trust." This "query" would produce a list of web pages that contain those words, possibly including the text of the case itself.

A search may turn up hundreds of entries, which you can view in successive lists of ten or 20. Because the entries usually are listed according to the frequency with which the words in your query appear, items at the top of the list tend to be the most helpful.

Glossary

abatement Cutting back certain gifts under a will when it's necessary to meet expenses, pay taxes, satisfy debts, or take care of other bequests that are given priority under law or under the will.

acknowledgment A statement in front of a person who's authorized to administer oaths (usually, a notary public) that a document bearing your signature was actually signed by you.

ademption The failure of a specific bequest of property to take effect because the will writer no longer owns the property at the time of his or her death.

administration (of an estate) The court-supervised distribution of the probate estate of a deceased person. The person who manages the distribution is called the executor if there's a will. If there's no will, the court appoints someone called the administrator. But in a few states, the person is called "personal representative" in either instance.

adopted child Any person, whether an adult or a minor, who is legally adopted as the child of another in a court proceeding.

adult Any person age 18 or older.

augmented estate A method used in a number of states following the common law ownership of property system to measure a person's estate for the purpose of determining whether a surviving spouse has been adequately provided for. Generally, the augmented estate consists of property left by the will plus certain property transferred outside of the will by such devices as gifts, joint tenancies, and living trusts. Some states include some or all of the separate property owned by the surviving spouse as well. In the states using this concept, a surviving spouse is generally considered to be adequately provided for if he or she receives at least one-third of the augmented estate.

beneficiary A person or organization who's legally entitled to receive benefits under a legal document such as a will or trust. Except when very small estates are involved, beneficiaries of wills receive their property only after the will is examined and approved by the probate court. Beneficiaries of trusts receive their property as provided in the trust instrument.

bequest An old legal term for a will provision leaving personal property (all types except real estate) to a specified person or organization. In this book it's called a "gift."

bond A document guaranteeing that a certain amount of money will be paid to people who lose money because a person occupying a position of trust doesn't carry out his or her legal and ethical responsibilities. For example, if an executor, trustee, or guardian who's bonded (covered by a bond) wrongfully deprives a beneficiary of his or her property (say by blowing it during a trip in Las Vegas), the bonding company will replace it, up to the limits of the bond. Bonding companies are normally divisions of insurance companies.

children For the purpose of *Nolo's Simple Will Book*, children are: (1) your biological offspring; (2) people you have legally adopted; (3) children born out of wedlock if you are the mother; (4) children born outside of marriage if you are the father and have acknowledged the child as being yours as required by the law of the particular state; or (5) children born to you after your will is made.

codicil A separate, signed, and properly witnessed legal document that changes an existing will.

common law marriage Valid in a minority of states. In those states, a specific law provides that if a couple lives together for a set time and holds themselves out as married, they become legally married, even if there was no legal marriage ceremony.

community and separate property A handful of states follow a system of marital property ownership called "community property." Very generally, all property acquired after marriage and before permanent separation is considered to belong equally to both spouses, except for gifts to and inheritances by one spouse, and, in some community property states, income from property owned by one spouse prior to marriage.

Items purchased during the marriage with the income earned by either spouse during the marriage are usually considered to be community property, unless the spouses have entered into an agreement to the contrary. If the property was purchased with the separate property of a spouse, it's separate property, unless it has been given to the community by gift or agreement.

If separate property and community property are mixed together (commingled) in a bank account and expenditures made from this bank account, the goods purchased are usually treated as community property unless they can be specifically linked with the separate property (this is called "tracing").

Under the law of community property states, a surviving spouse automatically keeps his or her one-half share of all community property. The other spouse has no legal power to affect this portion by will or otherwise. Thus, the property that a spouse can leave by will consists of his or her separate property and one-half of the community property.

conditional gift A gift that passes only under certain specified conditions or upon the occurrence of a specific event. For example, if you leave property to Aunt Millie provided she's living in Cincinnati when you die, and otherwise to Uncle Fred, you've made a "conditional gift." *Nolo's Simple Will Book* doesn't encourage or provide clauses for conditional bequests.

custodian A person named to care for property left to a minor under the Uniform Transfers to Minors Act.

decedent A person who has died.

devise An old legal term for real estate left by a will. In this book, it's called a "gift."

domicile The state, or country, where you have your primary home.

dower and curtesy The right of a surviving spouse to claim a set portion of the deceased spouse's property (usually one-third to one-half) if the surviving spouse isn't left at least that share and chooses to "take against the will." Dower refers to the title that a surviving wife gets, while curtesy refers to what a man receives. Until recently, these amounts differed in a number of states. However, since discrimination on the basis of sex is now considered to be illegal in most cases, states generally provide the same benefits regardless of sex.

encumbrances Debts (such as taxes, mechanics' liens, and judgment liens) and loans (such as mortgages, deeds of trust, and security interests) which use property as collateral for payment of the debt or loan. They encumber the property because they must be paid off before title to the property can pass from one owner to the next. Generally, the value of a person's ownership in such property (called the "equity") is measured by the market value of the property less the sum of all encumbrances.

equity The difference between the fair market value of your real estate and personal property and the amount you still owe on it, if any.

estate Generally, all the property you own when you die. There are different ways to measure your estate, depending on whether you're concerned with tax reduction (the taxable estate), probate avoidance (the probate estate), or net worth (the net estate).

estate planning The art and craft of continuing to prosper when you're alive, and passing your property to your loved ones with a minimum of fuss and expense after you die. Planning your estate may involve making a will, living trust, health care directives, durable power of attorney for finances, or other documents.

estate taxes Federal taxes imposed on property as it passes from the dead to the living.

executor The person named in your will to manage your estate, deal with the probate court, collect your assets, and distribute them as you've specified after your death. In some states, this person is called the "personal representative." If you die without a will, the probate court will appoint such a person, called the "administrator" of the estate.

financial guardian See "property guardian."

gifts In your will, a gift is property you leave to people or organizations at your death. A specific gift means an identified piece of property left to a named beneficiary.

The word "gift" can have another meaning: property you give to someone while you're alive.

guardian of the minor's property See "property guardian."

guardian of the person See "personal guardian."

heirs Persons who are entitled by law to inherit your estate if you don't leave a will.

holographic will A will that's not witnessed and that is completely handwritten by the person making it. While legal in many states, it's never advised except as a last resort.

inherit To receive property from one who dies.

inheritance taxes A tax imposed by a minority of states on the property of a deceased person.

inheritors Persons or organizations to whom you leave property.

inter vivos trusts See "living trusts."

intestate Someone who died without a will is said to have died "intestate."

intestate succession The method by which property is distributed when a person fails to distribute it by a will or other estate planning device. In such cases, the law of each state provides that the property be distributed in certain shares to the closest surviving relatives. In most states, these are a surviving spouse, children, parents, siblings, nieces and nephews, and next of kin, in that order. The intestate succession laws are also used if a child is found to be overlooked and entitled to inherit some of the estate.

joint tenancy A way to take title to jointly owned real estate or personal property. When two or more people own property as joint tenants, and one of the owners dies, the other owners automatically own the deceased owner's share. For example, if a parent and child own a house as joint tenants, and the parent dies, the child automatically becomes the full owner. Because of this "right of survivorship," a joint tenancy interest in property doesn't go through probate.

Instead, it goes directly to the surviving joint tenants once some tax and transfer forms are completed.

libel The communication of a written statement that makes a false claim, expressly stated or implied to be factual, that may harm the reputation of an individual, business, product, or group.

living trust A trust set up while you are alive and which remains under your control during the remainder of your life. Also referred to as "inter vivos trusts," living trusts are designed to avoid probate of the trust property.

marital deduction A deduction allowed by the federal estate tax law for all property passed to a surviving spouse who is a U.S. citizen. This deduction (which is really an exemption) allows anyone to pass his or her entire estate to a surviving spouse without any estate tax.

marriage A specific status conferred on a couple by a state. In most states, it's necessary to file papers with a county clerk and have a marriage ceremony conducted by an authorized individual in order to be married. However, in a minority of states that authorize "common law marriage," you may be considered married if you've lived together for a certain period of time and intended to be husband and wife. Unless you're considered legally married in the state where you claim your marriage occurred, you aren't legally married for purposes of *Nolo's Simple Will Book*.

minor A person under 18 years of age. All minors are required to be under the care of a competent adult (parent or guardian) unless they qualify as emancipated minors—that is, they are in the military, married, or living independently with court permission. Property left to a minor must be handled by a guardian, trustee or custodian until the minor becomes an adult under the laws of the state.

net taxable estate The value of all your property at death, less all encumbrances and your other liabilities.

pay-on-death bank account An account enabling you to name a beneficiary who will receive the funds in the account free of probate after your death. These are sometimes called "Totten trusts."

personal guardian An adult appointed by you, and confirmed by a court, to care for a minor child in the event no biological or adoptive parent (legal parent) of the child is able to do so. If one legal parent is alive when the other dies, however, the child will automatically go to that parent, unless it can be proved that that parent is harmful to the child, or (in some states) the court finds the child would suffer detriment.

personal property All property other than land and buildings attached to land. Cars, bank accounts, wages, securities, a small business, furniture, insurance policies, jewelry, pets, and season basketball tickets are all personal property.

power of attorney A legal document in which you authorize someone to act for you. A durable power of attorney allows someone to make health care or financial decisions for you if you become incapacitated.

pretermitted heir A child (or the child of a deceased child) who's either not named or (in some states) not provided for in a will. Most states presume that persons want their children to inherit. Accordingly, children, or the children of a child who has died before the person making the will (the "testator"), who aren't mentioned, or provided for in the will, are entitled to claim a share of the estate.

probate The court proceeding in which: (1) the authenticity of your will (if you made one) is established; (2) your executor or administrator is appointed; (3) your debts and taxes are paid; (4) your heirs are identified; and (5) your property in your probate estate is distributed according to your will (again, if there is a will).

probate estate All of your property that will pass through probate. Generally, this means all property owned by you at your death, less any property that has been placed in any probate avoidance device, such as a living trust or joint tenancy.

probate fees Fees paid to lawyers, courts, appraisers, and financial advisers during the probate process.

property guardian The person (or institution) selected in your will to care for property of your minor child. Also sometimes called "Guardian of the Minor's Estate" or "Financial Guardian." Usually the same person serves as personal and property guardian. However, it's possible to split these tasks.

proving a will Getting a probate court to accept the fact, after your death, that the document purporting to be your will really is your will. In many states, this can be done simply by introducing a properly executed will, especially if a "self-proving affidavit" is attached. In others, it's necessary to produce one or more witnesses (or their affidavits) in court, or offer some proof of your handwriting.

quasi–community property Property acquired by people during marriage in other states which is treated as community property if they move to Idaho, California, or Washington. Wisconsin recognizes a similar type of property, called "deferred marital property."

real estate Land and property permanently attached to it, such as buildings, houses, stationary mobile homes, fences, and trees. In legalese, "real property." All property that isn't "real property" is personal property.

residue, residuary estate All property left by your will to your residuary beneficiary after all specific gifts of property (real and personal) have been made—that is, what's left.

spouse The person to whom you're legally married at the time you sign your will. If you later remarry, you'll need to make a new will.

taking against the will The choice by a surviving spouse or domestic partner to claim a statutorily allotted share of the deceased spouse's estate instead of the share specified in his or her will. In most common law property states, a surviving spouse can claim a certain percentage of the other spouse's estate—commonly between one-third and one-half. If the spouse chooses to accept the share specified in the will, it's called "taking under the will."

taxable estate The portion of your estate, if any, that's subject to federal and state estate taxes.

tenancy in common A way of sharing ownership of property. The ownership shares needn't be equal. Each owner's share can be left to whomever he or she chooses.

testator The person making the will.

transfer-on-death registration A form of ownership of certain property that allows it to be transferred to the beneficiary outside of probate.

trust A legal arrangement under which one person or institution (called a "trustee") controls property given by the trust grantor for the benefit of a third person (called a "beneficiary").

Uniform Transfers to Minors Act A series of statutes, adopted by almost all states, that provides a method for appointing an adult (called a custodian) to manage property left to a minor.

will A document in which you specify what is to be done with your property when you die and name your executor. You can also use your will to name a guardian and property manager for your young children.

How to Use the CD-ROM

The tear-out forms in Appendix B are included on a CD-ROM in the back of the book. This CD-ROM, which can be used with Windows computers, installs files that you use with software programs that are already installed on your computer. It is not a stand-alone software program. Please read this appendix and the README.TXT file included on the CD-ROM for instructions on using the Forms CD.

Note to Mac users: This CD-ROM and its files should also work on Macintosh computers. Please note, however, that Nolo cannot provide technical support for non-Windows users.

How to View the README File

If you do not know how to view the file README.TXT, insert the Forms CD-ROM into your computer's CD-ROM drive and follow these instructions:

- **Windows 2000, XP, and Vista:** (1) On your PC's desktop, double click the My Computer icon; (2) double click the icon for the CD-ROM drive into which the Forms CD-ROM was inserted; (3) double click the file README.TXT.

- **Macintosh:** (1) On your Mac desktop, double click the icon for the CD-ROM that you inserted; (2) double click on the file README.TXT.

While the README file is open, print it out by using the Print command in the File menu.

Installing the Form Files Onto Your Computer

Word processing forms that you can open, complete, print, and save with your word processing program (see "Using the Word Processing Files to Create Documents," below) are contained on the CD-ROM. Before you can do anything with the files on the CD-ROM, you need to install them onto your hard disk. In accordance with U.S. copyright laws, remember that copies of the CD-ROM and its files are for your personal use only.

Insert the Forms CD and do the following.

Windows 2000, XP, and Vista Users

Follow the instructions that appear on the screen. (If nothing happens when you insert the Forms CD-ROM, then (1) double click the My Computer icon; (2) double click the icon for the CD-ROM drive into which the Forms CD-ROM was inserted; and (3) double click the file WELCOME.EXE.)

By default, all the files are installed to the \Nolo's Forms folder in the \Program Files folder of your computer. A folder called "Nolo's Will Forms" is added to the Programs folder of the Start menu.

Macintosh Users

Step 1: If the "Nolo's Will CD" window is not open, open it by double clicking the "Nolo's Will CD" icon.

Step 2: Select the "Nolo's Will CD" folder icon.

Step 3: Drag and drop the folder icon onto the icon of your hard disk.

Using the Word Processing Files to Create Documents

This section concerns the files for forms that can be opened and edited with your word processing program.

All word processing forms come in rich text format. These files have the extension ".RTF."

For example, the Property Worksheet discussed in Chapter 4 is on the file PROPWORK.rtf. All forms, their file names, and file formats are listed at the end of this appendix.

RTF files can be read by most recent word processing programs including all versions of MS Word for Windows and Macintosh, WordPad for Windows, and recent versions of WordPerfect for Windows and Macintosh.

To use a form from the CD to create your documents you must: (1) open a file in your word processor or text editor; (2) edit the form by filling in the required information; (3) print it out; and (4) rename and save your revised file.

The following are general instructions. However, each word processor uses different commands to open, format, save, and print documents. Please read your word processor's manual for specific instructions on performing these tasks.

Do not call Nolo's technical support if you have questions on how to use your word processor or your computer.

Step 1: Opening a File

There are three ways to open the word processing files included on the CD-ROM after you have installed them onto your computer.

- Windows users can open a file by selecting its "shortcut" as follows: (1) Click the Windows "Start" button; (2) open the "Programs" folder; (3) open the "Nolo's Will CD" subfolder; and (4) click on the shortcut to the form you want to work with.

- Both Windows and Macintosh users can open a file directly by double clicking on it. Use My Computer or Windows Explorer (Windows 2000, XP, and Vista) or the Finder (Macintosh) to go to the folder you installed or copied the CD-ROM's files to.

Then, double click on the specific file you want to open.

- You can also open a file from within your word processor. To do this, you must first start your word processor. Then, go to the File menu and choose the Open command. This opens a dialog box where you will tell the program (1) the type of file you want to open (*.RTF); and (2) the location and name of the file (you will need to navigate through the directory tree to get to the folder on your hard disk where the CD's files have been installed).

Where Are the Files Installed?

Windows Users

- RTF files are installed by default to a folder named \Nolo's Will Forms in the \Program Files folder of your computer.

Macintosh Users

- RTF files are located in the "Nolo's Will Forms."

Step 2: Editing Your Document

Fill in the appropriate information according to the instructions and sample agreements in the book. Underlines are used to indicate where you need to enter your information, frequently followed by instructions in brackets. Be sure to delete the underlines and instructions from your edited document. You will also want to make sure that any signature lines in your completed documents appear on a page with at least some text from the document itself.

Step 3: Printing Out the Document

Use your word processor's or text editor's "Print" command to print out your document.

Step 4: Saving Your Document

After filling in the form, use the "Save As" command to save and rename the file. Because all the files are "read-only," you will not be able to use the "Save" command. This is for your protection. If you save the file without renaming it, the underlines that indicate where you need to enter your information will be lost, and you will not be able to create a new document with this file without recopying the original file from the CD-ROM.

Forms on the CD-ROM

The following files are in rich text format (RTF):

File Name	Form Title
Worksheets	
PROPWORK	Property Worksheet
BENEWORK	Beneficiary Worksheet
EXECWORK	Executor Worksheet
PRSGWORK	Personal Guardian Worksheet
UTMAWORK	UTMA Custodians Worksheet
TRUSWORK	Child's Trust Worksheet
FAMIWORK	Family Pot Trust Worksheet
PRPGWORK	Child's Property Guardian Worksheet
GIFTWORK	Gifts Left to Others' Children Worksheet
Fill-in-the-Blank Wills	
FORM1	Will for a Married Person Leaving All or Bulk of Property to Spouse
FORM2	Will for a Single Person With No Minor Children
FORM3	Will for a Single Person With Minor Children
FORM4	Will for a Married Person With No Minor Children
FORM5	Will for a Married Person With Minor Children
FORM6	Will for an Unmarried Person With a Partner and No Minor Children
FORM7	Will for an Unmarried Person With a Partner and Minor Children
TEXAS	Special Executor's Clause for Texas
Custom Wills	
MYWILL	Clause A, B, C, & AA
CLAUSED	Clause D: Personal Information
CLAUSEE	Clause E: Disinheritance
CLAUSEF	Clause F: Specific Gifts
CLAUSEG	Clause G: Debts Forgiven

CLAUSEH	Clause H: Real Estate Encumbrances
CLAUSEI	Clause I: Personal Property Encumbrances
CLAUSEJ	Clause J: Shared Gifts
CLAUSEK	Clause K: Residuary Estate
CLAUSEL	Clause L: Survivorship Period
CLAUSEM	Clause M: Abatement
CLAUSEN	Clause N: Payment of Death Taxes
CLAUSEO	Clause O: Payment of Debts
CLAUSEP	Clause P: Nomination of Executor
CLAUSEQ	Clause Q: Executor's Powers
CLAUSER	Clause R: Personal Guardian
CLAUSES	Clause S: Gifts to Minors Under the Uniform Transfers to Minors Act
CLAUSET	Clause T: Family Pot Trust
CLAUSEU	Clause U: Child's Trusts
CLAUSEV	Clause V: General Trust Administrative Provisions
CLAUSEW	Clause W: Property Guardian
CLAUSEX	Clause X: No-Contest Clause
CLAUSEY	Clause Y: Simultaneous Death
CLAUSEZ	Clause Z: Pets
Self-Proving Affidavits	
SP_AFF1	Self-Proving Affidavit: Form 1
SP_AFF2	Self-Proving Affidavit: Form 2
SP_TEXAS	Self-Proving Affidavit: Texas
SP_PENN	Self-Proving Affidavit: Pennsylvania
CODICIL	First Codicil

Tear-Out Forms

Property Worksheet

Beneficiary Worksheet

Executor Worksheet

Personal Guardian Worksheet

UTMA Custodians Worksheet

Child's Trust Worksheet

Family Pot Trust Worksheet

Child's Property Guardian Worksheet

Gifts Left to Others' Children Worksheet

Will Form 1: Will for a Married Person Leaving All or Bulk of Property to Spouse

Will Form 2: Will for a Single Person With No Minor Children

Will Form 3: Will for a Single Person With Minor Children

Will Form 4: Will for a Married Person With No Minor Children

Will Form 5: Will for a Married Person With Minor Children

Will Form 6: Will for an Unmarried Person With a Partner and No Minor Children

Will Form 7: Will for an Unmarried Person With a Partner and Minor Children

Self-Proving Affidavit: Form 1

Self-Proving Affidavit: Form 2

Self-Proving Affidavit: Texas

Self-Proving Affidavit: Pennsylvania

First Codicil

Property Worksheet

I. Assets

Column 1 Description of Your Property	Column 2 Type of Shared Ownership	Column 3 Percentage You Own	Column 4 Net Value of Your Ownership

A. Liquid Assets

1. cash (dividends, etc.)

2. savings accounts

3. checking accounts

4. money market accounts

5. certificates of deposit

6. mutual funds

Column 1	Column 2	Column 3	Column 4
	Type of Shared	Percentage	Net Value of
Description of Your Property	Ownership	You Own	Your Ownership

7. retirement accounts

_____ _____ _____ _____
_____ _____ _____ _____
_____ _____ _____ _____

8. tradeable stocks and bonds

_____ _____ _____ _____
_____ _____ _____ _____
_____ _____ _____ _____
_____ _____ _____ _____

9. trust income

_____ _____ _____ _____
_____ _____ _____ _____
_____ _____ _____ _____
_____ _____ _____ _____

B. Other Personal Property (all your property except liquid assets, business interests, and real estate: houses, buildings, apartments, etc.)

1. small company (unlisted)

_____ _____ _____ _____
_____ _____ _____ _____
_____ _____ _____ _____
_____ _____ _____ _____

2. government bonds

_____ _____ _____ _____
_____ _____ _____ _____
_____ _____ _____ _____

3. automobiles and other vehicles, including planes, boats, and recreational vehicles

_____ _____ _____ _____
_____ _____ _____ _____
_____ _____ _____ _____

4. precious metals

_____ _____ _____ _____
_____ _____ _____ _____
_____ _____ _____ _____

Column 1	Column 2	Column 3	Column 4
	Type of Shared Ownership	Percentage You Own	Net Value of Your Ownership
Description of Your Property			

5. household goods

_____ _____ _____ _____

_____ _____ _____ _____

_____ _____ _____ _____

6. clothing

_____ _____ _____ _____

_____ _____ _____ _____

_____ _____ _____ _____

7. jewelry and furs

_____ _____ _____ _____

_____ _____ _____ _____

_____ _____ _____ _____

8. artworks, collectibles, and antiques

_____ _____ _____ _____

_____ _____ _____ _____

_____ _____ _____ _____

9. tools and equipment

_____ _____ _____ _____

_____ _____ _____ _____

_____ _____ _____ _____

10. valuable livestock/animals

_____ _____ _____ _____

_____ _____ _____ _____

_____ _____ _____ _____

11. money owed you (personal loans, etc.)

_____ _____ _____ _____

_____ _____ _____ _____

_____ _____ _____ _____

12. vested interest in profit sharing plan, stock options, etc.

_____ _____ _____ _____

_____ _____ _____ _____

_____ _____ _____ _____

Property Worksheet

13. limited partnerships

_____

_____

_____

_____

14. vested interest in retirement plans, IRAs, death benefits, annuities

_____

_____

_____

_____

15. life insurance

_____

_____

_____

_____

16. frequent flyer miles

_____

_____

_____

_____

17. miscellaneous (any personal property not listed above, including trust property you can leave to others)

_____

_____

_____

_____

C. Business Personal Property

1. patents, copyrights, domain rights, trademarks, and royalties

_____

_____

_____

_____

Column 1	Column 2	Column 3	Column 4
	Type of Shared	Percentage	Net Value of
Description of Your Property	Ownership	You Own	Your Ownership

2. business ownerships
   (partnerships, sole proprietorships, corporations, etc.; list separately and use a separate sheet of paper if you need to elaborate)
   name and type of business

   _____   _____   _____   _____
   _____   _____   _____   _____
   _____   _____   _____   _____

   name and type of business

   _____   _____   _____   _____
   _____   _____   _____   _____
   _____   _____   _____   _____

3. miscellaneous receivables (mortgages, deeds of trust, or promissory notes held by you; any rents due from income property owned by you; and payments due for professional or personal services or property sold by you that are not fully paid by the purchaser)

   _____   _____   _____
   _____   _____   _____
   _____   _____   _____
   _____   _____   _____
   _____   _____   _____

D. Real Estate
   address

   _____   _____   _____   _____
   _____   _____   _____   _____
   _____   _____   _____   _____

   address

   _____   _____   _____   _____
   _____   _____   _____   _____
   _____   _____   _____   _____

   address

   _____   _____   _____   _____
   _____   _____   _____   _____
   _____   _____   _____   _____

address

_____   _____   _____   _____
_____   _____   _____   _____
_____   _____   _____   _____

address

_____   _____   _____   _____
_____   _____   _____   _____
_____   _____   _____   _____

address

_____   _____   _____   _____
_____   _____   _____   _____
_____   _____   _____   _____
_____   _____   _____   _____

address

_____   _____   _____   _____
_____   _____   _____   _____
_____   _____   _____   _____

E. TOTAL NET VALUE OF ALL YOUR ASSETS $ _____

II. Liabilities (what you owe)

Many of your liabilities will already have been accounted for because you listed the net value of your property in Part I of this chart. For example, to determine the net value of your interest in real estate, you deducted the amount of all mortgages and encumbrances on that real estate. Similarly, the value of a small business is the value after business debts and other obligations are subtracted. For this reason, the only liabilities you need list here are those not previously covered. Don't bother with the small stuff (such as the phone bill or what you owe on your credit card this month), which changes frequently. Just list all major liabilities not previously accounted for, so you can get a clearer picture of your net worth.

Column 1	Column 2
	Net Amount of
To Whom Debt Is Owed	Debt You Owe

A. Personal Property Debts
1. personal loans (banks, major credit cards, etc.)

_____   _____
_____   _____
_____   _____
_____   _____
_____   _____

Column 1	Column 2
To Whom Debt Is Owed	**Net Amount of Debt You Owe**

2. other personal debts

_____ _____

_____ _____

_____ _____

_____ _____

_____ _____

B. **Taxes** (include only taxes past and currently due. Do not include taxes due in the future or estimated estate taxes)

_____ _____

_____ _____

_____ _____

_____ _____

_____ _____

C. **Any Other Liabilities** (legal judgments, accrued child support, etc.) _____

D. **TOTAL LIABILITIES** (excluding those liabilities already deducted in Section I) $ _____

III. **NET WORTH** (Total Net Value of All Your Assets (Section I. E)
minus Total Liabilities (Section II. D)) $ _____

Beneficiary Worksheet

1. Beneficiaries of Specific Gifts

_____ to

Item

_____

Beneficiary(ies)

_____

Alternate Beneficiary(ies)

_____ to

Item

_____

Beneficiary(ies)

_____

Alternate Beneficiary(ies)

_____ to

Item

_____

Beneficiary(ies)

_____

Alternate Beneficiary(ies)

_____ to

Item

_____

Beneficiary(ies)

_____

Alternate Beneficiary(ies)

_____ to

Item

_____

Beneficiary(ies)

_____

Alternate Beneficiary(ies)

_____ to

Item

_____

Beneficiary(ies)

_____

Alternate Beneficiary(ies)

_____ to _____

Item _____

Beneficiary(ies) _____

Alternate Beneficiary(ies) _____

_____ to _____

Item _____

Beneficiary(ies) _____

Alternate Beneficiary(ies) _____

_____ to _____

Item _____

Beneficiary(ies) _____

Alternate Beneficiary(ies) _____

_____ to _____

Item _____

Beneficiary(ies) _____

Alternate Beneficiary(ies) _____

_____ to _____

Item _____

Beneficiary(ies) _____

Alternate Beneficiary(ies) _____

_____ to _____

Item _____

Beneficiary(ies) _____

Alternate Beneficiary(ies) _____

2. Debts Forgiven

_____ to _____

Amount Forgiven   Debtor

_____

Date of Loan

_____ to _____
Amount Forgiven   Debtor

_____
Date of Loan

_____ to _____
Amount Forgiven   Debtor

_____
Date of Loan

_____ to _____
Amount Forgiven   Debtor

_____
Date of Loan

_____ to _____
Amount Forgiven   Debtor

_____
Date of Loan

3. Residuary Beneficiary or Beneficiaries

Residuary Beneficiary(ies) (and percentage each one receives):

_____

_____

_____

_____

Alternate Residuary Beneficiaries

Alternate Residuary Beneficiary(ies) _____

_____

for _____

Alternate Residuary Beneficiary(ies) _____

_____

for _____

Alternate Residuary Beneficiary(ies) _____

_____

for _____

Alternate Residuary Beneficiary(ies) _____

_____

for _____

Alternate Residuary Beneficiary(ies) _____

_____

for _____

Alternate Residuary Beneficiary(ies) _____

_____

for _____

Second Level or Alternate Alternate Residuary Beneficiary(ies) (Chapter 11 wills only)

Second Level or Alternate Alternate Residuary Beneficiary(ies) _____

_____

for _____
                          Alternate Residuary Beneficiary

Second Level or Alternate Alternate Residuary Beneficiary(ies) _____

_____

for _____
                          Alternate Residuary Beneficiary

Second Level or Alternate Alternate Residuary Beneficiary(ies) _____

_____

for _____
                          Alternate Residuary Beneficiary

Second Level or Alternate Alternate Residuary Beneficiary(ies) _____

_____

for _____
                          Alternate Residuary Beneficiary

Second Level or Alternate Alternate Residuary Beneficiary(ies) _____

_____

for _____
                          Alternate Residuary Beneficiary

Executor Worksheet

Single Executor

_____
Executor's Name

_____
Alternate Executor's Name

Coexecutors

_____
First Coexecutor's Name

_____
Second Coexecutor's Name

_____
Third Coexecutor's Name

_____
Alternate Executor's Name

Ancillary Executor

_____
Ancillary Executor's Name

_____
State Where This Executor May Act

Personal Guardian Worksheet

One Personal Guardian for All Your Children

_____
Personal Guardian

_____
Alternate Personal Guardian

Different Personal Guardians for Different Children

_____
Personal Guardian

For: _____
               Children's Names

_____

_____
Alternate Personal Guardian for These Children

_____
Personal Guardian

For: _____
               Children's Names

_____

_____
Alternate Personal Guardian for These Children

Explaining Your Choices

Here, you can set out your reasons for your choice of personal guardian. Don't be afraid to erase, edit, and rewrite. You want your explanation to be as persuasive and pithy as you can make it.

_____

_____

_____

_____

_____

_____

_____

UTMA Custodians Worksheet

Child _____

Age child is to receive gift
(if state law lets you
choose the age) _____

Custodian _____

Alternate Custodian _____

Child _____

Age child is to receive gift
(if state law lets you
choose the age) _____

Custodian _____

Alternate Custodian _____

Child _____

Age child is to receive gift
(if state law lets you
choose the age) _____

Custodian _____

Alternate Custodian _____

Child _____

Age child is to receive gift
(if state law lets you
choose the age) _____

Custodian _____

Alternate Custodian _____

Child _____

Age child is to receive gift
(if state law lets you
choose the age) _____

Custodian _____

Alternate Custodian _____

Child's Trust Worksheet

Here you can list the pertinent information for creating one or more child's trusts.

Child _____ Age at which trust terminates _____

Trustee _____

Successor Trustee _____

Child _____ Age at which trust terminates _____

Trustee _____

Successor Trustee _____

Child _____ Age at which trust terminates _____

Trustee _____

Successor Trustee _____

Child _____ Age at which trust terminates _____

Trustee _____

Successor Trustee _____

Child _____ Age at which trust terminates _____

Trustee _____

Successor Trustee _____

Child _____ Age at which trust terminates _____

Trustee _____

Successor Trustee _____

Child _____ Age at which trust terminates _____

Trustee _____

Successor Trustee _____

Child _____ Age at which trust terminates _____

Trustee _____

Successor Trustee _____

Child _____ Age at which trust terminates _____

Trustee _____

Successor Trustee _____

Child _____ Age at which trust terminates _____

Trustee _____

Successor Trustee _____

Child _____ Age at which trust terminates _____

Trustee _____

Successor Trustee _____

Child _____ Age at which trust terminates _____

Trustee _____

Successor Trustee _____

Family Pot Trust Worksheet

Here you can list the pertinent information for creating a family pot trust.

Children who are beneficiaries of family pot trust:

_____

_____

_____

_____

_____

_____

_____

_____

_____

_____

_____

_____

_____

_____

Trustee: _____

_____

Successor Trustee: _____

Child's Property Guardian Worksheet

One Property Guardian for All Your Children

_____
Property Guardian

_____
Alternate Property Guardian

Different Property Guardians for Different Children

_____
Property Guardian

For: _____
           Children's Names

_____

_____
Alternate Property Guardian for These Children

_____
Property Guardian

For: _____
           Children's Names

_____

_____
Alternate Property Guardian for These Children

_____
Property Guardian

For: _____
           Children's Names

_____

_____
Alternate Property Guardian for These Children

_____
Property Guardian

For: _____
           Children's Names

_____

_____
Alternate Property Guardian for These Children

Property Guardian

_____

For: _____
         Children's Names

_____

Alternate Property Guardian for These Children

_____

Property Guardian

_____

For: _____
         Children's Names

_____

Alternate Property Guardian for These Children

_____

Property Guardian

_____

For: _____
         Children's Names

_____

Alternate Property Guardian for These Children

_____

Property Guardian

_____

For: _____
         Children's Names

_____

Alternate Property Guardian for These Children

_____

Property Guardian

_____

For: _____
         Children's Names

_____

Alternate Property Guardian for These Children

Gifts Left to Others' Children Worksheet

Child _____

Age child is to receive gift _____

Transfer Method _____

Adult Property Manager _____

Child _____

Age child is to receive gift _____

Transfer Method _____

Adult Property Manager _____

Child _____

Age child is to receive gift _____

Transfer Method _____

Adult Property Manager _____

Child _____

Age child is to receive gift _____

Transfer Method _____

Adult Property Manager _____

Child _____

Age child is to receive gift _____

Transfer Method _____

Adult Property Manager _____

Child _____

Age child is to receive gift _____

Transfer Method _____

Adult Property Manager _____

Child _____

Age child is to receive gift _____

Transfer Method _____

Adult Property Manager _____

Child
_____

Age child is to receive gift
_____

Transfer Method
_____

Adult Property Manager
_____

Child
_____

Age child is to receive gift
_____

Transfer Method
_____

Adult Property Manager
_____

Child
_____

Age child is to receive gift
_____

Transfer Method
_____

Adult Property Manager
_____

Child
_____

Age child is to receive gift
_____

Transfer Method
_____

Adult Property Manager
_____

Child
_____

Age child is to receive gift
_____

Transfer Method
_____

Adult Property Manager
_____

Child
_____

Age child is to receive gift
_____

Transfer Method
_____

Adult Property Manager
_____

Child
_____

Age child is to receive gift
_____

Transfer Method
_____

Adult Property Manager
_____

Will for a Married Person Leaving All or Bulk of Property to Spouse

Will of _____
your name

I, _____, a resident of
your name

_____, _____, _____,
city   *county*   *state*

declare that this is my will.

1. **Revocation of Prior Wills.** I revoke all wills and codicils that I have previously made.

2. **Personal Information.** I am married to _____,
spouse's name

and all references in this will to my _____ are to _____.
      husband/wife   *him/her*

3. **Children.** I have _____ _____ whose name(s) and date(s) of birth _____:
      number   *child/children*   *is/are*

_____   _____
name   *date of birth*

_____   _____
name   *date of birth*

_____   _____
name   *date of birth*

_____   _____
name   *date of birth*

_____   _____
name   *date of birth*

(repeat as needed)

There _____ _____ living _____ of my deceased child _____:
   is/are   *number*   *child/children*   *name*

_____   _____
name of grandchild   *date of birth*

_____   _____
name of grandchild   *date of birth*

_____   _____
name of grandchild   *date of birth*

(repeat as needed)

If I do not leave property in this will to a child or grandchild listed above, my failure to do so is intentional.

4. **Specific Gifts.** I leave the following specific gifts:

I leave _____
description of gift(s)

to _____ or, if _____
      beneficiary/beneficiaries   *she/he/they*

_____ not survive me, to _____.
does/do   *alternate beneficiary/beneficiaries*

I leave _____
                                              description of gift(s)

to _____ or, if _____
                              beneficiary/beneficiaries   *she/he/they*

_____ not survive me, to _____ .
does/do   *alternate beneficiary/beneficiaries*

I leave _____
                                              description of gift(s)

to _____ or, if _____
                              beneficiary/beneficiaries   *she/he/they*

_____ not survive me, to _____ .
does/do   *alternate beneficiary/beneficiaries*

5. Residuary Estate. I leave my residuary estate, that is, the rest of my property not otherwise specifically and

validly disposed of by this will or in any other manner, including lapsed or failed gifts, to my spouse,

_____, or, if my spouse fails to survive me, to my _____
                     name of spouse   *child/children*

_____
         name(s)

_____

as alternate residuary _____ in equal shares.
                                              beneficiary/beneficiaries

6. Beneficiary Provisions. The following terms and conditions shall apply to the beneficiary clauses of this will.

A. 45-Day Survivorship Period. As used in this will, the phrase "survive me" means to be alive or in existence as an

organization on the 45th day after my death. Any beneficiary, except any alternate residuary beneficiary, must survive me

to inherit under this will. If there are no surviving beneficiaries for a specific gift, that gift shall become part of my residuary

estate.

B. Shared Gifts. If I leave property to be shared by two or more beneficiaries, it shall be shared equally between them

unless this will provides otherwise.

If any beneficiary of a shared specific gift left in a single paragraph of the Specific Gifts clause, above, does not survive

me, that deceased beneficiary's portion of the gift shall be given to the surviving beneficiaries in equal shares.

If there is more than one alternate residuary beneficiary, they shall take property in equal shares. If any alternate

residuary beneficiary fails to survive me, that beneficiary's share shall be shared equally by the surviving alternate residuary

beneficiaries.

C. Encumbrances. All property that I leave by this will shall pass subject to any encumbrances or liens on the

property.

7. Executor. The following terms and conditions shall apply to the executor of this will.

A. Nomination of Executor. I nominate _____
                                                                                  executor's name

as executor, to serve without bond. If _____ shall for any reason fail to qualify or cease to act as executor,
                                                             she/he

I nominate _____
                                       alternate executor's name

as executor, also to serve without bond.

B. Executor's Powers. I direct that my executor take all actions legally permissible to have the probate of my will conducted as simply and as free of court supervision as possible, including filing a petition in the appropriate court for the independent administration of my estate.

I grant to my personal representative the following powers, to be exercised as he or she deems to be in the best interests of my estate:

1. To pay, as my executor decides is best (unless state law requires a specific method for payment), all my debts and taxes that may, by reason of my death, be assessed against my estate or any portion of it.

2. To retain property without liability for loss or depreciation resulting from such retention.

3. To dispose of property by public or private sale, or exchange, or otherwise, and receive or administer the proceeds as a part of my estate.

4. To vote stock, to exercise any option or privilege to convert bonds, notes, stocks, or other securities belonging to my estate into other bonds, notes, stocks, or other securities, and to exercise all other rights and privileges of a person owning similar property in his or her own right.

5. To lease any real property that may at any time form part of my estate.

6. To abandon, adjust, arbitrate, compromise, sue on, defend, or otherwise deal with and settle claims in favor of or against my estate.

7. To continue, maintain, operate, or participate in any business which is a part of my estate, and to effect incorporation, dissolution, or other change in the form of organization of the business.

8. To do all other acts, which in his or her judgment may be necessary or appropriate for the proper and advantageous management, investment, and distribution of my estate.

The foregoing powers, authority, and discretion are in addition to the powers, authority, and discretion vested in him or her by operation of law and may be exercised as often as is deemed necessary or advisable without application to or approval by any court in any jurisdiction.

8. Personal Guardian. If at my death any of my children are minors, and a personal guardian is needed, I nominate

_____
personal guardian's name

to be appointed personal guardian of my minor children. If _____ cannot serve as personal guardian,
                                                              she/he

I nominate _____
                          alternate personal guardian's name

to be appointed personal guardian.

I direct that no bond be required of any personal guardian.

9. Property Guardian. If at my death any of my children are minors, and a property guardian is needed, I appoint

_____
property guardian's name

as the property guardian of my minor children. If _____ cannot serve as property guardian, I appoint
she/he

_____ as property guardian.
alternate property guardian's name

I direct that no bond be required of any property guardian.

[Include only ONE Clause 10, below. Choose Uniform Transfers to Minors Act, the Family Pot Trust, OR the Child's Trust.]

10. Gifts Under the Uniform Transfers to Minors Act. All property left by this will to _____
minor's name

_____ shall be given to _____
custodian's name

as custodian for _____ under the Uniform Transfers to
minor's name

Minors Act of _____. If _____
your state   *custodian's name*

cannot serve as custodian, _____ shall serve as custodian.
alternate custodian's name

(repeat as needed)

10. Family Pot Trust. All property I leave by this will to the children listed in Section A below shall be held for them in a single trust, the family pot trust.

 A. Trust Beneficiaries

 _____
child's name

 _____
child's name

 _____
child's name

 _____
child's name

If all of the beneficiaries of the family pot trust are age 18 or older at my death, no family pot trust shall be established, and the property left to them shall be distributed to them outright.

If a beneficiary survives me but dies before the family pot trust terminates, that beneficiary's interest in the trust shall pass to the surviving beneficiaries of the family pot trust.

 B. Trustee of the Family Pot Trust. The trustee shall be _____
trustee's name

_____ or, if _____ cannot serve as trustee, the trustee shall be
she/he

_____.
successor trustee's name

 No bond shall be required of any trustee.

Will Form 1

NOLO www.nolo.com   Page 4 of 8

C. Duties of the Family Pot Trust Trustee

1. The trustee may distribute trust assets (income or principal) as the trustee deems necessary for a beneficiary's health, support, maintenance, and education. Education includes, but is not limited to, college, graduate, postgraduate, and vocational studies, plus reasonably related living expenses.

2. In deciding whether or not to make distributions, the trustee shall consider the value of the trust assets, the relative current and future needs of each beneficiary, and each beneficiary's other income, resources, and sources of support. In doing so, the trustee has the discretion to make distributions that benefit some beneficiaries more than others or that completely exclude others.

3. Any trust income that is not distributed by the trustee shall be accumulated and added to the principal.

D. Termination of the Family Pot Trust. When the youngest surviving beneficiary of this family pot trust reaches 18, the trustee shall distribute the remaining trust assets to the surviving beneficiaries in equal shares.

If none of the trust beneficiaries survives to the age of 18, the trustee shall distribute the remaining trust assets to my heirs at the death of the last surviving beneficiary.

E. Powers of the Trustee. In addition to all other powers granted a trustee in any portion of this will, the trustee of the family pot trust shall have the power to make distributions to the beneficiaries directly or to other people or organizations on behalf of the beneficiaries.

10. Child's Trusts. All property I leave by this will to a child listed in Section A below shall be held for that child in a separate trust.

A. Trust Beneficiaries and Age Limits. Each trust shall end when the beneficiary becomes 35, except as otherwise specified in this section.

Trust for	Shall end at age
_____	_____
_____	_____
_____	_____
_____	_____
_____	_____
_____	_____
_____	_____

B.   Trustees. The trustee of each child's trust shall be _____
trustee's name

_____ or, if _____ cannot serve as trustee, the trustee shall be
she/he

_____.
successor trustee's name

No bond shall be required of any trustee.

C. Duties of the Trustee

1. The trustee may distribute trust assets (income or principal) as the trustee deems necessary for the beneficiary's health, support, maintenance, and education. Education includes, but is not limited to, college, graduate, postgraduate, and vocational studies, plus reasonably related living expenses.

2. In deciding whether or not to make a distribution, the trustee may take into account the beneficiary's other income, resources, and sources of support.

3. Any trust income that is not distributed by the trustee shall be accumulated and added to the principal of that child's trust.

D. Termination of Trust. A child's trust shall terminate when any of the following events occurs:

1. The beneficiary becomes the age specified in Section A of this trust clause;

2. The beneficiary dies before becoming the age specified in Section A of this trust clause;

3. The trust is exhausted through distributions allowed under these provisions.

If a trust terminates for reason one, the remaining principal and accumulated net income of the trust shall pass to the beneficiary. If a trust terminates for reason two, the remaining principal and accumulated net income of the trust shall pass to the trust beneficiary's heirs.

E. Powers of the Trustee. In addition to all other powers granted the trustee in this will, the trustee shall have the power to make distributions to a child's trust beneficiary directly or to other people or organizations on behalf of that child.

[Delete Clause 11 if in Clause 10 you selected Gifts Under the Uniform Transfers to Minors Act.]

13. General Trust Administrative Provisions. Any trust established under this will shall be managed subject to the following provisions.

A. Intent. It is my intent that any trust established under this will be administered independently of court supervision to the maximum extent possible under the laws of the state having jurisdiction over the trust.

B. No Assignment. The interests of any beneficiary of any trust established under this will shall not be transferable by voluntary or involuntary assignment or by operation of law and shall be free from the claims of creditors and from attachment, execution, bankruptcy, or other legal process to the fullest extent permitted by law.

C. Trustee's Powers. In addition to other powers granted the trustee in this will, the trustee shall have all the powers generally conferred on trustees by the laws of the state having jurisdiction over this trust and the powers to:

1. Invest and reinvest trust funds in every kind of property and every kind of investment, provided that the trustee acts with the care, skill, prudence, and diligence under the prevailing circumstances that a prudent person acting in a similar capacity and familiar with such matters would use.

2. Receive additional property from any source and acquire or hold properties jointly or in undivided interests or in partnership or joint venture with other people or entities.

3. Enter, continue, or participate in the operation of any business, and incorporate, liquidate, reorganize, or otherwise change the form or terminate the operation of the business and contribute capital or loan money to the business.

4. Exercise all the rights, powers, and privileges of an owner of any securities held in the trust.

5. Borrow funds, guarantee or indemnify in the name of the trust, and secure any obligation, mortgage, pledge, or other security interest, and renew, extend, or modify any such obligations.

6. Lease trust property for terms within or beyond the term of the trust.

7. Prosecute, defend, contest, or otherwise litigate legal actions or other proceedings for the protection or benefit of the trust; pay, compromise, release, adjust, or submit to arbitration any debt, claim, or controversy; and insure the trust against any risk and the trustee against liability with respect to other people.

8. Pay himself or herself reasonable compensation out of trust assets for ordinary and extraordinary services, and for all services in connection with the complete or partial termination of this trust.

9. Employ and discharge professionals to aid or assist in managing the trust and compensate them from the trust assets.

D. Severability. If any provision of any trust is held invalid, that shall not affect other trust provisions that can be given effect without the invalid provision.

E. "Trustee" Defined. The term "trustee" shall include all successor trustees.

Signature

I subscribe my name to this will the _____ day of _____, _____, at

month *year*

_____, _____, _____,
city *county* *state*

and do hereby declare that I sign and execute this instrument as my last will and that I sign it willingly, that I execute it as my free and voluntary act for the purposes therein expressed and that I am of the age of majority or otherwise legally empowered to make a will, and under no constraint or undue influence.

_____
your signature

Witnesses

On this _____ day of _____, _____, _____
month *year* *your name*
declared to us, the undersigned, that this instrument was _____ will and requested us to act as witnesses
his/her
to it. _____ thereupon signed this will in our presence, all of us being present at the same time. We now, at
He/She
_____ request, in _____ presence and in the presence of each other, subscribe our names as
his/her *his/her*
witnesses and declare we understand this to be _____ will, and that to the best of our knowledge the
his/her

testator is of the age of majority, or is otherwise legally empowered to make a will, and under no constraint or undue influence.

We declare under penalty of perjury that the foregoing is true and correct, this _____ day of

_____, _____, at _____.
     month   *year*   *city and state*

_____
            witness's signature

_____ residing at _____,
     witness's typed name   *address*

_____, _____, _____.
        city   *county*   *state*

_____
            witness's signature

_____ residing at _____,
     witness's typed name   *address*

_____, _____, _____.
        city   *county*   *state*

_____
            witness's signature

_____ residing at _____,
     witness's typed name   *address*

_____, _____, _____.
        city   *county*   *state*

Will for a Single Person With No Minor Children

Will of

_____
your name

I, _____, a resident of
your name

_____, _____, _____,
city   *county*   *state*

declare that this is my will.

1. **Revocation of Prior Wills.** I revoke all wills and codicils that I have previously made.

2. **Personal Information.** I am a single adult.

3. **Children.** I have _____ _____ whose name(s) and date(s) of birth _____:
   number   *child/children*   *is/are*

   _____   _____
   name   *date of birth*

   _____   _____
   name   *date of birth*

   _____   _____
   name   *date of birth*

   _____   _____
   name   *date of birth*

   _____   _____
   name   *date of birth*

(repeat as needed)

There _____ _____ living _____ of my deceased child _____:
   is/are   *number*   *child/children*   *name*

   _____   _____
   name of grandchild   *date of birth*

   _____   _____
   name of grandchild   *date of birth*

   _____   _____
   name of grandchild   *date of birth*

(repeat as needed)

If I do not leave property in this will to a child or grandchild listed above, my failure to do so is intentional.

4. **Specific Gifts.** I leave the following specific gifts:

   I leave _____
   description of gift(s)

to _____ or, if _____
   beneficiary/beneficiaries   *she/he/they*

_____ not survive me, to _____.
does/do   *alternate beneficiary/beneficiaries*

I leave _____
description of gift(s)

to _____ or, if _____
beneficiary/beneficiaries   *she/he/they*

_____ not survive me, to _____.
does/do   *alternate beneficiary/beneficiaries*

I leave _____
description of gift(s)

to _____ or, if _____
beneficiary/beneficiaries   *she/he/they*

_____ not survive me, to _____.
does/do   *alternate beneficiary/beneficiaries*

II leave _____
description of gift(s)

to _____ or, if _____
beneficiary/beneficiaries   *she/he/they*

_____ not survive me, to _____.
does/do   *alternate beneficiary/beneficiaries*

I leave _____
description of gift(s)

to _____ or, if _____
beneficiary/beneficiaries   *she/he/they*

_____ not survive me, to _____
does/do   *alternate beneficiary/beneficiaries*

5. Residuary Estate. I leave my residuary estate, that is, the rest of my property not otherwise specifically and validly disposed of by this will or in any other manner, including lapsed or failed gifts, to _____

_____
residuary beneficiary/beneficiaries

or, if _____ _____ not survive me, to _____.
    she/he/they   *does/do*   *alternate residuary beneficiary/beneficiairies*

6. Beneficiary Provisions. The following terms and conditions shall apply to the beneficiary clauses of this will.

A. 45-Day Survivorship Period. As used in this will, the phrase "survive me" means to be alive or in existence as an organization on the 45th day after my death. Any beneficiary, except any alternate residuary beneficiary, must survive me to inherit under this will. If there are no surviving beneficiaries for a specific gift, that gift shall become part of my residuary estate.

B. Shared Gifts. If I leave property to be shared by two or more beneficiaries, it shall be shared equally between them unless this will provides otherwise.

If any beneficiary of a shared specific gift left in a single paragraph of the Specific Gifts clause, above, does not survive me, that deceased beneficiary's portion of the gift shall be given to the surviving beneficiaries in equal shares.

If any residuary beneficiary of a shared residuary gift does not survive me, that deceased beneficiary's portion of the residue shall be given to the surviving residuary beneficiaries in equal shares.

C. Encumbrances. All property that I leave by this will shall pass subject to any encumbrances or liens on the property.

7. Executor. The following terms and conditions shall apply to the executor of this will.

    A. Nomination of Executor. I nominate _____

                                                            executor's name

as executor, to serve without bond. If _____ shall for any reason fail to qualify or cease to act as executor,
                                              she/he

I nominate _____
                                alternate executor's name

as executor, also to serve without bond.

    B. Executor's Powers. I direct that my executor take all actions legally permissible to have the probate of my will conducted as simply and as free of court supervision as possible, including filing a petition in the appropriate court for the independent administration of my estate.

I grant to my personal representative the following powers, to be exercised as he or she deems to be in the best interests of my estate:

    1. To pay, as my executor decides is best (unless state law requires a specific method for payment), all my debts and taxes that may, by reason of my death, be assessed against my estate or any portion of it.

    2. To retain property without liability for loss or depreciation resulting from such retention.

    3. To dispose of property by public or private sale, or exchange, or otherwise, and receive or administer the proceeds as a part of my estate.

    4. To vote stock, to exercise any option or privilege to convert bonds, notes, stocks, or other securities belonging to my estate into other bonds, notes, stocks, or other securities, and to exercise all other rights and privileges of a person owning similar property in his or her own right.

    5. To lease any real property that may at any time form part of my estate.

    6. To abandon, adjust, arbitrate, compromise, sue on, defend, or otherwise deal with and settle claims in favor of or against my estate.

    7. To continue, maintain, operate, or participate in any business which is a part of my estate, and to effect incorporation, dissolution, or other change in the form of organization of the business.

    8. To do all other acts, which in his or her judgment may be necessary or appropriate for the proper and advantageous management, investment, and distribution of my estate.

The foregoing powers, authority, and discretion are in addition to the powers, authority, and discretion vested in him or her by operation of law and may be exercised as often as is deemed necessary or advisable without application to or approval by any court in any jurisdiction.

Signature

I subscribe my name to this will the _____ day of _____, _____, at
                                                            month   *year*

_____, _____, _____
           city   *county*   *state*

and do hereby declare that I sign and execute this instrument as my last will and that I sign it willingly, that I execute it as my free and voluntary act for the purposes therein expressed and that I am of the age of majority or otherwise legally empowered to make a will, and under no constraint or undue influence.

_____
your signature

Witnesses

On this _____ day of _____, _____, _____
                                    month   *year*   *your name*

declared to us, the undersigned, that this instrument was _____ will and requested us to act as witnesses
                                                                                  his/her

to it. _____ thereupon signed this will in our presence, all of us being present at the same time. We now, at
           He/She

_____ request, in _____ presence and in the presence of each other, subscribe our names as
   his/her   *his/her*

witnesses and declare we understand this to be _____ will, and that to the best of our knowledge the
                                                         his/her

testator is of the age of majority, or is otherwise legally empowered to make a will, and under no constraint or undue influence.

We declare under penalty of perjury that the foregoing is true and correct, this _____ day of

_____, _____, at _____.
        month   *year*   *city and state*

_____
witness's signature

_____ residing at _____,
           witness's typed name   *address*

_____, _____, _____.
        city   *county*   *state*

_____
witness's signature

_____ residing at _____,
           witness's typed name   *address*

_____, _____, _____.
        city   *county*   *state*

_____
witness's signature

_____ residing at _____,
           witness's typed name   *address*

_____, _____, _____.
        city   *county*   *state*

Will for a Single Person With Minor Children

Will of _____
your name

I, _____, a resident of
your name

_____, _____, _____,
city   *county*   *state*

declare that this is my will.

1. **Revocation of Prior Wills.** I revoke all wills and codicils that I have previously made.

2. **Personal Information.** I am a single adult.

3. **Children.** I have _____ _____ whose name(s) and date(s) of birth _____:
   number   *child/children*   *is/are*

   _____   _____
   name   *date of birth*

   _____   _____
   name   *date of birth*

   _____   _____
   name   *date of birth*

   _____   _____
   name   *date of birth*

   _____   _____
   name   *date of birth*

(repeat as needed)

There _____ _____ living _____ of my deceased child _____:
   is/are   *number*   *child/children*   *name*

   _____   _____
   name of grandchild   *date of birth*

   _____   _____
   name of grandchild   *date of birth*

   _____   _____
   name of grandchild   *date of birth*

(repeat as needed)

If I do not leave property in this will to a child or grandchild listed above, my failure to do so is intentional.

4. **Specific Gifts.** I leave the following specific gifts:

   I leave _____
   description of gift(s)

   to _____ or, if _____
   beneficiary/beneficiaries   *she/he/they*

   _____ not survive me, to _____.
   does/do   *alternate beneficiary/beneficiaries*

   I leave _____
   description of gift(s)

   to _____ or, if _____
   beneficiary/beneficiaries   *she/he/they*

   _____ not survive me, to _____.
   does/do   *alternate beneficiary/beneficiaries*

I leave _____
description of gift(s)

to _____ or, if _____
beneficiary/beneficiaries   *she/he/they*

_____ not survive me, to _____.
does/do   *alternate beneficiary/beneficiaries*

I leave _____
description of gift(s)

to _____ or, if _____
beneficiary/beneficiaries   *she/he/they*

_____ not survive me, to _____.
does/do   *alternate beneficiary/beneficiaries*

I leave _____
description of gift(s)

to _____ or, if _____
beneficiary/beneficiaries   *she/he/they*

_____ not survive me, to _____.
does/do   *alternate beneficiary/beneficiaries*

5. **Residuary Estate.** I leave my residuary estate, that is, the rest of my property not otherwise specifically and validly disposed of by this will or in any other manner, including lapsed or failed gifts, to _____

_____
residuary beneficiary/beneficiaries

or, if _____ _____ not survive me, to _____.
she/he/they   *does/do*   *alternate residuary beneficiary/beneficiairies*

6. **Beneficiary Provisions.** The following terms and conditions shall apply to the beneficiary clauses of this will.

A. 45-Day Survivorship Period. As used in this will, the phrase "survive me" means to be alive or in existence as an organization on the 45th day after my death. Any beneficiary, except any alternate residuary beneficiary, must survive me to inherit under this will. If there are no surviving beneficiaries for a specific gift, that gift shall become part of my residuary estate.

B. Shared Gifts. If I leave property to be shared by two or more beneficiaries, it shall be shared equally between them unless this will provides otherwise.

If any beneficiary of a shared specific gift left in a single paragraph of the Specific Gifts clause, above, does not survive me, that deceased beneficiary's portion of the gift shall be given to the surviving beneficiaries in equal shares.

If any residuary beneficiary of a shared residuary gift does not survive me, that deceased beneficiary's portion of the residue shall be given to the surviving residuary beneficiaries in equal shares.

C. Encumbrances. All property that I leave by this will shall pass subject to any encumbrances or liens on the property.

7. Executor. The following terms and conditions shall apply to the executor of this will.

    A. Nomination of Executor. I nominate _____

executor's name

as executor, to serve without bond. If _____ shall for any reason fail to qualify or cease to act as executor,

she/he

I nominate _____

alternate executor's name

as executor, also to serve without bond.

    B. Executor's Powers. I direct that my executor take all actions legally permissible to have the probate of my will conducted as simply and as free of court supervision as possible, including filing a petition in the appropriate court for the independent administration of my estate.

    I grant to my personal representative the following powers, to be exercised as he or she deems to be in the best interests of my estate:

    1. To pay, as my executor decides is best (unless state law requires a specific method for payment), all my debts and taxes that may, by reason of my death, be assessed against my estate or any portion of it.

    2. To retain property without liability for loss or depreciation resulting from such retention.

    3. To dispose of property by public or private sale, or exchange, or otherwise, and receive or administer the proceeds as a part of my estate.

    4. To vote stock, to exercise any option or privilege to convert bonds, notes, stocks, or other securities belonging to my estate into other bonds, notes, stocks, or other securities, and to exercise all other rights and privileges of a person owning similar property in his or her own right.

    5. To lease any real property that may at any time form part of my estate.

    6. To abandon, adjust, arbitrate, compromise, sue on, defend, or otherwise deal with and settle claims in favor of or against my estate.

    7. To continue, maintain, operate, or participate in any business which is a part of my estate, and to effect incorporation, dissolution, or other change in the form of organization of the business.

    8. To do all other acts, which in his or her judgment may be necessary or appropriate for the proper and advantageous management, investment, and distribution of my estate.

    The foregoing powers, authority, and discretion are in addition to the powers, authority, and discretion vested in him or her by operation of law and may be exercised as often as is deemed necessary or advisable without application to or approval by any court in any jurisdiction.

8. Personal Guardian. If at my death any of my children are minors, and a personal guardian is needed, I nominate

_____

personal guardian's name

to be appointed personal guardian of my minor children. If _____ cannot serve as personal guardian,

she/he

I nominate _____
alternate personal guardian's name

to be appointed personal guardian.

I direct that no bond be required of any personal guardian.

9. Property Guardian. If at my death any of my children are minors, and a property guardian is needed, I appoint

_____
property guardian's name

as the property guardian of my minor children. If _____ cannot serve as property guardian, I appoint
she/he

_____ as property guardian.
alternate property guardian's name

I direct that no bond be required of any property guardian.

[Include only ONE Clause 10, below. Choose Uniform Transfers to Minors Act, the Family Pot Trust, OR the Child's Trust.]

10. Gifts Under the Uniform Transfers to Minors Act. All property left by this will to _____
minor's name

_____ shall be given to _____
custodian's name

as custodian for _____ under the Uniform Transfers to
minor's name

Minors Act of _____. If _____
your state   *custodian's name*

cannot serve as custodian, _____ shall serve as custodian.
alternate custodian's name

(repeat as needed)

10. Family Pot Trust. All property I leave by this will to the children listed in Section A below shall be held for them in a single trust, the family pot trust.

    A. Trust Beneficiaries

_____
child's name

_____
child's name

_____
child's name

_____
child's name

If all of the beneficiaries of the family pot trust are age 18 or older at my death, no family pot trust shall be established, and the property left to them shall be distributed to them outright.

If a beneficiary survives me but dies before the family pot trust terminates, that beneficiary's interest in the trust shall pass to the surviving beneficiaries of the family pot trust.

    B. Trustee of the Family Pot Trust. The trustee shall be _____
trustee's name

_____ or, if _____ cannot serve as trustee, the trustee shall be
she/he

_____.
successor trustee's name

No bond shall be required of any trustee.

C. Duties of the Family Pot Trust Trustee

1. The trustee may distribute trust assets (income or principal) as the trustee deems necessary for a beneficiary's health, support, maintenance, and education. Education includes, but is not limited to, college, graduate, postgraduate, and vocational studies, plus reasonably related living expenses.

2. In deciding whether or not to make distributions, the trustee shall consider the value of the trust assets, the relative current and future needs of each beneficiary, and each beneficiary's other income, resources, and sources of support. In doing so, the trustee has the discretion to make distributions that benefit some beneficiaries more than others or that completely exclude others.

3. Any trust income that is not distributed by the trustee shall be accumulated and added to the principal.

D. Termination of the Family Pot Trust. When the youngest surviving beneficiary of this family pot trust reaches 18, the trustee shall distribute the remaining trust assets to the surviving beneficiaries in equal shares.

If none of the trust beneficiaries survives to the age of 18, the trustee shall distribute the remaining trust assets to my heirs at the death of the last surviving beneficiary.

E. Powers of the Trustee. In addition to all other powers granted a trustee in any portion of this will, the trustee of the family pot trust shall have the power to make distributions to the beneficiaries directly or to other people or organizations on behalf of the beneficiaries.

10. Child's Trusts. All property I leave by this will to a child listed in Section A below shall be held for that child in a separate trust.

A. Trust Beneficiaries and Age Limits. Each trust shall end when the beneficiary becomes 35, except as otherwise specified in this section.

Trust for   **Shall end at age**

_____   _____

_____   _____

_____   _____

_____   _____

_____   _____

_____   _____

_____   _____

B. Trustees. The trustee of each child's trust shall be _____

trustee's name

_____ or, if _____ cannot serve as trustee, the trustee shall be

she/he

_____.

successor trustee's name

No bond shall be required of any trustee.

C. Duties of the Trustee

1. The trustee may distribute trust assets (income or principal) as the trustee deems necessary for the beneficiary's health, support, maintenance, and education. Education includes, but is not limited to, college, graduate, postgraduate, and vocational studies, plus reasonably related living expenses.

2. In deciding whether or not to make a distribution, the trustee may take into account the beneficiary's other income, resources, and sources of support.

3. Any trust income that is not distributed by the trustee shall be accumulated and added to the principal of that child's trust.

D. Termination of Trust. A child's trust shall terminate when any of the following events occurs:

1. The beneficiary becomes the age specified in Section A of this trust clause;

2. The beneficiary dies before becoming the age specified in Section A of this trust clause;

3. The trust is exhausted through distributions allowed under these provisions.

If a trust terminates for reason one, the remaining principal and accumulated net income of the trust shall pass to the beneficiary. If a trust terminates for reason two, the remaining principal and accumulated net income of the trust shall pass to the trust beneficiary's heirs.

E. Powers of the Trustee. In addition to all other powers granted the trustee in this will, the trustee shall have the power to make distributions to a child's trust beneficiary directly or to other people or organizations on behalf of that child.

[Delete Clause 11 if in Clause 10 you selected Gifts Under the Uniform Transfers to Minors Act.]

13. General Trust Administrative Provisions. Any trust established under this will shall be managed subject to the following provisions.

A. Intent. It is my intent that any trust established under this will be administered independently of court supervision to the maximum extent possible under the laws of the state having jurisdiction over the trust.

B. No Assignment. The interests of any beneficiary of any trust established under this will shall not be transferable by voluntary or involuntary assignment or by operation of law and shall be free from the claims of creditors and from attachment, execution, bankruptcy, or other legal process to the fullest extent permitted by law.

C. Trustee's Powers. In addition to other powers granted the trustee in this will, the trustee shall have all the powers generally conferred on trustees by the laws of the state having jurisdiction over this trust and the powers to:

1. Invest and reinvest trust funds in every kind of property and every kind of investment, provided that the trustee acts with the care, skill, prudence, and diligence under the prevailing circumstances that a prudent person acting in a similar capacity and familiar with such matters would use.

2. Receive additional property from any source and acquire or hold properties jointly or in undivided interests or in partnership or joint venture with other people or entities.

3. Enter, continue, or participate in the operation of any business, and incorporate, liquidate, reorganize, or otherwise change the form or terminate the operation of the business and contribute capital or loan money to the business.

4. Exercise all the rights, powers, and privileges of an owner of any securities held in the trust.

5. Borrow funds, guarantee or indemnify in the name of the trust, and secure any obligation, mortgage, pledge, or other security interest, and renew, extend, or modify any such obligations.

6. Lease trust property for terms within or beyond the term of the trust.

7. Prosecute, defend, contest, or otherwise litigate legal actions or other proceedings for the protection or benefit of the trust; pay, compromise, release, adjust, or submit to arbitration any debt, claim, or controversy; and insure the trust against any risk and the trustee against liability with respect to other people.

8. Pay himself or herself reasonable compensation out of trust assets for ordinary and extraordinary services, and for all services in connection with the complete or partial termination of this trust.

9. Employ and discharge professionals to aid or assist in managing the trust and compensate them from the trust assets.

D. Severability. If any provision of any trust is held invalid, that shall not affect other trust provisions that can be given effect without the invalid provision.

E. "Trustee" Defined. The term "trustee" shall include all successor trustees.

Signature

I subscribe my name to this will the _____ day of _____, _____, at
month<space><space><space><space><space><space><space><space><space><space>*year*

_____, _____, _____,
city<space><space><space><space><space><space><space><space><space><space><space><space>*county*<space><space><space><space><space><space><space><space><space><space><space><space>*state*

and do hereby declare that I sign and execute this instrument as my last will and that I sign it willingly, that I execute it as my free and voluntary act for the purposes therein expressed and that I am of the age of majority or otherwise legally empowered to make a will, and under no constraint or undue influence.

_____
your signature

Witnesses

On this _____ day of _____, _____, _____
month<space><space><space><space><space><space>*year*<space><space><space><space><space><space><space><space>*your name*

declared to us, the undersigned, that this instrument was _____ will and requested us to act as witnesses
his/her

to it. _____ thereupon signed this will in our presence, all of us being present at the same time. We now, at
He/She

_____ request, in _____ presence and in the presence of each other, subscribe our names as
his/her<space><space><space><space><space><space><space><space>*his/her*

witnesses and declare we understand this to be _____ will, and that to the best of our knowledge the
his/her

testator is of the age of majority, or is otherwise legally empowered to make a will, and under no constraint or undue influence.

We declare under penalty of perjury that the foregoing is true and correct, this _____ day of _____, _____, at _____.
        month   *year*   *city and state*

_____
              witness's signature

_____ residing at _____,
         witness's typed name   *address*

_____, _____, _____.
         city   *county*   *state*

_____
              witness's signature

_____ residing at _____,
         witness's typed name   *address*

_____, _____, _____.
         city   *county*   *state*

_____
              witness's signature

_____ residing at _____,
         witness's typed name   *address*

_____, _____, _____.
         city   *county*   *state*

Will for a Married Person With No Minor Children

Will of _____
your name

I, _____, a resident of
your name

_____, _____, _____,
     city   *county*   *state*

declare that this is my will.

1. **Revocation of Prior Wills.** I revoke all wills and codicils that I have previously made.

2. **Personal Information.** I am married to _____ ,
spouse's name

and all references in this will to my _____ are to _____ .
                               husband/wife   *him/her*

3. **Children.** I have _____ _____ whose name(s) and date(s) of birth _____:
           number   *child/children*   *is/are*

_____   _____
                           name   *date of birth*

_____   _____
                           name   *date of birth*

_____   _____
                           name   *date of birth*

_____   _____
                           name   *date of birth*

_____   _____
                           name   *date of birth*

(repeat as needed)

There _____ _____ living _____ of my deceased child _____ :
      is/are   *number*   *child/children*   *name*

_____   _____
                 name of grandchild   *date of birth*

_____   _____
                 name of grandchild   *date of birth*

_____   _____
                 name of grandchild   *date of birth*

(repeat as needed)

If I do not leave property in this will to a child or grandchild listed above, my failure to do so is intentional.

4. **Specific Gifts.** I leave the following specific gifts:

I leave _____
description of gift(s)

to _____ or, if _____
                      beneficiary/beneficiaries   *she/he/they*

_____ not survive me, to _____ ,
  does/do   *alternate beneficiary/beneficiaries*

I leave _____
description of gift(s)

to _____ or, if _____
                      beneficiary/beneficiaries   *she/he/they*

_____ not survive me, to _____.
    does/do   *alternate beneficiary/beneficiaries*

    I leave _____
                                   description of gift(s)

to _____ or, if _____
              beneficiary/beneficiaries   *she/he/they*

_____ not survive me, to _____.
    does/do   *alternate beneficiary/beneficiaries*

5. **Residuary Estate.** I leave my residuary estate, that is, the rest of my property not otherwise specifically and validly disposed of by this will or in any other manner, including lapsed or failed gifts, to _____

_____
                   residuary beneficiary/beneficiaries

or, if _____ _____ not survive me, to _____.
    she/he/they   *does/do*   *alternate residuary beneficiary/beneficiairies*

6. **Beneficiary Provisions.** The following terms and conditions shall apply to the beneficiary clauses of this will.

    A. 45-Day Survivorship Period. As used in this will, the phrase "survive me" means to be alive or in existence as an organization on the 45th day after my death. Any beneficiary, except any alternate residuary beneficiary, must survive me to inherit under this will. If there are no surviving beneficiaries for a specific gift, that gift shall become part of my residuary estate.

    B. Shared Gifts. If I leave property to be shared by two or more beneficiaries, it shall be shared equally between them unless this will provides otherwise.

    If any beneficiary of a shared specific gift left in a single paragraph of the Specific Gifts clause, above, does not survive me, that deceased beneficiary's portion of the gift shall be given to the surviving beneficiaries in equal shares.

    If any residuary beneficiary of a shared residuary gift does not survive me, that deceased beneficiary's portion of the residue shall be given to the surviving residuary beneficiaries in equal shares.

    C. Encumbrances. All property that I leave by this will shall pass subject to any encumbrances or liens on the property.

7. **Executor.** The following terms and conditions shall apply to the executor of this will.

    A. Nomination of Executor. I nominate _____
                                        executor's name

as executor, to serve without bond. If _____ shall for any reason fail to qualify or cease to act as executor,
                                    she/he

I nominate _____
                     alternate executor's name

as executor, also to serve without bond.

B. Executor's Powers. I direct that my executor take all actions legally permissible to have the probate of my will conducted as simply and as free of court supervision as possible, including filing a petition in the appropriate court for the independent administration of my estate.

I grant to my personal representative the following powers, to be exercised as he or she deems to be in the best interests of my estate:

1. To pay, as my executor decides is best (unless state law requires a specific method for payment), all my debts and taxes that may, by reason of my death, be assessed against my estate or any portion of it.

2. To retain property without liability for loss or depreciation resulting from such retention.

3. To dispose of property by public or private sale, or exchange, or otherwise, and receive or administer the proceeds as a part of my estate.

4. To vote stock, to exercise any option or privilege to convert bonds, notes, stocks, or other securities belonging to my estate into other bonds, notes, stocks, or other securities, and to exercise all other rights and privileges of a person owning similar property in his or her own right.

5. To lease any real property that may at any time form part of my estate.

6. To abandon, adjust, arbitrate, compromise, sue on, defend, or otherwise deal with and settle claims in favor of or against my estate.

7. To continue, maintain, operate, or participate in any business which is a part of my estate, and to effect incorporation, dissolution, or other change in the form of organization of the business.

8. To do all other acts, which in his or her judgment may be necessary or appropriate for the proper and advantageous management, investment, and distribution of my estate.

The foregoing powers, authority, and discretion are in addition to the powers, authority, and discretion vested in him or her by operation of law and may be exercised as often as is deemed necessary or advisable without application to or approval by any court in any jurisdiction.

Signature

I subscribe my name to this will the _____ day of _____, _____, at

month   year

_____, _____, _____,

city   county   state

and do hereby declare that I sign and execute this instrument as my last will and that I sign it willingly, that I execute it as my free and voluntary act for the purposes therein expressed and that I am of the age of majority or otherwise legally empowered to make a will, and under no constraint or undue influence.

_____

your signature

Witnesses

On this _____ day of _____, _____, _____

month   year   your name

declared to us, the undersigned, that this instrument was _____ will and requested us to act as witnesses

his/her

to it. _____ thereupon signed this will in our presence, all of us being present at the same time. We now, at

He/She

_____ request, in _____ presence and in the presence of each other, subscribe our names as

his/her   his/her

witnesses and declare we understand this to be _____ will, and that to the best of our knowledge the

his/her

testator is of the age of majority, or is otherwise legally empowered to make a will, and under no constraint or undue

influence.

We declare under penalty of perjury that the foregoing is true and correct, this _____ day of

_____, _____, at _____.

month   year   city and state

_____

witness's signature

_____ residing at _____,

witness's typed name   address

_____, _____, _____.

city   county   state

_____

witness's signature

_____ residing at _____,

witness's typed name   address

_____, _____, _____.

city   county   state

_____

witness's signature

_____ residing at _____,

witness's typed name   address

_____, _____, _____.

city   county   state

Will for a Married Person With Minor Children

Will of _____
your name

I, _____, a resident of
your name

_____, _____, _____,
city   *county*   *state*

declare that this is my will.

1. **Revocation of Prior Wills.** I revoke all wills and codicils that I have previously made.

2. **Personal Information.** I am married to _____ ,
spouse's name

and all references in this will to my _____ are to _____ .
husband/wife   *him/her*

3. **Children.** I have _____ _____ whose name(s) and date(s) of birth _____:
number   *child/children*   *is/are*

_____	_____
name	*date of birth*
_____	_____
name	*date of birth*
_____	_____
name	*date of birth*
_____	_____
name	*date of birth*
_____	_____
name	*date of birth*

(repeat as needed)

There _____ _____ living _____ of my deceased child _____ :
is/are   *number*   *child/children*   *name*

_____	_____
name of grandchild	*date of birth*
_____	_____
name of grandchild	*date of birth*
_____	_____
name of grandchild	*date of birth*

(repeat as needed)

If I do not leave property in this will to a child or grandchild listed above, my failure to do so is intentional.

4. **Specific Gifts.** I leave the following specific gifts:

I leave _____
description of gift(s)

to _____ or, if _____
beneficiary/beneficiaries   *she/he/they*

_____ not survive me, to _____ .
does/do   *alternate beneficiary/beneficiaries*

I leave _____
_____ description of gift(s) _____

to _____ or, if _____
_____ beneficiary/beneficiaries _____ she/he/they

_____ not survive me, to _____.
does/do _____ alternate beneficiary/beneficiaries

I leave _____
_____ description of gift(s) _____

to _____ or, if _____
_____ beneficiary/beneficiaries _____ she/he/they

_____ not survive me, to _____.
does/do _____ alternate beneficiary/beneficiaries

I leave _____
_____ description of gift(s) _____

to _____ or, if _____
_____ beneficiary/beneficiaries _____ she/he/they

_____ not survive me, to _____.
does/do _____ alternate beneficiary/beneficiaries

I leave _____
_____ description of gift(s) _____

to _____ or, if _____
_____ beneficiary/beneficiaries _____ she/he/they

_____ not survive me, to _____.
does/do _____ alternate beneficiary/beneficiaries

5. Residuary Estate. I leave my residuary estate, that is, the rest of my property not otherwise specifically and validly disposed of by this will or in any other manner, including lapsed or failed gifts, to _____

_____
residuary beneficiary/beneficiaries

or, if _____ _____ not survive me, to _____.
she/he/they *does/do* *alternate residuary beneficiary/beneficiairies*

6. Beneficiary Provisions. The following terms and conditions shall apply to the beneficiary clauses of this will.

A. 45-Day Survivorship Period. As used in this will, the phrase "survive me" means to be alive or in existence as an organization on the 45th day after my death. Any beneficiary, except any alternate residuary beneficiary, must survive me to inherit under this will. If there are no surviving beneficiaries for a specific gift, that gift shall become part of my residuary estate.

B. Shared Gifts. If I leave property to be shared by two or more beneficiaries, it shall be shared equally between them unless this will provides otherwise.

If any beneficiary of a shared specific gift left in a single paragraph of the Specific Gifts clause, above, does not survive me, that deceased beneficiary's portion of the gift shall be given to the surviving beneficiaries in equal shares.

If any residuary beneficiary of a shared residuary gift does not survive me, that deceased beneficiary's portion of the residue shall be given to the surviving residuary beneficiaries in equal shares.

C. Encumbrances. All property that I leave by this will shall pass subject to any encumbrances or liens on the property.

7. **Executor.** The following terms and conditions shall apply to the executor of this will.

    A. Nomination of Executor. I nominate _____

                                                  executor's name

as executor, to serve without bond. If _____ shall for any reason fail to qualify or cease to act as executor,

                                    she/he

I nominate _____

                                    alternate executor's name

as executor, also to serve without bond.

    B. Executor's Powers. I direct that my executor take all actions legally permissible to have the probate of my will conducted as simply and as free of court supervision as possible, including filing a petition in the appropriate court for the independent administration of my estate.

I grant to my personal representative the following powers, to be exercised as he or she deems to be in the best interests of my estate:

1. To pay, as my executor decides is best (unless state law requires a specific method for payment), all my debts and taxes that may, by reason of my death, be assessed against my estate or any portion of it.

2. To retain property without liability for loss or depreciation resulting from such retention.

3. To dispose of property by public or private sale, or exchange, or otherwise, and receive or administer the proceeds as a part of my estate.

4. To vote stock, to exercise any option or privilege to convert bonds, notes, stocks, or other securities belonging to my estate into other bonds, notes, stocks, or other securities, and to exercise all other rights and privileges of a person owning similar property in his or her own right.

5. To lease any real property that may at any time form part of my estate.

6. To abandon, adjust, arbitrate, compromise, sue on, defend, or otherwise deal with and settle claims in favor of or against my estate.

7. To continue, maintain, operate, or participate in any business which is a part of my estate, and to effect incorporation, dissolution, or other change in the form of organization of the business.

8. To do all other acts, which in his or her judgment may be necessary or appropriate for the proper and advantageous management, investment, and distribution of my estate.

The foregoing powers, authority, and discretion are in addition to the powers, authority, and discretion vested in him or her by operation of law and may be exercised as often as is deemed necessary or advisable without application to or approval by any court in any jurisdiction.

8. **Personal Guardian.** If at my death any of my children are minors, and a personal guardian is needed, I nominate

_____

                                    personal guardian's name

to be appointed personal guardian of my minor children. If _____ cannot serve as personal guardian,

                                    she/he

I nominate _____

                                    alternate personal guardian's name

to be appointed personal guardian.

I direct that no bond be required of any personal guardian.

9. Property Guardian. If at my death any of my children are minors, and a property guardian is needed, I appoint

_____
property guardian's name

as the property guardian of my minor children. If _____ cannot serve as property guardian, I appoint
she/he

_____ as property guardian.
alternate property guardian's name

I direct that no bond be required of any property guardian.

[Include only ONE Clause 10, below. Choose Uniform Transfers to Minors Act, the Family Pot Trust, OR the Child's Trust.]

10. Gifts Under the Uniform Transfers to Minors Act. All property left by this will to _____
minor's name

_____ shall be given to _____
custodian's name

as custodian for _____ under the Uniform Transfers to
minor's name

Minors Act of _____. If _____
your state   *custodian's name*

cannot serve as custodian, _____ shall serve as custodian.
alternate custodian's name

(repeat as needed)

10. Family Pot Trust. All property I leave by this will to the children listed in Section A below shall be held for them in a single trust, the family pot trust.

    A. Trust Beneficiaries

_____
child's name

_____
child's name

_____
child's name

_____
child's name

If all of the beneficiaries of the family pot trust are age 18 or older at my death, no family pot trust shall be established, and the property left to them shall be distributed to them outright.

If a beneficiary survives me but dies before the family pot trust terminates, that beneficiary's interest in the trust shall pass to the surviving beneficiaries of the family pot trust.

    B. Trustee of the Family Pot Trust. The trustee shall be _____
trustee's name

_____ or, if _____ cannot serve as trustee, the trustee shall be
she/he

_____.
successor trustee's name

No bond shall be required of any trustee.

C. Duties of the Family Pot Trust Trustee

1. The trustee may distribute trust assets (income or principal) as the trustee deems necessary for a beneficiary's health, support, maintenance, and education. Education includes, but is not limited to, college, graduate, postgraduate, and vocational studies, plus reasonably related living expenses.

2. In deciding whether or not to make distributions, the trustee shall consider the value of the trust assets, the relative current and future needs of each beneficiary, and each beneficiary's other income, resources, and sources of support. In doing so, the trustee has the discretion to make distributions that benefit some beneficiaries more than others or that completely exclude others.

3. Any trust income that is not distributed by the trustee shall be accumulated and added to the principal.

D. Termination of the Family Pot Trust. When the youngest surviving beneficiary of this family pot trust reaches 18, the trustee shall distribute the remaining trust assets to the surviving beneficiaries in equal shares.

If none of the trust beneficiaries survives to the age of 18, the trustee shall distribute the remaining trust assets to my heirs at the death of the last surviving beneficiary.

E. Powers of the Trustee. In addition to all other powers granted a trustee in any portion of this will, the trustee of the family pot trust shall have the power to make distributions to the beneficiaries directly or to other people or organizations on behalf of the beneficiaries.

10. Child's Trusts. All property I leave by this will to a child listed in Section A below shall be held for that child in a separate trust.

A. Trust Beneficiaries and Age Limits. Each trust shall end when the beneficiary becomes 35, except as otherwise specified in this section.

Trust for	Shall end at age
_____	_____
_____	_____
_____	_____
_____	_____
_____	_____
_____	_____
_____	_____

B. Trustees. The trustee of each child's trust shall be _____
trustee's name

_____ or, if _____ cannot serve as trustee, the trustee shall be
she/he

_____.
successor trustee's name

No bond shall be required of any trustee.

C. Duties of the Trustee

1. The trustee may distribute trust assets (income or principal) as the trustee deems necessary for the beneficiary's health, support, maintenance, and education. Education includes, but is not limited to, college, graduate, postgraduate, and vocational studies, plus reasonably related living expenses.

2. In deciding whether or not to make a distribution, the trustee may take into account the beneficiary's other income, resources, and sources of support.

3. Any trust income that is not distributed by the trustee shall be accumulated and added to the principal of that child's trust.

D. Termination of Trust. A child's trust shall terminate when any of the following events occurs:

1. The beneficiary becomes the age specified in Section A of this trust clause;

2. The beneficiary dies before becoming the age specified in Section A of this trust clause;

3. The trust is exhausted through distributions allowed under these provisions.

If a trust terminates for reason one, the remaining principal and accumulated net income of the trust shall pass to the beneficiary. If a trust terminates for reason two, the remaining principal and accumulated net income of the trust shall pass to the trust beneficiary's heirs.

E. Powers of the Trustee. In addition to all other powers granted the trustee in this will, the trustee shall have the power to make distributions to a child's trust beneficiary directly or to other people or organizations on behalf of that child.

[Delete Clause 11 if in Clause 10 you selected Gifts Under the Uniform Transfers to Minors Act.]

11. General Trust Administrative Provisions. Any trust established under this will shall be managed subject to the following provisions.

A. Intent. It is my intent that any trust established under this will be administered independently of court supervision to the maximum extent possible under the laws of the state having jurisdiction over the trust.

B. No Assignment. The interests of any beneficiary of any trust established under this will shall not be transferable by voluntary or involuntary assignment or by operation of law and shall be free from the claims of creditors and from attachment, execution, bankruptcy, or other legal process to the fullest extent permitted by law.

C. Trustee's Powers. In addition to other powers granted the trustee in this will, the trustee shall have all the powers generally conferred on trustees by the laws of the state having jurisdiction over this trust and the powers to:

1. Invest and reinvest trust funds in every kind of property and every kind of investment, provided that the trustee acts with the care, skill, prudence, and diligence under the prevailing circumstances that a prudent person acting in a similar capacity and familiar with such matters would use.

2. Receive additional property from any source and acquire or hold properties jointly or in undivided interests or in partnership or joint venture with other people or entities.

3. Enter, continue, or participate in the operation of any business, and incorporate, liquidate, reorganize, or otherwise change the form or terminate the operation of the business and contribute capital or loan money to the business.

4. Exercise all the rights, powers, and privileges of an owner of any securities held in the trust.

5. Borrow funds, guarantee or indemnify in the name of the trust, and secure any obligation, mortgage, pledge, or other security interest, and renew, extend, or modify any such obligations.

6. Lease trust property for terms within or beyond the term of the trust.

7. Prosecute, defend, contest, or otherwise litigate legal actions or other proceedings for the protection or benefit of the trust; pay, compromise, release, adjust, or submit to arbitration any debt, claim, or controversy; and insure the trust against any risk and the trustee against liability with respect to other people.

8. Pay himself or herself reasonable compensation out of trust assets for ordinary and extraordinary services, and for all services in connection with the complete or partial termination of this trust.

9. Employ and discharge professionals to aid or assist in managing the trust and compensate them from the trust assets.

D. Severability. If any provision of any trust is held invalid, that shall not affect other trust provisions that can be given effect without the invalid provision.

E. "Trustee" Defined. The term "trustee" shall include all successor trustees.

Signature

I subscribe my name to this will the _____ day of _____, _____, at
                                                month   *year*

_____, _____, _____,
         city   *county*   *state*

and do hereby declare that I sign and execute this instrument as my last will and that I sign it willingly, that I execute it as my free and voluntary act for the purposes therein expressed, and that I am of the age of majority or otherwise legally empowered to make a will, and under no constraint or undue influence.

_____
your signature

Witnesses

On this _____ day of _____, _____, _____
                         month   *year*   *your name*

declared to us, the undersigned, that this instrument was _____ will and requested us to act as witnesses
                                                 his/her

to it. _____ thereupon signed this will in our presence, all of us being present at the same time. We now, at
   He/She

_____ request, in _____ presence and in the presence of each other, subscribe our names as
   his/her   *his/her*

witnesses and declare we understand this to be _____ will, and that to the best of our knowledge the
                                              his/her

testator is of the age of majority, or is otherwise legally empowered to make a will, and under no constraint or undue influence.

We declare under penalty of perjury that the foregoing is true and correct, this _____ day of

_____, _____, at _____.
           month   *year*   *city and state*

_____
               witness's signature

_____ residing at _____,
           witness's typed name   *address*

_____, _____, _____.
         city   *county*   *state*

_____
               witness's signature

_____ residing at _____,
           witness's typed name   *address*

_____, _____, _____.
         city   *county*   *state*

_____
               witness's signature

_____ residing at _____,
           witness's typed name   *address*

_____, _____, _____.
         city   *county*   *state*

Will for an Unmarried Person With a Partner and No Minor Children

Will of _____
your name

I, _____, a resident of
your name

_____, _____, _____,
city   *county*   *state*

declare that this is my will.

1. Revocation of Prior Wills. I revoke all wills and codicils that I have previously made.

2. Personal Information. My _____ name is _____ ,
partner's   *name*

and all references in this will to my _____ are to _____.
partner   *him/her*

3. Children. I have _____ _____ whose name(s) and date(s) of birth _____:
number   *child/children*   *is/are*

_____   _____
name   *date of birth*

_____   _____
name   *date of birth*

_____   _____
name   *date of birth*

_____   _____
name   *date of birth*

_____   _____
name   *date of birth*

(repeat as needed)

There _____ _____ living _____ of my deceased child _____:
is/are   *number*   *child/children*   *name*

_____   _____
name of grandchild   *date of birth*

_____   _____
name of grandchild   *date of birth*

_____   _____
name of grandchild   *date of birth*

(repeat as needed)

If I do not leave property in this will to a child or grandchild listed above, my failure to do so is intentional.

4. Specific Gifts. I leave the following specific gifts:

I leave _____
description of gift(s)

to _____ or, if _____
beneficiary/beneficiaries   *she/he/they*

_____ not survive me, to _____.
does/do   *alternate beneficiary/beneficiaries*

I leave _____

description of gift(s)

to _____ or, if _____

beneficiary/beneficiaries   *she/he/they*

_____ not survive me, to _____.

does/do   *alternate beneficiary/beneficiaries*

I leave _____

description of gift(s)

to _____ or, if _____

beneficiary/beneficiaries   *she/he/they*

_____ not survive me, to _____.

does/do   *alternate beneficiary/beneficiaries*

I leave _____

description of gift(s)

to _____ or, if _____

beneficiary/beneficiaries   *she/he/they*

_____ not survive me, to _____.

does/do   *alternate beneficiary/beneficiaries*

I leave _____

description of gift(s)

to _____ or, if _____

beneficiary/beneficiaries   *she/he/they*

_____ not survive me, to _____.

does/do   *alternate beneficiary/beneficiaries*

5. Residuary Estate. I leave my residuary estate, that is, the rest of my property not otherwise specifically and validly disposed of by this will or in any other manner, including lapsed or failed gifts, to _____

_____

residuary beneficiary/beneficiaries

or, if _____ _____ not survive me, to _____.

she/he/they   *does/do*   *alternate residuary beneficiary/beneficiairies*

6. Beneficiary Provisions. The following terms and conditions shall apply to the beneficiary clauses of this will.

A. 45-Day Survivorship Period. As used in this will, the phrase "survive me" means to be alive or in existence as an organization on the 45th day after my death. Any beneficiary, except any alternate residuary beneficiary, must survive me to inherit under this will. If there are no surviving beneficiaries for a specific gift, that gift shall become part of my residuary estate.

B. Shared Gifts. If I leave property to be shared by two or more beneficiaries, it shall be shared equally between them unless this will provides otherwise.

If any beneficiary of a shared specific gift left in a single paragraph of the Specific Gifts clause, above, does not survive me, that deceased beneficiary's portion of the gift shall be given to the surviving beneficiaries in equal shares.

If any residuary beneficiary of a shared residuary gift does not survive me, that deceased beneficiary's portion of the residue shall be given to the surviving residuary beneficiaries in equal shares.

C. Encumbrances. All property that I leave by this will shall pass subject to any encumbrances or liens on the property.

7. Executor. The following terms and conditions shall apply to the executor of this will.

    A. Nomination of Executor. I nominate _____

executor's name

as executor, to serve without bond. If _____ shall for any reason fail to qualify or cease to act as executor,

she/he

I nominate _____

alternate executor's name

as executor, also to serve without bond.

    B. Executor's Powers. I direct that my executor take all actions legally permissible to have the probate of my will conducted as simply and as free of court supervision as possible, including filing a petition in the appropriate court for the independent administration of my estate.

I grant to my personal representative the following powers, to be exercised as he or she deems to be in the best interests of my estate:

1. To pay, as my executor decides is best (unless state law requires a specific method for payment), all my debts and taxes that may, by reason of my death, be assessed against my estate or any portion of it.

2. To retain property without liability for loss or depreciation resulting from such retention.

3. To dispose of property by public or private sale, or exchange, or otherwise, and receive or administer the proceeds as a part of my estate.

4. To vote stock, to exercise any option or privilege to convert bonds, notes, stocks, or other securities belonging to my estate into other bonds, notes, stocks, or other securities, and to exercise all other rights and privileges of a person owning similar property in his or her own right.

5. To lease any real property that may at any time form part of my estate.

6. To abandon, adjust, arbitrate, compromise, sue on, defend, or otherwise deal with and settle claims in favor of or against my estate.

7. To continue, maintain, operate, or participate in any business which is a part of my estate, and to effect incorporation, dissolution, or other change in the form of organization of the business.

8. To do all other acts, which in his or her judgment may be necessary or appropriate for the proper and advantageous management, investment, and distribution of my estate.

The foregoing powers, authority, and discretion are in addition to the powers, authority, and discretion vested in him or her by operation of law and may be exercised as often as is deemed necessary or advisable without application to or approval by any court in any jurisdiction.

Signature

I subscribe my name to this will the _____ day of _____, _____, at

                                                                       month   *year*

_____, _____, _____

            city   *county*   *state*

and do hereby declare that I sign and execute this instrument as my last will and that I sign it willingly, that I execute it as my free and voluntary act for the purposes therein expressed and that I am of the age of majority or otherwise legally empowered to make a will, and under no constraint or undue influence.

_____
your signature

Witnesses

On this _____ day of _____, _____, _____
                              month   *year*   *your name*

declared to us, the undersigned, that this instrument was _____ will and requested us to act as witnesses
                                                                           his/her

to it. _____ thereupon signed this will in our presence, all of us being present at the same time. We now, at
     He/She

_____ request, in _____ presence and in the presence of each other, subscribe our names as
    his/her   *his/her*

witnesses and declare we understand this to be _____ will, and that to the best of our knowledge the
                                                   his/her

testator is of the age of majority, or is otherwise legally empowered to make a will, and under no constraint or undue influence.

We declare under penalty of perjury that the foregoing is true and correct, this _____ day of

_____, _____, at _____.
       month   *year*   *city and state*

_____
           witness's signature

_____ residing at _____,
        witness's typed name   *address*

_____, _____, _____.
          city   *county*   *state*

_____
           witness's signature

_____ residing at _____,
        witness's typed name   *address*

_____, _____, _____.
          city   *county*   *state*

_____
           witness's signature

_____ residing at _____,
        witness's typed name   *address*

_____, _____, _____.
          city   *county*   *state*

Will for an Unmarried Person With a Partner and Minor Children

Will of _____
your name

I, _____, a resident of
your name

_____, _____, _____,
city   *county*   *state*

declare that this is my will.

1. **Revocation of Prior Wills.** I revoke all wills and codicils that I have previously made.

2. **Personal Information.** My _____ name is _____ ,
                                partner's   *name*

and all references in this will to my _____ are to _____.
                                            partner   *him/her*

3. **Children.** I have _____ _____ whose name(s) and date(s) of birth _____:
                        number   *child/children*   *is/are*

_____   _____
name   *date of birth*

_____   _____
name   *date of birth*

_____   _____
name   *date of birth*

_____   _____
name   *date of birth*

_____   _____
name   *date of birth*

(repeat as needed)

There _____ _____ living _____ of my deceased child _____:
       is/are   *number*   *child/children*   *name*

_____   _____
name of grandchild   *date of birth*

_____   _____
name of grandchild   *date of birth*

_____   _____
name of grandchild   *date of birth*

(repeat as needed)

If I do not leave property in this will to a child or grandchild listed above, my failure to do so is intentional.

4. **Specific Gifts.** I leave the following specific gifts:

I leave _____
description of gift(s)

to _____ or, if _____
                    beneficiary/beneficiaries   *she/he/they*

_____ not survive me, to _____.
does/do   *alternate beneficiary/beneficiaries*

Will Form 7

NOLO
www.nolo.com
     Page 1 of 8

I leave _____
description of gift(s)

to _____ or, if _____
       beneficiary/beneficiaries   *she/he/they*

_____ not survive me, to _____.
does/do   *alternate beneficiary/beneficiaries*

I leave _____
description of gift(s)

to _____ or, if _____
       beneficiary/beneficiaries   *she/he/they*

_____ not survive me, to _____.
does/do   *alternate beneficiary/beneficiaries*

I leave _____
description of gift(s)

to _____ or, if _____
       beneficiary/beneficiaries   *she/he/they*

_____ not survive me, to _____.
does/do   *alternate beneficiary/beneficiaries*

I leave _____
description of gift(s)

to _____ or, if _____
       beneficiary/beneficiaries   *she/he/they*

_____ not survive me, to _____.
does/do   *alternate beneficiary/beneficiaries*

5. Residuary Estate. I leave my residuary estate, that is, the rest of my property not otherwise specifically and validly disposed of by this will or in any other manner, including lapsed or failed gifts, to _____

_____
residuary beneficiary/beneficiaries

or, if _____ _____ not survive me, to _____.
  she/he/they   *does/do*   *alternate residuary beneficiary/beneficiairies*

6. Beneficiary Provisions. The following terms and conditions shall apply to the beneficiary clauses of this will.

    A. 45-Day Survivorship Period. As used in this will, the phrase "survive me" means to be alive or in existence as an organization on the 45th day after my death. Any beneficiary, except any alternate residuary beneficiary, must survive me to inherit under this will. If there are no surviving beneficiaries for a specific gift, that gift shall become part of my residuary estate.

    B. Shared Gifts. If I leave property to be shared by two or more beneficiaries, it shall be shared equally between them unless this will provides otherwise.

    If any beneficiary of a shared specific gift left in a single paragraph of the Specific Gifts clause, above, does not survive me, that deceased beneficiary's portion of the gift shall be given to the surviving beneficiaries in equal shares.

    If any residuary beneficiary of a shared residuary gift does not survive me, that deceased beneficiary's portion of the residue shall be given to the surviving residuary beneficiaries in equal shares.

    C. Encumbrances. All property that I leave by this will shall pass subject to any encumbrances or liens on the property.

7. Executor. The following terms and conditions shall apply to the executor of this will.

   A. Nomination of Executor. I nominate _____

   executor's name

as executor, to serve without bond. If _____ shall for any reason fail to qualify or cease to act as executor,

   she/he

I nominate _____

   alternate executor's name

as executor, also to serve without bond.

   B. Executor's Powers. I direct that my executor take all actions legally permissible to have the probate of my will conducted as simply and as free of court supervision as possible, including filing a petition in the appropriate court for the independent administration of my estate.

   I grant to my personal representative the following powers, to be exercised as he or she deems to be in the best interests of my estate:

   1. To pay, as my executor decides is best (unless state law requires a specific method for payment), all my debts and taxes that may, by reason of my death, be assessed against my estate or any portion of it.

   2. To retain property without liability for loss or depreciation resulting from such retention.

   3. To dispose of property by public or private sale, or exchange, or otherwise, and receive or administer the proceeds as a part of my estate.

   4. To vote stock, to exercise any option or privilege to convert bonds, notes, stocks, or other securities belonging to my estate into other bonds, notes, stocks, or other securities, and to exercise all other rights and privileges of a person owning similar property in his or her own right.

   5. To lease any real property that may at any time form part of my estate.

   6. To abandon, adjust, arbitrate, compromise, sue on, defend, or otherwise deal with and settle claims in favor of or against my estate.

   7. To continue, maintain, operate, or participate in any business which is a part of my estate, and to effect incorporation, dissolution, or other change in the form of organization of the business.

   8. To do all other acts, which in his or her judgment may be necessary or appropriate for the proper and advantageous management, investment, and distribution of my estate.

   The foregoing powers, authority, and discretion are in addition to the powers, authority, and discretion vested in him or her by operation of law and may be exercised as often as is deemed necessary or advisable without application to or approval by any court in any jurisdiction.

8. Personal Guardian. If at my death any of my children are minors, and a personal guardian is needed, I nominate

_____

personal guardian's name

to be appointed personal guardian of my minor children. If _____ cannot serve as personal guardian,

she/he

I nominate _____

alternate personal guardian's name

to be appointed personal guardian.

I direct that no bond be required of any personal guardian.

9. Property Guardian. If at my death any of my children are minors, and a property guardian is needed, I appoint

_____
property guardian's name

as the property guardian of my minor children. If _____ cannot serve as property guardian, I appoint
she/he

_____ as property guardian.
alternate property guardian's name

I direct that no bond be required of any property guardian.

[Include only ONE Clause 10, below. Choose Uniform Transfers to Minors Act, the Family Pot Trust, OR the Child's Trust.]

10. Gifts Under the Uniform Transfers to Minors Act. All property left by this will to _____
minor's name

_____ shall be given to _____
custodian's name

as custodian for _____ under the Uniform Transfers to
minor's name

Minors Act of _____. If _____
your state   *custodian's name*

cannot serve as custodian, _____ shall serve as custodian.
alternate custodian's name

(repeat as needed)

10. Family Pot Trust. All property I leave by this will to the children listed in Section A below shall be held for them in a single trust, the family pot trust.

    A. Trust Beneficiaries

    _____
                             child's name

    _____
                             child's name

    _____
                             child's name

    _____
                             child's name

If all of the beneficiaries of the family pot trust are age 18 or older at my death, no family pot trust shall be established, and the property left to them shall be distributed to them outright.

If a beneficiary survives me but dies before the family pot trust terminates, that beneficiary's interest in the trust shall pass to the surviving beneficiaries of the family pot trust.

    B. Trustee of the Family Pot Trust. The trustee shall be _____
                                                 trustee's name

_____ or, if _____ cannot serve as trustee, the trustee shall be
                                                 she/he

_____.
successor trustee's name

No bond shall be required of any trustee.

C. Duties of the Family Pot Trust Trustee

1. The trustee may distribute trust assets (income or principal) as the trustee deems necessary for a beneficiary's health, support, maintenance, and education. Education includes, but is not limited to, college, graduate, postgraduate, and vocational studies, plus reasonably related living expenses.

2. In deciding whether or not to make distributions, the trustee shall consider the value of the trust assets, the relative current and future needs of each beneficiary, and each beneficiary's other income, resources, and sources of support. In doing so, the trustee has the discretion to make distributions that benefit some beneficiaries more than others or that completely exclude others.

3. Any trust income that is not distributed by the trustee shall be accumulated and added to the principal.

D. Termination of the Family Pot Trust. When the youngest surviving beneficiary of this family pot trust reaches 18, the trustee shall distribute the remaining trust assets to the surviving beneficiaries in equal shares.

If none of the trust beneficiaries survives to the age of 18, the trustee shall distribute the remaining trust assets to my heirs at the death of the last surviving beneficiary.

E. Powers of the Trustee. In addition to all other powers granted a trustee in any portion of this will, the trustee of the family pot trust shall have the power to make distributions to the beneficiaries directly or to other people or organizations on behalf of the beneficiaries.

10. Child's Trusts. All property I leave by this will to a child listed in Section A below shall be held for that child in a separate trust.

A. Trust Beneficiaries and Age Limits. Each trust shall end when the beneficiary becomes 35, except as otherwise specified in this section.

Trust for	Shall end at age
_____	_____
_____	_____
_____	_____
_____	_____
_____	_____
_____	_____
_____	_____

B. Trustees. The trustee of each child's trust shall be _____

trustee's name

_____ or, if _____ cannot serve as trustee, the trustee shall be

she/he

_____.

successor trustee's name

No bond shall be required of any trustee.

C. Duties of the Trustee

1. The trustee may distribute trust assets (income or principal) as the trustee deems necessary for the beneficiary's health, support, maintenance, and education. Education includes, but is not limited to, college, graduate, postgraduate, and vocational studies, plus reasonably related living expenses.

2. In deciding whether or not to make a distribution, the trustee may take into account the beneficiary's other income, resources, and sources of support.

3. Any trust income that is not distributed by the trustee shall be accumulated and added to the principal of that child's trust.

D. Termination of Trust. A child's trust shall terminate when any of the following events occurs:

1. The beneficiary becomes the age specified in Section A of this trust clause;

2. The beneficiary dies before becoming the age specified in Section A of this trust clause;

3. The trust is exhausted through distributions allowed under these provisions.

If a trust terminates for reason one, the remaining principal and accumulated net income of the trust shall pass to the beneficiary. If a trust terminates for reason two, the remaining principal and accumulated net income of the trust shall pass to the trust beneficiary's heirs.

E. Powers of the Trustee. In addition to all other powers granted the trustee in this will, the trustee shall have the power to make distributions to a child's trust beneficiary directly or to other people or organizations on behalf of that child.

[Delete Clause 11 if in Clause 10 you selected Gifts Under the Uniform Transfers to Minors Act.]

11. General Trust Administrative Provisions. Any trust established under this will shall be managed subject to the following provisions.

A. Intent. It is my intent that any trust established under this will be administered independently of court supervision to the maximum extent possible under the laws of the state having jurisdiction over the trust.

B. No Assignment. The interests of any beneficiary of any trust established under this will shall not be transferable by voluntary or involuntary assignment or by operation of law and shall be free from the claims of creditors and from attachment, execution, bankruptcy, or other legal process to the fullest extent permitted by law.

C. Trustee's Powers. In addition to other powers granted the trustee in this will, the trustee shall have all the powers generally conferred on trustees by the laws of the state having jurisdiction over this trust and the powers to:

1. Invest and reinvest trust funds in every kind of property and every kind of investment, provided that the trustee acts with the care, skill, prudence, and diligence under the prevailing circumstances that a prudent person acting in a similar capacity and familiar with such matters would use.

2. Receive additional property from any source and acquire or hold properties jointly or in undivided interests or in partnership or joint venture with other people or entities.

3. Enter, continue, or participate in the operation of any business, and incorporate, liquidate, reorganize, or otherwise change the form or terminate the operation of the business and contribute capital or loan money to the business.

4. Exercise all the rights, powers, and privileges of an owner of any securities held in the trust.

5. Borrow funds, guarantee or indemnify in the name of the trust, and secure any obligation, mortgage, pledge, or other security interest, and renew, extend, or modify any such obligations.

6. Lease trust property for terms within or beyond the term of the trust.

7. Prosecute, defend, contest, or otherwise litigate legal actions or other proceedings for the protection or benefit of the trust; pay, compromise, release, adjust, or submit to arbitration any debt, claim, or controversy; and insure the trust against any risk and the trustee against liability with respect to other people.

8. Pay himself or herself reasonable compensation out of trust assets for ordinary and extraordinary services, and for all services in connection with the complete or partial termination of this trust.

9. Employ and discharge professionals to aid or assist in managing the trust and compensate them from the trust assets.

D. Severability. If any provision of any trust is held invalid, that shall not affect other trust provisions that can be given effect without the invalid provision.

E. "Trustee" Defined. The term "trustee" shall include all successor trustees.

Signature

I subscribe my name to this will the _____ day of _____, _____, at

                                           month   *year*

_____, _____, _____,

          city   *county*   *state*

and do hereby declare that I sign and execute this instrument as my last will and that I sign it willingly, that I execute it as my free and voluntary act for the purposes therein expressed and that I am of the age of majority or otherwise legally empowered to make a will, and under no constraint or undue influence.

_____

your signature

Witnesses

On this _____ day of _____, _____, _____

                  month   *year*   *your name*

declared to us, the undersigned, that this instrument was _____ will and requested us to act as witnesses

                                          his/her

to it. _____ thereupon signed this will in our presence, all of us being present at the same time. We now, at

    He/She

_____ request, in _____ presence and in the presence of each other, subscribe our names as

  his/her   *his/her*

witnesses and declare we understand this to be _____ will, and that to the best of our knowledge the

                                        his/her

testator is of the age of majority, or is otherwise legally empowered to make a will, and under no constraint or undue influence.

    We declare under penalty of perjury that the foregoing is true and correct, this _____ day of

_____, _____, at _____.
        month   *year*   *city and state*

_____
             witness's signature

_____ residing at _____,
        witness's typed name   *address*

_____, _____, _____.
         city   *county*   *state*

_____
             witness's signature

_____ residing at _____,
        witness's typed name   *address*

_____, _____, _____.
         city   *county*   *state*

_____
             witness's signature

_____ residing at _____,
        witness's typed name   *address*

_____, _____, _____.
         city   *county*   *state*

Self-Proving Affidavit

We, _____

and _____

, _____ and

_____, the testator and

the witnesses, whose names are signed to the attached or foregoing instrument in those capacities, personally appearing

before the undersigned authority and being first duly sworn, declare to the undersigned authority under penalty of perjury

that: 1) the testator declared, signed, and executed the instrument as his or her last will; 2) he or she signed it willingly

or directed another to sign for him or her; 3) he or she executed it as his or her free and voluntary act for the purposes

therein expressed; and 4) each of the witnesses, at the request of the testator, in his or her hearing and presence, and in the

presence of each other, signed the will as witness and that to the best of his or her knowledge the testator was at that time

18 years of age or older, of sound mind, and under no constraint or undue influence.

Testator:_____

Witness: _____

Address:_____

Witness: _____

Address:_____

Witness: _____

Address:_____

Subscribed, sworn, and acknowledged before me by _____ ,

the testator, and by _____ ,

_____ and

_____ , the witnesses, this

_____ day of _____ .

Signed: _____

_____
Official Capacity of Officer

Self-Proving Affidavit

STATE OF _____

COUNTY OF _____

    I, the undersigned, an officer authorized to administer oaths, certify that

_____ , the testator,

and _____ ,

_____ and

_____ , the witnesses, whose

names are signed to the attached or foregoing instrument and whose signatures appear below, having appeared together before me and having been first duly sworn, each then declared to me that: 1) the attached or foregoing instrument is the last will of the testator; 2) the testator willingly and voluntarily declared, signed, and executed the will in the presence of the witnesses; 3) the witnesses signed the will upon request by the testator, in the presence and hearing of the testator, and in the presence of each other; 4) to the best knowledge of each witness the testator was, at the time of the signing, 18 years of age or older (or otherwise legally competent to make a will), of sound mind and memory, and under no constraint or undue influence; and 5) each witness was and is competent and of the proper age to witness a will.

Testator: _____

Witness: _____

Address: _____

Witness: _____

Address: _____

Witness: _____

Address: _____

    Subscribed, sworn, and acknowledged before me by _____ ,

the testator, and by _____ ,

_____ and

_____ , the witnesses, this

_____ day of _____ .

Signed: _____

_____
Official Capacity of Officer

Self-Proving Affidavit

THE STATE OF TEXAS

COUNTY OF _____

Before me, the undersigned authority, on this day personally appeared _____

_____ ,

_____ and

_____ ,

known to me to be the testator and the witnesses, respectively, whose names are subscribed to the annexed

or foregoing instrument in their respective capacities, and, all of said persons being by me duly sworn, the said

_____ , testator, declared to me and to

the said witnesses in my presence that said instrument is his or her last will and testament, and that he or she had willingly

made and executed it as his or her free act and deed, and the said witnesses, each on his or her oath stated to me in the

presence and hearing of the said testator, that the said testator had declared to them that said instrument is his or her last

will and testament, and that he or she executed same as such and wanted each of them to sign it as a witness; and upon

their oaths each witness stated further that they did sign the same as witnesses in the presence of the said testator and at

his or her request; that he or she was at the time eighteen years of age or over (or being under such age, was or had been

lawfully married, or was then a member of the armed forces of the United States or an auxiliary thereof or of the Maritime

Service) and was of sound mind; and that each of said witnesses was then at least fourteen years of age.

Testator: _____   _____

Witness: _____

Witness: _____

    Subscribed, sworn, and acknowledged before me by _____ ,

the testator, and by _____ ,

_____ and

_____ , the witnesses, this

_____ day of _____ .

Signed: _____

_____
Official Capacity of Officer

Acknowledgment

THE STATE OF PENNSYLVANIA

COUNTY OF _____

I, _____ , the testator whose name is signed to the attached or foregoing

instrument, having been duly qualified according to law, do hereby acknowledge that I signed and executed the instrument

as my Last will; and that I signed it willingly and as my free and voluntary act for the purposes therein expressed.

    Sworn to or affirmed and acknowledged before me by _____ ,

the testator, this _____ day of _____ .

_____

(Testator)

_____

(Signature of officer)

(Seal and official capacity of officer)

Affidavit

THE STATE OF PENNSYLVANIA

COUNTY OF _____

We (or I), _____ and _____ , the witness(es) whose

name(s) are (is) signed to the attached or foregoing instrument, being duly qualified according to law, do depose and say

that we were (I was) present and saw the testator sign and execute the instrument as his Last Will; that the testator signed

willingly and executed it as his free and voluntary act for the purposes therein expressed; that each subscribing witness in

the hearing and sight of the testator signed the will as a witness; and that to the best of our (my) knowledge the testator

was at that time 18 or more years of age, of sound mind and under no constraint or undue influence.

Sworn to or affirmed and subscribed to before me by _____ and

_____ , witness(es), this _____ day of

_____ , 20_____ .

_____

Witness: Signature, Name, and Address

_____

Witness: Signature, Name, and Address

_____

(Signature of officer)

(Seal and official capacity of officer)

First Codicil to the Will of _____

I, _____ ,
your name

a resident of _____ , _____ ,
city   state

declare this to be the first codicil to my will dated _____ .
date of will

    FIRST: I revoke the provision of Clause _____ of my will that provided:

[Include the exact language you wish to revoke]

    SECOND: I add the following provision to Clause _____ of my will:

[Add whatever is desired]

    THIRD: In all other respects I confirm and republish my will dated _____ _____ , _____ .
month/day   year

    I subscribe my name to this codicil this _____ day of _____ , _____ ,
month   year

at _____ , _____ , _____ ,
city   county   state

and do hereby declare that I sign and execute this codicil willingly, that I execute it as my free and voluntary act for the

purposes therein expressed, and that I am of the age of majority or otherwise legally empowered to make a codicil and

under no constraint or undue influence.

your signature

    On this _____ day of _____ , _____ ,
month   year

_____ declared to us, the undersigned, that this
name

instrument was the codicil to _____ will and requested us to act as witnesses to it. _____ thereupon signed this
his/her   He/She

codicil in our presence, all of us being present at the same time. We now, at _____ request, in _____
his/her   his/her

presence, and in the presence of each other, subscribe our names as witness and declare we understand this to be

---

Page 1 of 2

_____ codicil and that to the best of our knowledge _____ is of the age of majority, or is otherwise
his/her   *he/she*

legally empowered to make a codicil and is under no constraint or undue influence.

    We declare under penalty of perjury that the foregoing is true and correct. This _____ day of

_____, _____, at _____.
            month   *year*   *city, state*

_____
                        witness's signature

_____ residing at _____
              witness's typed name   *address*

_____, _____, _____.
             city   *county*   *state*

_____
                        witness's signature

_____ residing at _____
              witness's typed name   *address*

_____, _____, _____.
             city   *county*   *state*

_____
                        witness's signature

_____ residing at _____
              witness's typed name   *address*

_____, _____, _____.
             city   *county*   *state*

CAUTION

You must retype this codicil for it to be valid. As explained in Chapter 13, a codicil, like a will, cannot contain handwritten material. Retype this entire form and sign it in front of witnesses, otherwise it will not be a legally valid codicil.

Index

Get the Latest in the Law

(1) **Nolo's Legal Updater**
We'll send you an email whenever a new edition of your book is published!
Sign up at **www.nolo.com/legalupdater**.

(2) **Updates at Nolo.com**
Check **www.nolo.com/update** to find recent changes in the law that
affect the current edition of your book.

(3) **Nolo Customer Service**
To make sure that this edition of the book is the most recent one, call us at
800-728-3555 and ask one of our friendly customer service representatives
(7:00 am to 6:00 pm PST, weekdays only). Or find out at **www.nolo.com**.

(4) **Complete the Registration & Comment Card ...**
... and we'll do the work for you! Just indicate your preferences below:

- -

Registration & Comment Card

NAME _____ DATE _____

ADDRESS _____

CITY _____ STATE _____ ZIP _____

PHONE _____ EMAIL _____

COMMENTS _____

WAS THIS BOOK EASY TO USE?   (VERY EASY)   5   4   3   2   1   (VERY DIFFICULT)

☐ Yes, you can quote me in future Nolo promotional materials. *Please include phone number above.*

☐ Yes, send me **Nolo's Legal Updater** via email when a new edition of this book is available.

Yes, I want to sign up for the following email newsletters:

   ☐ **NoloBriefs** (monthly)
   ☐ **Nolo's Special Offer** (monthly)
   ☐ **Nolo's BizBriefs** (monthly)
   ☐ **Every Landlord's Quarterly** (four times a year)

☐ Yes, you can give my contact info to carefully selected
partners whose products may be of interest to me.

SWIL7

NOLO

Nolo
950 Parker Street
Berkeley, CA 94710-9867
www.nolo.com

YOUR LEGAL COMPANION